ALONE
IN
COMMUNITY

Alone in Community

Journeys into Monastic Life
Around the World

William Claassen

Photographs by the Author

FOREST OF PEACE
Publishing

Suppliers for the Spiritual Pilgrim
Leavenworth, KS

Alone in Community

Library of Congress Cataloging-in-Publication Data

Claassen, William, 1948-
    Alone in community : journeys into monastic life around the world / William Claassen ; photographs by the author.
        p. cm.
    Includes bibliographical references and index.
    ISBN 0-939516-52-7 (pbk.)
        1. Retreats. 2. Monastic and religious life. 3. Monastic and religious life (Buddhism) 4. Monastic and religious life (Jainism) 5. Claassen, William, 1948---Journeys I. Title.

    BL628 .C57 2000
    291.6'57'09—dc21

                                        00-059314

published by   printed by
Forest of Peace Publishing, Inc.   Hall Commercial Printing
PO Box 269   Topeka, KS 66608-0007
Leavenworth, KS 66048-0269   USA
1-800-659-3227
www.forestofpeace.com

1st printing: August 2000

Cover design: Alma Landeros
Photography: William Claassen

To
My Family

Permissions

I gratefully acknowledge permission to quote from the following works.

CHADWICK, DAVID. *Thank You and OK! An American Zen Failure in Japan.* New York: Penguin, 1994.

DOSHI, SARYU. *Homage to Shravana Belgola.* Bombay: Marg Publications, 1981.

HARTSUIKER, DOLF. *Sadhus: Holy Men of India.* London: Thames and Hudson, 1993.

HEAT MOON, WILLIAM LEAST. *Blue Highways.* Boston: Little, Brown and Company, 1982.

LE MEE, KATHERINE. *Chant: The Origins, Form, Practice, and Healing Power of Gregorian Chant.* New York: Belltower, 1994.

MEINARDUS, OTTO F. A. *Monks and Monasteries of the Egyptian Deserts.* Cairo: American University in Cairo Press, 1961.

NISHIMURA, ESHIN. *Unsui: A Diary of Zen Monastic Life.* Honolulu: University Press of Hawaii, 1973.

STEVENS, JOHN. *The Marathon Monks of Mt. Hiei.* Boston: Shambhala Publications, Inc., 1988.

Contents

Photographs

Acknowledgments

Without the assistance of many, many people, both here in the United States and abroad, this book would not have come to fruition.

First, I wish to thank the Trappist brothers at Assumption Abbey, who have frequently welcomed me on retreat. Their insights, support and kindness have always been much appreciated. As well, a word of thanks goes to the Benedictine community of Conception Abbey for the use of their research library.

Next, I want to express my gratitude to Tim Williams, who was always willing to answer my never-ending list of questions. The resources he provided were a tremendous help in organizing my journeys to both Japan and Thailand.

Thanks go to those students from Japan, Thailand, Greece, Bulgaria, Turkey and India attending the University of Missouri-Columbia who assisted me on the project. Their help composing introductory letters to various monastic communities around the world, and translating correspondence that I received in return, was invaluable. My gratitude goes as well to the Stephens College Library staff for their cheerful assistance and encouragement.

It was a blessing to have had the enthusiastic support of Alice Anderson, Richard Baumann, Michael DiBenedetto, George Frissell, Tim Gallimore, Rocket Kirchner, Lisa Lapp, Ann McGinity, Steve Podry, Nonnie Pyle, Joel Rosenblit and Rick Truax. My thanks go to them for maintaining vigilance.

I want to thank Karen Robinson for her patience, insight and sense of humor. Her many skills and talents were demonstrated often during the preparation of the manuscript.

To my family, I offer my appreciation for their encouragement and willingness simply to be present. A special thanks goes to my father for his helpful comments after reviewing an early draft of the manuscript.

My gratitude goes to the brothers at Abbaye de la Trappe and Abbaye de Citeaux in France, Monasterio de Santo Domingo de Silos in Spain and Monastero di Sacro Speco in Italy. I thank them all for opening their doors to an outsider.

I wish to thank the Orthodox monks on Mt. Athos, Greece, for their hospitality and many spiritual gifts. I tried not to leave any footprints. In particular, I wish to express my appreciation to Andres, Artemus, Chris, Costas, Girosimos, Iakovos, Kosmos, Doug Lyttle and Robert Lloyd Parry.

The magic that Faunie created for me in her Greek home will not be forgotten. She made her religious icons come to life by example.

Dr. Isaac Fanous Youssef and Dr. Zakishanouda of the Coptic Institute of Studies in Cairo introduced me to a world I hardly knew existed. My thanks goes to the *abuna* at Dair as-Surian and Dair Anba Antunius in the Egyptian deserts. As well, my gratitude goes to Magued Baki, Haney, Haytham and Maha Kasseb for helping me find my way home.

I wish to thank my friends in Istanbul—the members of the Association of Galata Mevlevis—for inviting me into their houses of worship. And I am thankful for the diligence and trust of Ilham and the bookshop owner in the Old Book Bazaar.

A word of appreciation to James, Noel and Ryoei in Tokyo for making my stay in the city a much richer experience. And thank you to the Tendai monks at the Koji-rin Laypeople's Training Center on Mt. Hiei and to the Rinzai Zen monks of Sogenji. Their patience, tolerance and discipline gave me a renewed appreciation for living life mindfully.

I am grateful to those *ajahn, bhikkhu* and *mae-chii* in Thailand who permitted me to make retreats in their monastic communities. A special word of thanks to Pannavaddho, Sangwaro, Santikaro, Supin, Sister Wendy and Yantra.

My appreciation goes to V. H. Chudamani for setting me on the right path once I arrived in Mumbai (Bombay). I want to thank the faculty members of Mumbai's Bhavan College and the monks at the city's Ramakrishna Mission who offered me excellent advice; their recommendations held fast throughout my stay in India.

Dr. Ashok Kumar in Shravana Belgola shared his home, expertise and photographs. I trust he knows how encouraging his hospitality was for me. I am grateful to Maharaj and Neil Muji, at Kundakunda Bharati in New Delhi, for their time and understanding.

I want to express my gratitude to the administrators and Ramakrishna monks at Belar Math in Calcutta. My brief stay in their community was both restful and enlightening.

Finally, my appreciation goes to editors Sara Davis and Thomas Skorupa for their insights, suggestions and revisions. Their thorough review of my manuscript was very helpful.

You know when you've been found.
Something tells you this is where you belong.
That's what we mean when we say you're called to this life.
God finds you.

Brother Mac
Trappist Monk

INTRODUCTION

My first glimpse into monastic life was through Thomas Merton's autobiography, *The Seven Storey Mountain,* which was first published in the late 1940s. After boyhood years spent commuting with his father between Western Europe and the United States, Merton embarked upon a challenging academic career in New York. For Merton, academia was satisfying, yet it lacked something. I read with keen interest about his intense search for a spiritual and religious home and his eventual commitment to the contemplative life. He joined the Cistercian Order of the Strict Observance — more commonly called the Trappists — and some years later took permanent vows at the Abbey of Gethsemani in rural Kentucky.

I was intrigued by the story of Merton's spiritual journey, particularly his resolute commitment to life in a monastery. Who or what called him into religious community? Why would he choose such a life? How were his days structured? Were they filled with dramatic rituals? Who were the other men living behind the walls? Did his example have some bearing on my life?

These were but a few of the questions that dogged me over the years while I continued to read his voluminous output of religious tracts, commentaries on contemporary political issues and explorations into other religious traditions. These works sparked within me an intense desire to set out on my own monastic retreat. It would be the first of many.

In late December 1973, I arrived in Louisville, Kentucky. Inside a crowded, noisy bus depot, I waited anxiously for my ride. An hour later, I sat between two Trappist monks in the cab of an old Ford pickup headed for the Abbey of Gethsemani. Months earlier, I had applied for, and had been granted, permission by the monastery guestmaster to make a retreat at the community over the Christmas holiday. My new acquaintances soon made me feel at ease. There was good conversation and laughter shared during that bumpy truck ride. The heater didn't work properly, and the heavy snowfall from the night before crunched under the tires as we drove slowly over the country roads.

When I recall that first retreat, I can still visualize scenes that were an integral part of the experience. There was Christmas Eve Mass, where mysterious events unfolded amid the haze of incense and candlelight — my introduction to the antiphonal sounds of Gregorian chant emanating from the hooded, faceless figures who seemed to float through the sanctuary. A sparsely furnished room, with a cold bare floor, firm bed and a crucifix hanging on the wall, was where I fell asleep each night. And there were the long periods of silence throughout those winter days.

The solo walks into the dense Kentucky woods and the visits to the onetime hermitage of Thomas Merton remain in my memory. That simple, concrete-block abode was my daily pilgrimage site. Not once during those few days did I feel awkward, uncomfortable or out of place. I knew when I left the abbey that monastic retreats would become an important part of my life, a refuge of sorts. I had found a religious and spiritual community that understood my hunger for periods of silence and solitude, a community that strove for cooperation rather than competition. At one time, I briefly entertained the idea of seeking admission into a monastery, but I concluded that my place in the "contemplative life" was as a layman.

Over the years, I have taken many retreats in varied monastic settings, some in the United States and others abroad. There have been profound experiences with the Benedictine monks at Weston Priory in Vermont, where the day begins with monks and visitors sitting together on the floor for meditation and where liturgical dance is a common form of worship in the spring and summer months.

I've had the good fortune to stay at Trappist communities in the Oregon forest, the Iowa farmlands and the rolling hills of the Missouri Ozarks, among others. These monasteries maintain a tradition of offering hospitality to the seeker. Outside Yarmouth, Nova Scotia, I spent a long Easter holiday on retreat in the coed Christian monastic community of Nova Nada. The monastery, a former hunting lodge, provided one-room hermitages, originally hunter's cabins, for each member of the community and each visitor.

At the end of the Valle de Elqui, in a barren, mountainous region of northern Chile, I found a spiritual refuge with monks who integrated Hindu and Christian religious tradition and ritual. Inside a yurt, we observed daily prayer services sitting in a circle burning incense and ghee during the purification ceremonies. It was my introduction to monastic practices outside of Christianity.

The Chilean monastery is in a location known to be one of Earth's energy centers. There I experienced a gentle but constant energy surge running through my body by day, felt the warmth of the stars with my outstretched fingers by night, and skinny-dipped in an ice-cold stream early each morning. There was no question that I was led there to witness the beauty and power of nature and the universe.

At times I have welcomed the camaraderie of fellow seekers, and in other situations I have been thankful that there was no obligation to communicate or interrupt the richness of the silence. On some retreats, the emergence of powerful emotions has been a common occurrence, and self-searching has left me exhausted at the end of the day. But I have always left monastic retreats on better terms with myself and the world around me.

During the last two decades I have made an effort to broaden my knowledge of, and passion for, diverse religious communities and their rituals around the world. More specifically, I decided to document the daily life in Buddhist, Christian, Hindu, Jain and Sufi monastic communities to share with others.

Monastery, as defined by the *Oxford English Dictionary,* is "a place of residence of a community of persons living secluded from the world under religious vows; a monastic establishment. Chiefly, and now almost exclusively, applied to a house for monks; but applicable also to the house of any religious order, male or female." This definition, although at times loosely interpreted, is an appropriate description of the communities and individuals I visited.

In early spring 1994, I flew to Western Europe carrying only minimal provisions: a supply-filled backpack with a sleeping bag, blank journals and simple camera equipment. My starting point was a village built in the Pyrenees Mountains alongside El Camino de Santiago. A famous pilgrimage trail dating back to the eleventh century, El Camino extends all the way across northern Spain — an appropriate place to begin my journey.

During the next two and a half years, on a number of extended treks abroad, I arranged a series of monastic retreats. I visited more than forty communities of monks in nearly a dozen countries, seeking a better understanding of their chosen way of life. My intentions were to become more familiar with their history, to meet individuals within each community and to participate in the monks' daily lives as much as possible. A broadening of my own spiritual path would come with the territory.

When selecting the communities to describe in this book, I considered a number of factors: amount of time spent on specific retreats, availability of personal and literary resources, and the degree of my involvement with a monastery's daily rituals and traditions. My aim was to make each chapter a window into monastic practices in various religions around the world.

I was welcomed into Roman Catholic monasteries of Western Europe, Eastern Orthodox monastic communities of Greece and Coptic monasteries of the Egyptian deserts. They are the three primary monastic traditions within the Christian faith.

The Mevlevi Sufis, Muslim mystics better known as the "Whirling Dervishes," invited me into their Turkish prayer lodges as a fellow seeker. Although they no longer independently manage their training centers, called *tekkes,* they do continue the tradition of accepting novices into their order. Their religious and spiritual training is ongoing, and they continue to maintain a strong Sufi presence in the world.

In Japan, I stayed in Tendai and Zen Buddhist temple communities, and in Thailand, I was permitted access to the lives of Buddhist monks in "forest monasteries." There are two main branches of practice in the universe of Buddhism: Mahayana and Theravada. The Mahayana tradition is found in the Buddhist monastic communities of Japan, whereas Thai monks are most often associated with the Theravada tradition.

In southern India, members of the Jain community opened their hearts and temples to this traveler. They were the most ascetic group that I had the privilege of visiting. Their practice includes two major schools of monasticism, the Shvetambara and the older school, the Digambara. In other regions of India, an ancient and traditional order of Orthodox Hindu practitioners, known as Shaivites, laid out their welcome mats and never questioned my reason for coming. In contrast to that group's Orthodoxy, the Ramakrishna monks practice a very contemporary and nontraditional

Hindu monastic life. Through their teachings and daily practices, these monks demonstrated to me an acceptance of all world religions.

I have tried to record my journeys faithfully. Portions of many interviews are presented in this book. The quotations are drawn from my extensive notes and my memory and reproduce as accurately as possible both the statements and the manner of speaking of my hosts. Names of some individuals have been changed out of respect for their privacy. I have presented some events in religious groupings rather than chronological order to facilitate clarity and understanding. In one chapter, I have created an individual from the profiles of several to simplify my story. I have also incorporated an event experienced in one community into my story of another, similar community.

I hope this account of my experiences and encounters on these journeys will be enlightening and an aid to your own spiritual journey. To that end, I offer you their words and my witness.

Abbaye de la Trappe gate

Chapter One

COMES A VISITOR

Let all guests who arrive be received like Christ, for He is going to say, 'I came as a guest, and you received me.' And to all let due honor be shown, especially to the domestic of the faith and to pilgrims.

St. Benedict
sixth century

The white cross atop the lofty bell tower gleams as the sun breaks through the early morning cloud cover. Below is a cluster of buildings, enclosed by a tall stone wall, built in a monastic style that dates back to the Middle Ages. The setting is a valley in central Normandy, France, near the village of L'Aigle, where rolling green hills and freshly plowed fields accentuate the beauty of the area. The scent of rich, dark soil is heavy in the air.

~~~~~~~~~~

The Cistercian monastery of Abbaye de la Trappe was founded in the twelfth century. Since that time, it has been destroyed and rebuilt on several occasions. It is the home of Trappists — officially, Cistercian, Benedictine monks. A Trappist is a kind of Cistercian; a Cistercian is a type of Benedictine; and Benedictines are a type of Christian monk. The labels simply clarify the different orders of religious and their unique way of serving God.

In the seventeenth century, the spiritual leader at la Trappe initiated a reform movement. He and his followers sought a return to the simple, disciplined way of life advocated by St. Benedict, the "father" of Western monasticism. The movement was successful, and the reformers were later officially recognized as the Cistercian Order of the Strict Observance, or simply, Trappists.

~~~~~~~~~~

As my taxi pulls away, I approach a black, wrought-iron gate set into the monastery wall and find it locked. To one side is a gatehouse with lights on inside. I push the buzzer, the door opens with a click, and I am facing a tall, broad-shouldered, gray-haired man. Dressed in a red plaid shirt and blue jeans, he looks more like a rancher than a monastery gatekeeper. "Bonjour," he greets me.

"Bonjour," I reply, slipping off my backpack. I introduce myself, "Je m'appelle William Claassen," and hand him a letter from the abbey's guestmaster written almost entirely in French. In a moment of whimsy, the guestmaster had written at the bottom, in English, "P.S. I hope you are able to understand my French. Bye-bye!"

"Je m'appelle Jean Pierre," says the gatekeeper, offering a firm handshake. He takes the letter and reads it, then asks me to wait, "Je comprends, un moment," and turns to a switchboard to make a brief phone call. Jean Pierre glances back at me. "Parlez-vous Francais?" he asks.

"Non," I answer, showing him my French/English dictionary.

I ask if he speaks English, "Parlez-vous Anglais?"

"Je parle un peu l'Anglais," he replies, revealing that he speaks a little English.

Does he speak Spanish, I ask, "Parlez-vous Español?"

"Oui," says Jean Pierre. "Si, hablo Español." We have found a common language.

He explains that he has called the guestmaster and that I am welcome into the monastery. Then he directs me to the guest quarters. I walk down a driveway and past a barn, turn right, and there they are, just beside the soaring, gray stone church.

Guestmaster Frere (Brother) Jean greets me at the door and leads me into the entryway, which smells of cinnamon and baked apples. The brown-robed brother, short and stout, smiles and offers a vigorous handshake with both hands. Although I quickly discover that he speaks very little English and no Spanish, I am nevertheless confident that we will have no problem communicating. Frere Jean enters his office briefly and soon returns with a key in hand. I follow him up a winding staircase for one floor, where he grabs a towel and a bar of soap, then we continue to the top floor.

He leads me down a dark hallway. Suddenly stopping in front of a door, the brother shows me the brass plate mounted on it. Engraved on the plate is the name "St. Nivard." He points to the name, then to me, then back to the name. Apparently, Nivard will be my guardian during the stay, my friend, confidant and keeper here at Abbaye de la Trappe.

(Later, I'm pleased to discover that the saint was a highly regarded twelfth-century monk who had taken his vows at a Cistercian monastery established near Clairvaux-les-Lacs, France.) Unlocking the door, Jean hands over my towel, a bar of soap, a key and a copy of the daily schedule. He then bids me "au revoir" and leaves, shutting the door quietly behind him.

Nivard's room is large, with high ceilings and an arch-shaped window that allows light to fill the room. A worn French Bible has been placed on top of the sturdy wooden desk that sits in front of the window. From there, I can look out over the countryside. Against one wall sits a twin bed, above which hangs a crucifix, and along the opposite wall stands a wardrobe smelling of cedar. The circular, multicolored throw rug in the middle of the room is an island of warmth in the space. I empty my backpack and sort through my clothes, hanging up the items I'll need during my stay. Then I sit down on the bed to review the daily schedule, one that is quite familiar because of past monastic retreats.

There are seven periods of worship or divine office observed each day. *The Rule of St. Benedict* refers to them as the "Opus Dei," the work of God. At la Trappe, the first one, vigils, begins at 4:15 A.M., with compline drawing the day to a close at 8:15 P.M. Each service is based on the Psalter, a collection of the 150 Psalms that are sung or recited within a particular cycle determined by this community. The psalms are always accompanied with scriptural readings and prayers.

Daily Schedule					
Vigils	4:15	*Terce*	9:30	*Vespers*	18:15
Lauds	7:00	*Sext*	12:15	*Dinner*	18:55
Eucharist	7:30	*Lunch*	12:30	*Compline*	20:15
Breakfast	8:30	*None*	14:15		

While I am copying the schedule into my journal, the church bells begin ringing, announcing sext. I quickly find my way back to the entrance, then take a long, unfamiliar hallway that appears to lead to the church. When I reach the gothic stone structure, I take a seat in the empty front pew. Through a side door enter the white-robed monks with lowered heads and folded arms. Bowing toward the front of the sanctuary, the men move quietly into the ornate wooden choir stalls built on either side of the heavy, marble altar.

It's cold and damp inside the church, the kind of cold that lingers and is not warded off by an extra layer of clothing. On each side of the pews are walls broken by archways; above, a vaulted ceiling seemingly ties the structure together. A trinity of elongated stained glass windows, high above and far behind the altar, spills a rainbow of colors onto the polished wooden floor below.

After the simple prayer service, those of us who are guests quickly retreat to the warm dining room and take our places, in silence, along the wooden tables. Jean Pierre, my Spanish-speaking acquaintance, stands by my side. After the kitchen monk offers a prayer, we join in with a collective "amen" and sit down. Noticing that people are talking quietly as the food platters are passed around, I turn to Jean Pierre, "What is your relationship to this community?"

"I have been making retreats here for many years," he tells me. "The monastery has become my second home. Now that I am retired, I visit for longer periods of time and help the monks in one capacity or another."

"And do you live nearby?"

"Well, near enough. My home is in Paris." The city is to the east, a few hours by train. He is, in essence, part of the extended family of the monastery: a layperson who has developed a special relationship with the brothers. In the United States, monastic communities call these family members "oblates."

When the main course of pork roast, rice and mushrooms is served, I'm somewhat surprised by the inclusion of meat. "Jean Pierre, the monks are vegetarians, aren't they?"

"Oh, yes," he answers. "*The Rule of St. Benedict* directs the monks to keep a vegetarian diet except in cases of illness. However, they usually offer meat to the guests at the main meal of the day." When fruit and cheeses follow the main course, I get up to fetch a cup of coffee for both of us.

"You know, you have come at a very special time," my tablemate informs me.

"Why is this a special time?"

"Oh, you didn't know? Well, the reliquary of Ste. Therese de Lisieux is coming to la Trappe." I still don't understand, but I am not able to ask him for clarification because another guest begins talking with him.

After the meal, all of us take our dishes into the kitchen. Two people volunteer to wash them; a few guests grab dishtowels and line up for duty, while others grab wet sponges to wipe off the tabletops. Picking up a broom, I begin sweeping the dining hall. Everyone participates in the collective effort, seemingly enjoying the sense of community.

After cleanup, while I'm finishing a second cup of coffee, Frere Jean drops by to check on me. He has arranged for a younger monk, Frere Hueg, to meet with me a little later in the afternoon. But for now, Jean encourages me to rest and settle in. Taking his advice, I venture out for a leisurely walk around the monastery grounds and come upon the community cemetery: nameless unadorned crosses planted closely together behind the church. Just beyond is a trail leading to a small pond and behind that a tree-covered hillside overlooking the complex, a large parcel of property that includes fertile farmland and acreage for cattle to graze.

At the designated time, Frere Hueg — wearing the typical dress of a Trappist, a white habit with a hooded black scapular and a wide leather belt — finds me in front of the guest quarters. His crew cut, ruddy cheeks and solid build give him the appearance of a college athlete or an ROTC cadet. "You know, my English is not so good," he says during introductions. Hueg explains that there is only a half hour for our discussion, so we immediately begin walking and talking. While struggling to keep up with him, I ask if there are still distinctions made today between monks who are priests and those who are brothers.

"You know of the Second Vatican Council in the 1960s, yes?" he asks. I nod my head. "Well, during the Council the distinction between the two was eliminated along with the Latin Mass. There were also revisions to the rigid rules concerning sleep, diet and conversation in the Trappist Order."

He talks about the "rule of silence" outsiders so often equate with the Trappists. "There has never been a vow of silence," explains Hueg. "It's a misconception. Although silence is still valued, it is not an absolute."

I know that at one time monks often communicated through sign during the day, and I ask if it's still used.

"Some of the older monks still use it occasionally, but there really isn't any reason to."

He reveals that there are presently forty monks at la Trappe, but at

*Community
cemetery*

*Childhood photo of
Ste. Therese on a
side door*

24

the community's peak, there were twice that number. Aside from those men who have taken permanent vows, there are now a few postulants and novices, as well as two men who have taken temporary vows.

Traditionally, once a candidate is received into the monastery, he spends the first six months as a postulant, following the monastic schedule but wearing laymen's clothes. If, at the end of that time, the man decides to renew his commitment, he enters the novitiate for two years of training and is given the Trappists' white habit to wear. A novice who has completed his training and wishes to continue is permitted to take temporary vows, a commitment of three years or more, and is presented with a black scapular and the traditional wide leather belt. At the end of this period, he takes solemn, perpetual vows.

"Almost all of the labor here is done by the brothers," Hueg explains as we pass one of the dairy barns. "But we have hired some farmworkers that come in on a daily basis, and there are a few families that live and work in the community." At one time, the idea of a lay family living within the monastic walls would have been unthinkable.

"Obviously your income is from many sources," I say.

"As you can see, we have dairy and beef cattle," he replies. "We sell the beef locally and produce yogurt, milk and cottage cheese from the dairy cattle. Some of our land we farm, and the rest we rent out to our neighbors."

Our conversation is ended by the ringing of the church bells announcing vespers. We walk together into the church. I sink into a pew in the back of the sanctuary, while Frere Hueg takes his appointed place in the front choir with his brothers. This is my favorite service of the day, a time for brief reflection. In his book *Blue Highways,* William Least Heat Moon aptly expresses my feelings when describing his experience at a Trappist vesper service:

> There was nothing but song and silences. No sermon, no promise of salvation, no threat of damnation, no exhortation to better conduct. I'm not an authority, God knows, but if there is a way to talk into the Great Primal Ears — if ears there be — music and silence must be the best way."

Afterward, the guests return to the refectory for a simple evening meal of vegetable soup, bread and fruit — a menu more familiar to my

25

monastic experiences. Our meal is shared in silence.

That night at compline, with flickering candles near the altar providing the only light, the sanctuary is remarkably transformed into a much more intimate space. At the conclusion of the service, the monks close the day by turning to the statue of Mary and singing the *Salve Regina, Mater Misericordiae* as monks have done each evening for hundreds of years. "To you do we send up our sighs, mourning and weeping in this veil of tears," they sing in unison. When the brothers finally file out into the darkness, the abbot blesses each man and sprinkles him with holy water. Watching him repeat the ritual as the guests pass by, one by one, I envision a collective baptism, a reminder of membership within this international community of believers.

Back in Nivard's room, I take time to catch up in my journal before turning in, but I don't sleep long. A series of vivid dreams awakens me, breathless and sweating, a little after midnight. Unable to fall back asleep, I roll out of bed and return to my journal while the dreams are still fresh in my memory, scribbling down as much as can be recalled:

Ambling through the nearby village of L'Aigle, I come upon a long, unwound piece of white cloth saturated with blood; maybe a wound dressing. Picking it up and dragging the cloth behind me, I go in search of an explanation, but all the homes are built high up in the trees beyond my reach. The deserted sidewalks and driveways end at the base of each tree trunk.

But out in the street, breaking up through the asphalt and moving skyward into the sunlight, are sleeping adults loosely tied to circular telephone poles. They are not in pain. It's as if they are being reborn again. The scene then shifts.

Sitting in a Shaker rocking chair in the middle of my la Trappe room, I stare out the arch-shaped window. The space, otherwise empty, is painted a warm, inviting, pastel yellow.

I begin feeling extremely anxious and start rocking slowly and then gradually faster and faster until the chair is moving at breakneck speed. There's a feeling of being totally out of control; it's impossible to stop! "Help me, help me!" I yell out.

The demons have been temporarily exorcised with pen and paper. Sleep comes easier now.

When I wake again a few hours later, one of the monks, probably Frere Jean, is shuffling down the long hallway. The sound of his habit brushing against itself complements the rhythm of his footsteps. I can't go back to sleep. So I lie still, staring up at the ceiling, until time to attend lauds and the Eucharist.

Back down in the church, I happily join my voice to scores of others in Gregorian chant and become part of a tradition that has prevailed for more than a thousand years. There is something very soothing about the repetitive words and the steady rhythm that eventually leads to the receiving of the bread and wine — the body and blood of Christ. Peter Matthiessen's words from *The Circle of Life: Rituals from the Human Family Album* ring out in my mind:

> To this day, I am drawn joyfully to cathedrals in every land — mosques and temples, too — the stone, the light, the soaring naves, the murmuring and mystery and quiet. With gratitude, I kneel and lose myself amidst the bent humanity crouched in the pews. In the great hush, we breathe as one.

Later, I find an English edition of *The Rule of St. Benedict,* and I begin thumbing through the many, many chapters in which Benedict carefully outlines the organization for Christian monastic life in the West. His detailed plan addresses every aspect of a monk's daily life, from mealtimes and diet to periods of community prayer and elections for the abbot. The volume is as relevant to monastic life today as it was thirteen hundred years ago. In his prologue, St. Benedict writes,

> This message of mine is for you, then, if you are ready to give up your own will, once and for all, and armed with the strong and noble weapons of obedience to do battle for the true King, Christ the Lord.

At the midday meal, Jean Pierre informs me that he, too, has arranged a meeting for me with another monk, Frere Gregoire, who speaks English and grew up in the United States. So, I wait in the dining room after lunch. A big man, over six feet tall, exuding tremendous energy and wearing a full black beard, appears and strides toward me.

"I never speak English here at the monastery," the monk tells me after introducing himself. "In fact, my French is much better." He leans his head a bit to the right as he talks, suggesting a sense of curiosity. We quickly decide to hike up the hill behind the pond and talk along the way. He sets off at a fast pace, and I fall in behind.

Frere Gregoire grew up in a French-speaking family in northern Maine, so even in his parent's home English was always the second language. After graduating from college, he taught school in Poland for a few years. On his way back to the United States, he stopped to make a retreat at la Trappe. Because he was so taken by the experience, Gregoire eventually returned and asked to join the monastery. "We younger monks are bringing a new life into the community," he says proudly.

He repeats what Frere Hueg told me yesterday, that "all the monks wear many hats in this community." Some days Gregoire labors as an electrician or farmhand; on others, he works in the laundry and assists in the kitchen. The young brother obviously enjoys the diversity.

He explains how Trappists integrate individual prayer and meditation into their daily lives. "There is time in the early morning set aside for a meditative practice we call *lectio divina,* when we read and reflect on scriptural texts," says Gregoire. "The reflection might be on a word or two or maybe a sentence in the scripture."

When we reach the top of the hill, we stand awkwardly silent, looking out over the holdings of la Trappe. When hiking back down, we agree to visit the Stations of the Cross along the way, symbolic of the stops that Christ made on his way to be crucified outside of Jerusalem. At each station, Gregoire whispers something gently, but unintelligibly. I do not inquire as to the words; these moments seem intensely personal to the transplanted American. After we pass the last station, Frere Gregoire mentions Ste. Therese de Lisieux's reliquary. I've been waiting to ask about this. "I didn't realize that Catholic monks honored relics of the dead as do your Orthodox and Coptic brothers."

"Oh, sure," responds the monk. "There is a closed chapel here at la Trappe with many relics. This community even has a relic of St. Benedict." When we reach the monastery, we go to the monks' refectory to continue our conversation. We prepare cups of mint tea and sit down opposite each other at one of the tables.

"Have you taken your temporary vows yet, or are you still in the novitiate?" I begin.

"I have been in the monastery for three years and have taken my temporary vows."

"So, Gregoire is not your family name, but rather the name you have taken on here at la Trappe?"

"That's right. The brothers are my family now," says the man, blowing over the surface of the hot tea, then taking a sip.

I ask about the vows taken by Trappists.

"There are a number of vows that we honor," he explains, tilting his head as he did when we met. "One is the vow of stability, a commitment to living here permanently. Then there are the vows of poverty and chastity. And finally, we agree to obey our superiors and *The Rule of St. Benedict*." But he says they are not the most difficult aspects of monastic life.

"What is the most difficult part of living in community?"

He hesitates for a moment and then answers, "When I don't get along with another member of the community. Then I have to remember that the primary reason for being here is service to God. That supersedes even personal issues." Before we part, he agrees to send me a cassette recording of his community singing Gregorian chant. He remembers, and I receive it months later.

After compline, the brothers invite me to join them for a special event in the Chapter Room, a space below the church where the community meets weekly to discuss issues and make decisions. In honor of their special guest arriving tomorrow, they are showing a documentary about Ste. Therese's life. Eagerly crowding around the movie screen as the film begins, we pass a large bowl of buttered popcorn back and forth, grabbing handfuls as it goes by. I am reminded that the brothers are like family; it is a feeling I have often experienced in a monastic setting.

At noon the following day, the festivities begin when the arrival of the reliquary is announced by the ringing of the heavy church bells. Watching as the two novices, holding tight to the bell ropes, are lifted into the air, I join the laughter of others at this amusing and unfamiliar spectacle. The tolling bells mark the time and establish the daily rhythm of life here at la Trappe.

Sunshine pours in as the massive wooden doors of the church are pushed open and all the monks excitedly rush outside to welcome their guest. A minivan backs up to the front gate, and several brothers lift out the heavy, ornate, gold-embossed reliquary containing the remains of

Monks and novices carrying Ste. Therese's reliquary to the church

Ste. Therese, and lead the extended procession back into the building. Their stern-looking abbot, wearing a gold lamé and red satin cape and carrying a shepherd's crook, leads the procession behind Therese. He is the shepherd of this flock, the Christ figure in the community.

The narrator in last night's film explained that Therese, a Carmelite nun, joined her order as a teenager and was the model of late-nineteenth-century piety. In her early twenties, she died of tuberculosis and was canonized some years later. According to the narrator, it was her book, titled *Little Way*, a unique restatement of basic Christian truths, that drew so much attention.

By the time we return, the church is overflowing with restless visitors, and the local bishop, dressed in all his finery, has taken his place up front behind the altar. It is a celebratory gathering with incense filling the air and everyone joining in song to welcome one of their own to this place of worship. At the close of the ceremony, the monks, dressed in their hooded white robes, form a half-circle behind the altar and joyfully chant words of appreciation for this special event.

Returning to the sanctuary for solitary meditation in the evening, I discover that the reliquary has been placed on a table in front of the altar; on either side, a monk sits, enveloped in candlelight, silently reading scripture. In the tradition of the Trappists, members of the community will remain with her for the duration of the visit as a demonstration of respect and a way of honoring the deceased.

It feels so very right spending the final evening at la Trappe reflecting on my stay in the company of the Carmelite sister and two of the brothers.

A few days later I board a train in Paris, bound for the village of Nuits St. George, south of Dijon. From there I hitchhike to the Abbaye de Citeaux, the "motherhouse" of la Trappe. The driver of the car lets me out about a half mile from Citeaux, where the outline of the buildings is barely visible through the heavy fog that blankets the French countryside. Only when I finally come upon a road sign that bears a monk's silhouette and the words *ACCES RESERVE AUX MOINES* (Access Reserved for the Monks) am I sure of reaching my destination.

Up the gravel road, past some barns, stands a multistory, rectangular, stone block building. It's very institutional looking, like a government facility, with a circular drive leading up to the front doors. A fountain and a tall, imposing, black metal cross dominate the front yard. Off to one side is a simple church with an unimposing clock tower. It's smallish and very plain with exterior walls of pastel brown stucco. What a dramatic contrast to the traditional monastic architecture of Abbaye de la Trappe.

A Benedictine abbot founded the Abbaye de Citeaux in the late eleventh century. Because he had failed to bring about significant monastic reform at his former monastery in a nearby region, the abbot left, taking with him more than twenty of his fellow monks, and settled in this one-time wooded wilderness of Citeaux. Here, the group of men determinedly reinstituted the vows advocated by St. Benedict — stability, fidelity to monastic life and obedience to his "Rule" — as their Trappist brothers would do hundreds of years later.

Citeaux has had quite a colorful and dark history, like so many other European monasteries. During the fourteenth century, the Black Death and the Hundred Years' War disrupted life significantly at the abbey. Two hundred years later, the community was pillaged and burned to the ground during the Wars of Religion and rebuilt only to be plundered once again by imperial troops in the early seventeenth century. During the French Revolution, one hundred years later, the monks were forced to flee for their lives, and the buildings were sold and later destroyed. In 1846, a Frenchman built a home and school for juvenile delinquents on this very property. Half a century later, the Cistercian Order repurchased the land with the buildings included.

After entering the church through a side door, I wait in an entryway while the monks complete their prayers. When I proceed into the plain, brown-walled sanctuary after they finish, Frere Jean Claude — a tall, thin, handsome man with a gray, flattop haircut — offers his assistance after I introduce myself. "Have you had lunch?"

"I prepared a sack lunch; it's in my bag."

"Well, follow me and I'll show you to the guest refectory. You can eat there while I notify Frere Christopher of your arrival." Over in the dining room, Jean Claude provides hot water for packaged soup and tea and then quickly departs. Sitting at one of the long, wooden tables and running my hands over the thick sheets of clear plastic covering the flowered tablecloths, I begin to feel ill at ease in this drab room and consider leaving. I wonder if it was a mistake to come here. The gray day outside the windows adds to the solemn mood of the place.

Prior to coming to Citeaux, I had called ahead and was informed that the guesthouse was closed during the month of January so that the monks can take their own retreat without visitors. However, it felt very important to come, even if just for a day, and I asked for and received permission to visit.

After finishing my lunch, I wander out into the hall of the first floor. I don't hear or see anyone. The interior of the building is even more institutional looking than the exterior, with its pale green walls and gray tile floor. Returning to the dining room and picking up my coat and shoulder bag, I begin to exit just as Frere Christopher walks in. Short and thin, he wears a pair of tiny wire-rimmed glasses. The white habit, black scapular and leather belt appear to be weighing him down.

"Welcome, Monsieur William," Christopher greets me. "Let's go to the study and talk." He speaks English as if it is his native language. "I apologize for not being able to provide a space to stay. But as I explained, we are closed down in January," he says along the way.

The nearby study is a much more inviting room with richly colored carpets and dark wood paneling. Christopher begins talking, explaining that one of his jobs is teaching theology to the novices who have only taken temporary vows, and reveals some of his observations without any prompting. "This process, in my opinion, is like a hot air balloon," says the monk, drawing his chair closer to mine. "In the novitiate, the men throw the sandbags out to their teachers to lighten their loads. But after temporary vows the bags are put back in the carrier and they have to deal with them." I like his analogy. He is straightforward and seems easy to talk with, comfortable sharing his individual experiences.

"It was after ten years that I became resolved to the monk's life and finally settled into it." Stopping for a minute, he looks down at the floor. "The ten-year mark is a significant one for many monks," the guestmaster says, looking up again. Christopher has been a monk for thirteen years.

"I come from a bourgeois family in Paris," he reveals with a slight smile. "They've been in the city for many years. As you might imagine, they were quite surprised at my decision to become a monk."

Christopher then turns the table and begins asking me questions. He inquires about my family and educational background, as well as my work experiences, which I only briefly talk about because I imagine we're pressed for time. But it's his subsequent question, "Is your life focused on the search for God?" that hangs in midair. Is that what this journey is really all about — my search for God, I ask myself silently, looking out the window at the grayness.

Flashing back to a Mass at St. Andrew's Catholic Church in Portland, Oregon, I recall an event that took place more than a dozen years ago. A few of us were reading aloud a poem by Francis Thompson, *The Hound of Heaven*, in front of the congregation.

> I fled Him, down the nights and down the days;
> I fled Him, down the arches of the years;
> I fled Him, down the labyrinthe ways of my own mind;
>   and in the mist of tears;
> I hid from Him, and under running laughter.
> Up vistaed hopes I sped . . . .

"Is prayer an important part of your work and journey?" he asks quietly, putting his hand lightly on my shoulder as a way of drawing me back into our conversation.

"Uh, at times," I reply, returning my attention to Christopher. "And, you know, sometimes I wonder if my life has been a search for God." We sit for a long time in a comfortable silence.

When getting up to leave, I comment on the unusual architecture of the monastery. Christopher understands and smiles. "The facility we're in was built for juvenile delinquents, as you may know, and at one time there were nearly one thousand youths here. Now, there are thirty-eight monks! In 1998 we will celebrate our 100th anniversary of living in the present facility, and being at Citeaux for nine hundred years," Christopher pauses. "Amazing, isn't it. You must come back and participate in our celebration."

Chapter Two

CHANTING AS WORSHIP

Puer natus est nobis, et filius datus est nobis: Cuius imperium super humerum eius, et vocabitur nomen eius magni consilii angelus.

(A child is born to us, a son is given to us: His shoulders shall bear princely power, and his name shall be called Angel of Great Counsel.)

Chant
Silos Benedictines

The bus slows, passing through the tiny Spanish village of Silos. It is running ninety minutes behind schedule. Perhaps the driver thinks he can pick up time by skipping a stop, but my destination was clearly written on the ticket I presented a few hours earlier.

"Pasada, Pasada!" Stop, I yell from the back. Any seasoned backpacker knows it's a mistake to sit at the rear of the bus. "Silos! Silos!" The driver is acting surprised. Running up the aisle, dragging my pack behind me, I ask loudly as I go, "Donde esta el monestario, señor?" Where is the monastery?

"Alla, alla," he says, pointing back toward the village. Hopping off the bus, I begin walking, thinking that if the monks' final prayer service was early in the evening, then I might have to sleep outside in the cold.

With a full moon lighting the way, I follow the cobblestone road back into the village, where I soon come upon a stone wall, then a locked iron gate. And there's no buzzer in sight. So I move along the wall until it ends at a church. The building's heavy wooden doors are unlocked. Once I'm through them and in the entryway, I see a second set of doors and hear deep male voices singing Gregorian chant from the other side. I slip off my backpack, lean it up against the wall and carefully squeeze through one of the doors into an immense, cream-colored sanctuary.

At the far end of the austere, neoclassical interior, standing near the dark marble altar, are the Benedictine monks of Silos in their hooded black habits. Alone in the pews sit an elderly couple, huddling together, perhaps for warmth, and whispering to each other. I stand still in the back, not wanting to disrupt the chanting of the monks or the conversation of the couple.

The deep sanctuary has an extraordinarily high ceiling and, thus, marvelous acoustics. It's probably possible to carry on a conversation in a normal tone of voice with the men at the other end of the church. I close my eyes and concentrate on the meditative Latin music. The tempo of Gregorian chant is so dependable and unchanging. There are no musical surprises.

Pope Gregory I, the dominant authority in the Roman Catholic Church from the late sixth through the early seventh centuries, was primarily responsible for this monodic style of liturgical music. He commanded that the Church find a way to gather and preserve the monks' chanting, thus putting Christian scripture to notation.

The monks of Monasterio de Santo Domingo are internationally known for their recordings of Gregorian chant, which rose to the top of *Billboard*'s classical and pop charts in the early 1990s. Katharine LeMee, in her book *Chant*, writes that by 1994, almost four million of their recordings had been sold in more than forty countries. She points out that:

> ...the press took up and embellished the story of the black-robed Benedictines and their phenomenal success: their singing was "Preparation for the Millennium," "Monk Rock," "Nothing short of en-chanting," "A Hit 1,000 Years in the Making." Glorious sounds, pure and simple, sung in a language most could not understand, widely attracted the attention of even the younger generation, who flocked to record stores to pick up their copy.

The compline service I've been listening to is ending. Proceeding down the center aisle, two by two, with heads bowed and hands clasped, the "blackrobes" slowly make their way to a side chapel. Each man stops briefly in front of a roughly carved sarcophagus and then walks into the darkness. The old couple also exits, shuffling arm in arm toward the doors, acknowledging me along the way. I watch them walk out into the chilly night air.

Soon one of the monks returns, approaching me hurriedly. He is about my height, with dark blue eyes and thinning gray hair. The man greets me, "Buenos noches, señor."

"Buenos noches, hermano. Me llamo Guillermo Claassen." I call the man brother and introduce myself.

"Muy bien. Me llamo Padre Salgado." Father Salgado extends his hand, offering a welcoming handshake.

I apologize for addressing him as brother, but he just chuckles.

"No importa, no importa," he says. "Tiene una bolsa?"

"Si, si, si," and I rush to retrieve my backpack.

"Venga, venga," the padre commands, motioning for me to follow him. He charges through a maze of long corridors and runs up and down stone staircases. Salgado pauses to unlock gates and doors, ushers me through, and then locks them again. On the way, he explains that my room is on the second floor of the guest quarters.

The place has the feel of a sprawling Spanish villa, complete with dark, ornate wooden chests, high-back chairs covered in red velvet, and wall hangings everywhere, some vividly depicting the Crucifixion. Upon arriving at the guest quarters, the padre points out the dining room and a stairway leading up to my room, then he hands over a set of keys and a daily schedule printed in Spanish. In essence, the schedule is a duplicate of the one at Abbaye de la Trappe.

"Tiene unas preguntas?" he asks. I have no questions, so the monk bids me a good night and dashes away.

I carefully edge up the darkened stairway, fumbling for a light switch along the way. I find a knob on the second floor, and when I turn it full circle, lights along the corridor flicker on, one after another. Midway down the white stuccoed hallway is my room, a large space furnished in a similar fashion to the one at la Trappe. But here, a pair of shuttered doors opens out onto a narrow balcony that overlooks the moonlit countryside. While putting my things away, I hear muffled voices coming from the hallway. But soon the conversation trails off, two doors open, then close, one after the other, and silence returns.

Despite setting my internal alarm clock for early morning vigils, I awaken late, with just enough time to shower and shave before breakfast. I hurry down to the dining room and join two other men, who are eating at a table set for four. "Buenos dias," we greet each other. The food has been laid out on a long cabinet near the kitchen door: coffee with hot milk, hard, sweet biscuits and thick slices of freshly baked whole wheat bread with butter and strawberry preserves.

"Me llamo Guillermo." After giving my name, I begin chowing down because my last meal was yesterday's lunch. They, in turn, introduce themselves as Victor and Jesus. Longhaired Victor wears glasses with thick lenses and is short and slight. A black mustache dominates his face. In contrast, Jesus sits tall, is clean shaven and sports a crew cut. They look to be in their mid-thirties.

"I am a lawyer in a small town not too far from here," Victor reveals when I ask about his profession. This is his first monastic retreat, encouraged by his friend Jesus. "Understand that I am not a religious man, but I am curious about this way of life," he explains almost defensively. "Besides, I am considering leaving my job and making major changes in my life, and need some quiet time to think things over."

Jesus says that he's made frequent retreats here. Religion is an important part of his life, and he appreciates the opportunity to visit the monastery whenever possible. "My family owns a trattoria in Segovia, and I work there full time. The restaurant has been in our family for more than seventy years."

Both men are "muy amable," very friendly, and although they speak some English, the three of us agree to converse primarily in Spanish. After finishing the meal, we meander over to the church, passing through a quadrangle called the cloister, a two-tiered structure with intricate stone carvings on each frieze of the multitude of columns. It's not familiar from last night, probably because I was focused on keeping up with the padre. But in the gentle morning light, its beauty and craftsmanship are striking. The second tier is reserved for the monks, and looking up, we see a procession of hooded black robes quietly moving through the space in single file.

"If you were Spanish," whispers Jesus, "you would know this monastery for its famous Romanesque cloister more than for its music. This cloister is what remains standing from the original monastery." As we walk, he explains that its stone artwork dates back to the eleventh and twelfth centuries.

Romanesque cloister
of Monasterio de
Santo Domingo

Cloister walkway

In the sanctuary, we join a few other laypeople scattered among the pews. The feel of the space seems hardly changed from the night before. The only natural light comes in through a few round windows located high up on the exterior wall. Inviting us to join them in celebrating Communion are the twenty-one Benedictine monks that populate this Christian monastic collective. This act of solidarity among believers, as practiced here, is a simple ritual of eating a piece of bread torn from a small wheat loaf and sipping dry red wine from a common silver goblet.

Padre Salgado approaches me following the Eucharist. "Is everything in order?" he inquires. "Anything I can help you with?"

"Is it possible to meet with one of the monks during my stay?" Salgado hesitates, then says he'll try to make some arrangements and darts away again. Remaining a while longer in the sanctuary, I naturally ponder my first impressions of Silos and how they differ from my view of la Trappe. This community seems so much more reserved at the outset, more protective of its privacy. The architectural style alone suggests that this place is an impenetrable edifice.

I exit the sanctuary to track down a book on Silos, then excitedly return to the quadrangle and continue exploring with reference in hand. According to my information, the cloister in traditional Western monastic architecture was always the center of community life. All daily activities converged upon and then moved out from this square. For example, in the original Silos monastery, the church was constructed north of the cloister, and to the east was the chapter house, where community business took place. The kitchen and the refectory were located to the south, and the monks' cells were built to the west. Because it was always a place for walking and thinking, a space for contemplation, great care and attention were given to the aesthetics of the cloister.

In this quadrangle, atop the columns and carved into each frieze, are depictions of plants and animals amidst elaborate geometrical designs. On the ground floor stand honey-colored stone panels with low-relief depictions of Christ's life, including the Crucifixion and the Entombment, the Ascension and then the Pentecost. All of the carvings are simple and elegant. Scallop shells in one of the designs probably indicates that Monasterio de Santo Domingo was near a connecting route to the eleventh-century El Camino de Santiago, a famous pilgrimage road leading to the city of Santiago de Compostela in northwestern Spain.

James, one of the closest of Christ's disciples, was rumored to have been buried there.

Four walkways converge in the center of the cloister where there sits a circular stone fountain and a popular birdbath, and in one corner grows a tall, dark green cypress tree. In Christian symbology the cypress is a representation of life, one of many to be found in Christian monasteries throughout the world.

In another section of the monastery is a replica of the monk's pharmacy that has been on the site for hundreds of years. At one time, the monastery was a community medical clinic as well as a place to worship; a specialized botanical garden, providing herbs for medicinal use, grew inside its walls.

The extensive history at Santo Domingo is a reminder of the crucial role that similar religious communities played in the development of art and music, as well as in practical education for laypeople and in homeopathic medical care. History also reveals the sometimes negative roles played by Christian monasteries throughout the centuries: Some became fiefdoms; abbots held tremendous wealth and power, and religious practices were the lowest priority for many of the monks in leadership positions.

As happened at Abbaye de la Trappe and Abbaye de Citeaux, there was a period when the monks from Silos had to flee for their lives. After a Spanish government minister decreed disentailment in the early nineteenth century, Santo Domingo remained empty for almost fifty years. During that time many valuable artworks and manuscripts disappeared from the monastic archives.

I return to the guest dining room for lunch and find it empty because Jesus and Victor have gone out for a day hike. Vegetarian fare has been left on the buffet table by the kitchen monk. Not far from the guest dining room is the monks' refectory, where the daily custom at midday meal warrants that each man periodically takes a turn reading from the lectern while his brothers eat in silence. Reading material, usually selected by the monks and approved by the abbot, will vary from contemporary novels to works based on the Bible.

Leaving the monastery in the early afternoon, I exit through the unfamiliar front entrance into a square enclosure. Confronting me is an appropriate wooden sign lettered distinctly in white: *SILENCIO, ZONA MONASTICA*. Built into the monastery wall, not far from the sign, is an old water fountain, protected from above by a carved scallop shell — again the symbol associated with the old Spanish pilgrimage trail, El Camino de Santiago. It was customary to offer religious pilgrims and other passersby a water source so that they might stop to rest and refresh themselves on the route.

From the top of a nearby hill, rocky and spotted with brush, I can look out over the brown, parched land for miles and miles. The red clay tiles on the roof of the monastery stand out amongst nature's muted colors. A few acres of garden plots are visible inside the walls of the three-story, rectangular structure; the complex is fortresslike. Located in a small valley in the north central Castillian plain, the monastery has a rural location, as advocated by St. Benedict. It is a long way from the nearest city.

Returning late in the afternoon, I make a point of attending vespers. I have always found something comforting in the communal prayer services observed daily in a Christian monastery. They provide a sort of touchstone; a constant reminder of community and Creator, they are as dependable and unchanging as the natural rhythms of the day.

By dinnertime, my comrades have returned, and we share the evening meal. None of us talk much; we simply enjoy one another's company. Padre Salgado joins us briefly, and breaking the silence, he asks, "Do you still wish to talk with one of the monks?"

"Yes, if it's not too much of a problem," I reply.

"Well, I have spoken with Padre Pablo who will be happy to meet with you late tomorrow morning. You can gather in the conference room down the hall." When Salgado leaves, I ask Victor and Jesus if they'd care to join me in the morning.

Jesus declines, "No, thank you. I have had many conversations with the monks here." However, Victor accepts the invitation. "Maybe Padre Pablo can give me some insight as to the changes in my life," he comments thoughtfully.

In the early morning, the three of us attend lauds, the service meaning "to sing praises to," and sit in the front pew as the monks enter and take their places in the choir stalls. Then something very unusual occurs. One of the young monks slowly descends the stairs from the

42

Monastery entrance, the silent zone

altar and invites us to join them in the stalls for chanting. I feel honored by the invitation and readily accept. Jesus does as well, but Victor is reluctant and remains seated in the pew.

What a difference it makes to actually participate with the brothers in the sung service, the antiphonal form of this liturgical music dating back to medieval times. No single voice stands out; we are all one, asking and answering in song. The chanting is mantralike — a time for looking inward. An anonymous and particularly apt quotation for this experience says that "A monk is he who separates from everyone in order to unite with all."

I can still feel that sense of exhilaration later, when Victor and I are waiting in the conference room for Padre Pablo, who arrives a few minutes past the scheduled time. Apologizing, he drapes himself over a chair and adjusts his black habit. Pablo's glasses and receding hairline give him the appearance of an academic; a somewhat reserved manner adds to the impression. We introduce ourselves, then briefly explain the reasons for our retreats. I begin by talking about my work, and Victor follows, speaking of the difficult transitions in his life. His boldness takes me by surprise; two hours ago he didn't feel comfortable enough to chant with the monks.

Moving on to the topics we want to ask about, we comment on how small the community is for such a large facility. Pablo admits that it was built for three or four times the number of men currently here. "It's the state of monastic life in the West," he says.

I'm interested in knowing whether or not Santo Domingo has had a history of establishing other branch communities in Spain or elsewhere. "Does this monastery have any 'daughterhouses'?"

"In the past, there were two daughterhouses," the Padre replies. "There was one in Mexico and another in Argentina. However, we no longer maintain that relationship."

"Why is that?"

"There are many reasons, but the primary one is that it's no longer practical." The costs are prohibitive in these days of shrinking monastic populations in the Roman Catholic world.

On a more personal note, I ask about his life in the monastery. "I have been here for ten years," he says haltingly.

"In a recent conversation with a monk at Abbaye de Citeaux, he told me that his tenth year was a decisive one; it was clear only then that he would fully embrace the monastic life. Does that apply to you as well?"

Pablo is silent for a moment, "I think he probably has something there," he allows but then makes no further comment on the matter. It's clear to me that he is uncomfortable talking about his personal life, so I return to discussion of the community.

"I suspect that you're frequently asked about the Gregorian chant recordings. Would you object to talking briefly about the development of the recording business here at the monastery?"

Sitting up straight in the chair, he answers in a very businesslike manner, "Well, let me say this. The brothers are certainly pleased with the recent reception of our recordings outside of Spain. You may not know this, but we have been recording since the early 1970s. However, only in 1994 did our music become available outside of this country." Pausing for a moment and removing his glasses, he rubs his eyes, drawing my attention to the dark circles beneath them, and then continues. "Let me also say that our community has other sources of income, such as our scriptorium and enamel workshop, so we are not solely dependent on the sale of our recordings." Settling into a more relaxed position, Pablo again throws one arm over the back of the chair and crosses his legs.

"Was the first collection, *Chant,* recorded all at once, or is it a collection of previous recordings?"

"The collection is a compilation of works from the last twenty years," he replies. That surprises me, because all the cuts on the recording blend together so well.

I can't help asking whether he is familiar with a particular spiritual writer, one of my favorites, from the United States. I suspect that he will recognize the name. "In my country, there was a Trappist monk named Thomas Merton, a prolific writer who was partially responsible for creating an international dialogue between Christian and Buddhist monks. Do you know of the man and his work?"

"Oh, yes. I am very familiar with him," Pablo's dark eyes light up at the mention of Merton. "As a matter of fact, I help organize an international conference promoting dialogue between Buddhist and Christian monks every four years. We call it the Monastic Interreligious Dialogue. I will give you a copy of our newsletter."

My introduction to this Christian/Buddhist dialogue was years ago.

It was during a retreat at Weston Priory, a Benedictine monastery in Vermont, where the monks observe their early morning prayer service by sitting together on the floor in meditation.

"My plans include a visit to Subiaco, Italy," I tell the padre. Subiaco is where St. Benedict began formulating his book, *The Rule of St. Benedict (Rule for Monasteries)*. "It seems absolutely necessary in my exploration of Western monastic history."

Pablo encourages me. "I think a trip to Subiaco is crucial, too. You will be going to the source." I've asked all my questions, so I quietly withdraw, leaving Pablo and Victor to their personal discussion.

That night at supper, Victor talks excitedly about our morning interview. He was obviously impressed and found his dialogue with the monk very helpful. In fact, he is now considering returning for more retreats and possibly spiritual guidance from Padre Pablo.

I ask if he feels he's already found answers to some of his questions, "Have you come to any conclusions about changing jobs and redirecting your life during this short stay?"

"No, I haven't," he admits. "But I am now more comfortable with the idea of the impending changes."

The next day, Jesus leaves for Segovia after breakfast, and my plan is to catch a bus to the city of Burgos. To my surprise, Victor has decided overnight to remain on retreat an additional few days and graciously offers to walk me to the bus stop. Before boarding the bus, I ask Victor, partly in jest and partly out of curiosity, "If I come back to visit Santo Domingo in a few years, will you be wearing the black robes of a monk?"

"Well, who knows. Come back and find out," he replies with a grin, and he wishes me a good journey, "Que le via bien."

After weeks of on-again, off-again road travel, my journey takes me to the village of Subiaco, Italy, which is folded into a low mountainous region an hour east of Rome. I catch a bus to the village, but I am anxious to reach my destination, the Monastero di Sacro Speco, as soon as possible. Rather than waiting for other transport, I begin hiking up a winding, one-lane paved road but soon cut off onto an obscure path that is nothing but a steep dirt trail overgrown with thick brush.

Pope St. Gregory the Great, in his series of four books titled *Dialogues* written in the late sixth and early seventh centuries, revealed that St. Benedict began his monastic life here in Subiaco. According to Gregory's account, Benedict moved to this area from Rome after Christianity had been accepted as the local religious practice. Upon his arrival, Benedict met a local monk who told him of a hermit's cave near his monastery (then uninhabited), where the future saint took up residence for a few years, surviving on the food his new friend would lower to him in a basket.

Following the years of solitude, some of the local monks insisted that Benedict serve as their abbot, which he did. But over time he was thought too severe, according to Pope St. Gregory, and his brothers tried unsuccessfully to poison him. So, Benedict left but remained in the area, establishing a dozen monasteries. He then moved further south, where he founded a community later to be called Abbey of Monte Cassino. There he continued writing his ideas on monastic life, which were eventually compiled and entitled *The Rule of St. Benedict*. Today, the Monastero di Sacro Speco is built over the supposed cave, or grotto, where Benedict lived a solitary life for those first few years.

~~~~~~~~~~~~~

When I arrive, there is a sign on the entrance door of the monastery announcing that visiting hours begin mid-afternoon, in less than half an hour. While sitting on a wall, waiting, I watch an elderly bearded monk, dressed in a tattered black robe and hoeing a small garden plot beside a lower level of the monastery. A weathered fresco on the wall near the old man looks like a smeared watercolor from this distance. There's no humming or whistling to lighten his load, just a steady work pace with the tool. Peering up at me briefly, he nods ever so slightly and returns to the task at hand.

The Monastero di Sacro Speco is architecturally unique. It perches on, and actually drapes over, the narrow ledge of a sheer rock wall that rises from the valley below. It is built of stone blocks, on multiple levels, molding itself to the contorted rock formations.

At the appointed time, the plain, oval wooden door creaks open, and an old monk bids me good afternoon, then quickly disappears into the bowels of the structure. I follow through a stone arch, and once inside, I am overwhelmed, not only by the architecture but also by the intricately designed, green, black and white marble floors. Colorful frescoes with religious themes, some dating back to the seventh-century Byzantine period, cover every available space on the walls and ceilings.

There is a primitive fresco of St. Francis on one wall, reportedly the first image made of the man. Looking like an awkward folk art figure, he is depicted in fading blues, reds and light browns. Nearby is a series of sometimes-violent biblical scenes painted by members of the internationally known Italian Sienese School. Directly above me, on the domed ceiling, are depicted decomposing bodies in three coffins painted in scarlet, yellows and greens. When I swing around, an angry-looking skeleton riding horseback in pursuit of sinners confronts me. All of these paintings were the texts used to teach the scriptures to the illiterate, when visions of heaven and hell were strongly imprinted upon the minds of the converted or those soon to be converted.

Following the vivid scenes that merge one into another, I wind down through the multiple levels of the monastery until I reach the grotto of St. Benedict, where the opening is cold and damp. Further back, the narrow cave works its way deeper into the mountainside where Benedict may have sought shelter from harsh weather conditions.

On another level, faint chanting can be heard coming from the afternoon prayer service wafting out from behind a closed door. I begin to open it but hesitate and walk away. There is an element of delicious mystery here, an eerie feeling in this enclosed time capsule.

~~~~~~~~~~~

Months later on a return trip, there's an opportunity to meet Padre O'Shaunnesy, the guestmaster of the grotto, who introduces himself simply as John. When first talking with the monk in the morning, I find him abrupt, curt and unpleasant, as if he can't be bothered. However, later in the day, John is cordial and communicative.

Standing erect in his black habit, wearing a black cap pulled tightly down over his head, John's red, bulbous nose and ruddy complexion give him a look of health and vitality. After inviting me into a meeting room labeled "Private" for our conversation, he closes the door behind us. Sitting down opposite me at a wooden table, he begins talking. "I'm an Irishman from Australia," he reveals with a detectable accent. "And I think I know what your first question will be." I don't say a word, but only smile cautiously.

"I requested to come here," he declares. There must be an incredulous

*Guestmaster
Father O'Shaunnesy*

*Sacro Speco clinging
to the mountainside*

49

look on my face because he says it again. "Yes, that's right, I requested to come here." He's enjoying this. There's no hesitation when talking about his history. The man is seemingly an open book. "I have been on location for more than thirty years. And I speak Italian and German, and a smattering of other languages when need be."

Interrupting for a moment I ask, "So, much of your daily labor has to do with taking visitors through Sacro Speco?"

"Yes, that's right, William." He prefers William to Bill. "Eighty thousand people come here every year."

His day begins before dawn and ends with compline after dark. "Following the midday meal, there is a short recreation period when the boys get together, chat and have coffee," he reports. "There are only five of us up here now. But we're part of a larger monastery close by." It occurs to me, when watching O'Shaunnesy, that he resembles a Merchant Marine I once knew — his manner, style and sense of humor. I keep the revelation to myself, but in retrospect I think he would have appreciated my comparison.

"As you know, we follow the teachings of the great St. Benedict. Otherwise, we wouldn't be here, would we?" he comments wryly.

Returning soon to the first-floor chapel, we meet a retired German couple who joins us for the brief walk around the space. O'Shaunnesy is now in fine form, switching from English to German and then back to English once again. He invites us over to an opening on one side of the chapel. When straining to look through the metal bars that cover a room carved into the rock wall, we discover a most peculiar-looking black fresco of the devil. A light has been positioned so as to highlight Satan's face.

"William, that's a reminder of a period of temptation in St. Benedict's solitary life in the grotto. It must have been particularly effective with those that could not read, don't you think?" he asks, raising his bushy eyebrows and grinning.

After we shake hands and say our good-byes, the brother leaves me at the oval door with a parting quote, a simple one from St. Benedict. O'Shaunnesy gives me a wink and in his best Irish/Australian brogue admonishes, "By labor of obedience we go to God. By means of patience we become partakers in the passion of Christ."

Chapter Three

A MONK'S REPUBLIC

*No single man is sufficient to receive all spiritual gifts, but
according to the proportion of the faith that is in each man the
supply of the Spirit is given; consequently, in the common
monastic life, the private gift of each man becomes the common
property of his fellows.*

St. Basil
fourth century

Wandering down from the village to the narrow strip of beach in the
warm early evening, I discover a majestic Byzantine watchtower rising
up from the sand and rocks. In years past, it was an outpost for one of the
twenty Eastern Orthodox monasteries on Mt. Athos, known as the Holy
Mountain. More recently, it was a makeshift home for an English Quaker
couple working in the area under the sponsorship of an international relief
organization.

This coastal village of Oureanopolis, located in the very northeastern
region of Greece and situated a mile from the border of Mt. Athos, has
gone through numerous incarnations over the years. The present community,
half a day's bus ride from Thessaloniki, was designated by the League of
Nations to serve as a center for exchanging populations, following one of
many political shifts between Turkey and Greece in the early part of the
twentieth century. Today, it is a fishing village, an inexpensive weekend
retreat for the natives and a departure point for men making a pilgrimage
to the Holy Mountain.

Later, just before going to bed, I pack a shoulder bag with a change
of clothes, a rain poncho, my shaving kit, one blank journal and a water
bottle. The manager of the hostel where I've been staying has agreed to
store my backpack and other equipment until my return.

Next morning, I rise early, grab an orange, a bread roll and two
cups of strong Greek coffee at the local cafe and jog excitedly down to

the dock. There is a line for the ferry. Scores of other men, almost all Greek, stand anxiously awaiting permission to board. Two lines of folding tables have been set up by government authorities to process our papers. When my turn comes, they take my passport and check it against their records, then ask for a nominal fee. In return, they give me the *diamonitirion:* an official-looking document granting permission to stay on the Holy Mountain for a period of four days.

By midmorning, boarding is complete, and the ferry slowly pulls away from the dock. Beneath a clear blue sky, we head out into the Aegean Sea. "This must be the finest day I've experienced since boating over to the Holy Mountain," exclaims a short, white-bearded gentleman, leaning over the railing beside me. A sailor's cap is pulled down over his head, probably to protect him from the sun. Today the water is calm, but he tells me, "You know, the waters of the Aegean can be very choppy at times, even dangerous."

"So you've been over to Athos a number of times before?"

"Oh, yes. My first spiritual pilgrimage here was twenty years ago. And I've come back many times since." He is a photographer from the United States who has made arrangements to take portraits of each of the abbots during this visit.

"What are some of the changes that you've seen over the years?"

"Well, I have witnessed the rebirth and restoration of Mt. Athos from the 1970s through the 1980s. Now, you know, all the monasteries are cenobitic again."

Cenobitism is a form of monastic life in which the monks live in one complex, hold all property in common and honor a vow of obedience to a superior. Meals and worship services are always community activities. In the sixteenth century, some of the Athonite monasteries adopted an idiorrhythmic style of community whereby the monks were permitted to own private property, eat meals alone and annually elect a committee of their own to govern the monastery. In the years since, they have reverted to cenobitism.

"So, you must be part of the family by now."

"Oh, yes. I've made many friends on the mountain," he replies proudly. "And I always look forward to the reunion."

From where we are standing, the peak of Mt. Athos, outlined by thin streaks of white haze, can be seen clearly. This stretch of land,

ΙΕΡΑ ΕΠΙΣΤΑΣΙΑ
ΑΓΙΟΥ ΟΡΟΥΣ
ΑΘΩ

ΚΑΡΥΑΙ, ΤΗ 2 2 ΜΑΙ 1994 199

Δ/Α № 36809 *

ΔΙΑΜΟΝΗΤΗΡΙΟΝ

Προς

ΤΑΣ ΕΙΚΟΣΙΝ ΙΕΡΑΣ ΚΑΙ ΣΕΒΑΣΜΙΑΣ ΜΟΝΑΣ
ΤΟΥ ΑΓΙΟΥ ΟΡΟΥΣ
ΑΘΩ

Ὁ κομιστὴς τοῦ παρόντος Ἱεροκοινοσφραγίστου καὶ ἐνυπογράφου γράμματος ἡμῶν

ὁ κ. CLAASSEN CORNELIUS

Α.Δ. 070838791

συνιστάμενος ἡμῖν ὑπὸ τοῦ .... μὲ ἄδειαν παραμονῆς ἡμερῶν (4) ΤΕΣΣΑΡΩΝ

ἀφίκετο πρὸς ἐπίσκεψιν τῶν Ἱερῶν σκηναμάτων καὶ προσκύνησιν τῶν ἐν Αὐτοῖς ἀποκειμένων Ἱερῶν καὶ Ὁσίων τῆς Πίστεως ἡμῶν.

Παρακαλεῖσθε ὅθεν, ὅπως παράσχητε αὐτῷ, πρὸς τῇ φιλόφρονι ὑποδοχῇ καὶ πᾶσαν ἅμα δυνατὴν φιλοξενίαν καὶ περιποίησιν πρὸς ἐκπλήρωσιν τοῦ δι' ὃν ἔρχεται αὐτόσε σκοποῦ.

Ἐφ' ᾧ διατελοῦμεν λίαν φιλαδέλφως ἐν Χριστῷ ἀδελφοὶ

ΟΙ ΕΠΙΣΤΑΤΑΙ ΤΗΣ ΙΕΡΑΣ ΚΟΙΝΟΤΗΤΟΣ ΤΟΥ ΑΓΙΟΥ ΟΡΟΥΣ ΑΘΩ

Ὁ ΧΙΛΑΝΔΑΡΙΟΥ ΠΡΩΤΟΕΠΙΣΤΑΤΗΣ

Ὁ ΙΒΗΡΟΠΟΤΑΜΟΥ ΕΠΙΣΤΑΤΗΣ Γέρων Χρυσόστομος

Ὁ ΑΓΙΟΥ ΠΑΥΛΟΥ » Γέρων Νικόδημος

Ὁ ΟΣΙΟΥ ΓΡΗΓΟΡΙΟΥ » Ἱερομ. Ἰγνάτιος

Author's diamonitirion

53

measuring more than thirty miles long and five miles wide at its broadest point, is one of three peninsulas jutting into the Aegean Sea from the northeastern mainland of Greece.

There is a legend regarding the introduction of Christianity on the Holy Mountain in the middle of the first century. (I hear variations on the basic tale many times during my stay.) The biblical figure Lazarus, whom Christ had reportedly raised from the dead, was then the sitting Christian bishop of Cyprus. Lazarus was a friend of Christ's mother, and he had invited Mary to visit. She joyfully accepted his invitation, so the story goes, and the Cyprian bishop sent a ship to Palestine to fetch her. But during the return trip, the ship was blown off course and landed on the densely forested Athonite coast instead of at Cyprus. At that time, Athos was renowned for its pagan culture and was known in mythology as the home of the Greek gods before they moved to Mt. Olympus. According to the legend, when Mary stepped ashore and declared the mountain "holy ground," all the pagan statues and idols came crashing to the earth. The local populace rushed down to the coast, *en masse*, to meet Mary and convert to Christianity.

In terms of recorded history, Christian anchorites were drawn to Mt. Athos as early as the ninth century. The first cenobitic Orthodox monastery, Megisti Lavra, or the Great Lavra Monastery, was built in the middle of the tenth century at the tip of the peninsula, where it still stands today.

By the mid-eleventh century, Emperor Constantine IX had solidified monastic control of the peninsula with an edict forbidding women from setting foot on the peninsula, reportedly in honor of Mary. Since Mary had ordained the peninsula a Christian place, she was to be honored as the only female presence on the thirty-mile stretch of land. His edict also prohibited the military from interfering with the lives of the monks.

Under the continued protection of the Byzantine emperors, monastic life here reached its zenith in the fifteenth century, when all but one of the monasteries existing today were built, and the population swelled to nearly twenty thousand monks. After that, the number dwindled steadily due to conflicts among the monastic communities, frequent political upheavals outside the peninsula, natural disasters and frequent pirate attacks on the defenseless monasteries.

Even in modern times, the communities on Mt. Athos have enjoyed unusual privilege. In the mid-1920s, the Greek authorities decreed that Mt. Athos was officially part of Greece but permitted it to remain autonomous. This decision, in essence, made it the first and only "republic of monks" in the world. In the last three decades there has been a rejuvenation on the Holy Mountain. Young men, not only from Greece, but also from Europe and North America, have been taking vows in increasing numbers. Today, the population is estimated at between eighteen hundred and two thousand men.

These communities, "living museums of Byzantine culture," use the Julian calendar, placing them thirteen days behind the rest of the world, and begin each day at sunset. The monks' hours are filled with labor and private meditation as well as communal prayer and the tasks necessary to providing the hospitality traditionally extended to men traveling to Mt. Athos for — it is to be hoped — a spiritual pilgrimage.

By noontime the Oureanopolis ferry has arrived at Daphni, the primary port on the Holy Mountain, where most of us disembark, including a group of black-robed Athonite monks returning from attending to their business concerns. Waiting to transport us into the central village is an aging yellow school bus, the only one on the peninsula. It fills quickly, and there is standing room only by the time I hop aboard; each of the monks has been given a seat.

"Karyes!" yells the bus driver out the window. Karyes is the seat of government here. The driver starts the tired engine, and we begin the journey over rough terrain, following a dirt road — apparently the only road — that cuts through the forest and across the peninsula. Within half an hour, the dirt gives way to cobblestones. We have reached our destination.

On either side of the long, winding street is a collection of humble shops. Three monks with salt-and-pepper hair stand talking in front of the hardware store, their hands moving as quickly as their lips. Each wears a black outer garment that extends down to the shoes and is cinched at the waist with a wide leather belt. Long, loose sleeves hang to their wrists. Black, cylindrical hats, under which they tuck their long, braided hair, complete their religious garb.

Resting on the curb for a moment, I am struck by the peacefulness of this village. There are no barking dogs threatening to bite my heels, no radios or boom boxes blaring music out into the street, no honking automobiles spewing fumes. Noticeably, there are no women or children either.

Walking deeper into the village, passing a few simple hostels, a cafe and a bakery smelling of fresh bread, I come upon the Protaton, the oldest standing basilica on Mt. Athos, dating back to the tenth century. Unlike any Orthodox basilica in my limited experience, it's designed in the form of a cross, with two stories of arched windows tucked into the brownstone walls and a two-tiered roof covered with red clay tiles. Inside, the dark interior is overlaid with large, colorful fourteenth-century frescoes depicting stern-looking, golden-haloed biblical figures.

The flickering light of the white votives scattered through six rows of holders in a metal stand draws me into the center of the church. Picking up a handful of candles from the wooden box on the floor and leaving some change, I step to the stand, carefully place the votives into the empty holders and whisper a different name as I light each one.

Back out in the bright sunshine, I decide to spend my first night at Monastery Koutloumousiou, a mere twenty-minute hike away. Checking my map for the head of the proper trail, I follow a dirt path that first winds through thick brush and brambles then continues under a canopy of greenery growing in a valley. Approaching the monastery from a distance, I can see the stone tower in one corner of Koutloumousiou and the central dome of the basilica jutting skyward above the walls. Soon I'm standing outside the four-story monastery, where partial wooden rooms with porches extend out from sections on the top two floors. Behind me is a small, open, four-sided brick-and-marble dome that protects a drinking fountain for passersby, a traditional gesture of hospitality amongst the communities here.

The entranceway into the monastery, supported by marble columns, leads to a short tunnel that goes through the thick exterior walls and opens into a courtyard. When walking through, I see a bearded monk beckoning me into a cavelike room on one side, which serves as a place of hospitality for visiting pilgrims. Standing behind a counter, he says something in Greek, motioning for me to take a seat at one of two small wooden tables, and in a matter of minutes is serving me a shot glass of raki and a cup of cool water. A tray of chewy candies and a cup of strong Greek coffee

Preparing to dock at Mt. Athos

Docking at Mt. Athos

follow. The refreshments are a tradition of Athonite hospitality. I hand him my diamonitirion after accepting the coffee, and he enters my name, the date and the document number into a ledger kept behind the counter.

Meanwhile, two other laymen have walked in and taken seats at my table. The taller of the two introduces himself as George and says that he comes from Athens. He has been here before, and he explains that after having refreshments, we must walk up to the third floor in the west wing, find the guestmaster and get room assignments.

Once out into the courtyard, I have a distinct feeling of being cloistered — enclosed inside the walled complex. Throughout the four floors of the interior are a series of open galleries that look down onto the principal *katholikon*, the basilica, in the center of the community. Climbing up to the third floor I seek out a young man named Costas, an eager assistant guestmaster wearing a dark blue sweatshirt over a pair of black pants, with a blue wool cap pulled tightly over his head. His skin is quite pale, as if sunlight seldom touches it.

"Follow me and I'll show you to your room," he says in English, walking down the open gallery, the old wooden planks creaking beneath his feet. "If there are no more single guests tonight, it will be yours alone."

The room is dark with a low ceiling, but I am thankful to see that a window opens out onto the open gallery, allowing some light and fresh air to enter. There are two low, narrow beds, each with a pair of weathered leather slippers beside it. An oil lamp has been placed on the desk in the corner. On the walls hang Orthodox icons of Mary and the Christ child and two saints; one somber face is recognizable as that of St. Anthony. All the paintings are yellow with age.

After washing up in the communal bathroom, I meet Costas back in my room, and he gives me a book titled *Saint Arsenios of Cappadocia*. "This is a good introduction to the life of an Orthodox monk," he explains. "If you wish more reading material during your stay, please just let me know."

"Do you have time to walk me around the monastery?" I ask.

"Yes, of course I have time," says Costas, escorting me out into the hallway. We go back down the steps to the courtyard and begin wandering around the grounds, where two of the interior walls are partially covered with scaffolding, and the white marbled font, a basin for holy water, is under repair.

"How long has the renovation work been going on here?"

"For a few years now," he answers. "You will see renovation work in almost every monastery on Athos. Let's stop here at the katholikon for a moment," says Costas, and we enter an extended outer porch built across the front of the church. This porch gives us access to the doors of the basilica, but they are locked and partially covered by a heavy red velvet curtain hanging from a thick silver rod.

He tells me that the doors are locked following each service. Orthodox services are what Catholic monks might refer to as community worship periods, or divine office, throughout the day.

"Give me your pen for a moment," he says, pulling a torn piece of paper out of his pocket. "I'll draw you a floor plan of the basilica." Costas carefully sketches and labels the building's four distinct sections. "We are now in the *exonarthex*," he explains. The glassed-in porch has carved stone benches extending along either side. "This is where monks or visitors can take a rest from a service if necessary." In some monasteries, the ceilings and walls come alive with religious frescoes, while in others the religious artwork doesn't begin until you pass through the basilica doors.

Another area he's labeled is the *esonarthex*. "This is where you will go during the services," he explains. "There are choir stalls lining the walls, and you will be standing and sitting as do the other monks."

"So, the esonarthex is the seating area for those who are not Orthodox?"

"Correct. But the monks can sit in any of the sections," he adds.

"Will there ever be a time for me to walk into the central area of the basilica?"

"Yes, when we are not having a service you can visit the interior briefly before the doors are locked again."

Costas explains that the monks and Orthodox pilgrims sit in the choir stalls on either side of the nave, the central space in the basilica.

"You see this dotted line?" he asks, pointing down at the paper. "This is the *iconostasis*. In most katholikons it is a wall built of wood, but sometimes marble, from which the holy icons hang." He pauses while I sketch his floor plan into my journal. "In the center of the iconostasis is what we call the 'heavenly gate,' which opens into the sanctuary and the altar behind the curtain. Only the priest and his assistants are permitted into the holy sanctuary." Before leaving me, Costas explains that the next service is just prior to the second meal of the day. "Listen for a tapping sound rather than a bell," he says, walking away.

Returning to my room, I light the oil lamp, more for novelty than out of necessity, and continue recording the recent conversation into my journal. The smell of the burning oil filling the retreat space reinforces the sense of taking a step back in time. When a loud tapping sound breaks my concentration, I walk out onto the gallery to investigate, peering down from the third floor. A monk is holding a varnished wooden board about eight feet long and maybe ten inches wide at either end with a narrow place in the middle so that it can be grasped with one hand: a *semantron*. In his other hand he carries a mallet, beating out a distinct Athonite rhythm, calling the community to the worship service. As he quickly circles the katholikon three times, the rhythm grows faster and louder, then abruptly stops.

Constantine Cavarnos, in his book *Anchored In God*, translates the sound of the rhythm into words using capital letters to denote the strongest beats: "To talanton, To talanton, To tala-tala-talanton." It's a rhythm now imprinted on my brain. According to Athonite legend, this tapping symbolizes Noah calling the animals into the ark to save them from the flood. Likewise, the semantron calls the monks into a spiritual ark, saving them from worldly temptations.

Moving slowly down the steps and through the courtyard into the exonarthex then the esonarthex, I find an empty choir stall. The wood has been intricately carved with figures and the walls are painted with frescoes, but I can just barely make out the images. Religious symbols surround me in an environment filled with sweet incense, and scores of flickering hanging lamps create oversized shadows on the walls. I can hear but not see the brief service taking place in the nave. Afterward, the wool-capped Costas meets me back in the courtyard and escorts me over to the refectory.

"Normally, you would take your meal separately with the other non-Orthodox," he explains unapologetically, "but since you are the only pilgrim this evening you can join the monks." Taking a seat at a table separated from those of the monks, I am the lone non-Orthodox visitor, who appreciates being ignored. My isolation allows me time to absorb this new and mystical environment at my own pace.

A hearty green salad with olive oil, freshly baked whole wheat bread and crunchy green beans smothered with cold gravy make up my first Athonite meal. I pace myself by observing the silent, self-contained monks a short distance away. At a lectern in the corner of the refectory stands one of the men, reading scripture aloud in an expressionless voice, a practice observed for centuries. In less than half an hour, the abbot rings his bell, and everyone stops eating immediately. Following a prayer, we silently exit the dark refectory, and some of us venture outside the monastery for a leisurely stroll around the cloister walls.

We haven't been out long when the tangerine sun begins dropping, and the already familiar rhythm of the semantron beckons us back inside the walls. Much to my surprise, just as I reenter, the gatekeeper closes and locks the heavy wooden doors. They won't be opened again until sunrise. Costas tells me later that only sheer luck and my desire to attend the day's final service kept me from spending the night alone outside the impenetrable walls.

Returning to the esonarthex for the late service, I seek out a choir stall where it's possible to see into part of the nave. The officiating priest, attired in a white brocade robe and carrying a censer, begins the ritual at the heavenly gate in the center of the iconostasis. Swinging the metal incense holder, he regally moves from the gate toward the monks sitting in the nave, blessing each one with the voluminous sweet smoke. The sound of tiny, tinkling bells, decorating the censer, fills the air. Proceeding into the esonarthex, the priest repeats the blessing as each of us humbly bows from our individual choir stalls. The purifying incense washes over me as the priest passes by. "The incense does to the worshipper, through the sense of smell, what the sacred icon does to him through the sense of sight, and what sacred music does through that of hearing," writes Cavarnos in *Anchored in God.*

The next morning, just before the meal, I return to Karyes to request an extension of my permit. Although the Greek authorities commonly allow each pilgrim a maximum stay of four days, the photographer from New York has told me that an extension can be granted under unusual circumstances. An Athonite guard meets me at the front door of the building where the central governing body of Mt. Athos regularly gathers to take care of business. He escorts me to an office on the first floor. In a space just barely large enough for its desk and chair sits a middle-aged monk. The man is clearly busy and addresses me without looking up from his work. "Yes, what is it you need?" he asks in a startlingly deep voice.

I explain that I wish to request an extension of six additional days and briefly describe my journey. I want to visit many of the monasteries in order to gain a better appreciation for life on the Holy Mountain.

"It's very difficult to get an extension," he warns me, continuing to look down at the papers on his desk.

"Yes. That's what I've been told."

Finally looking up, he says, "Leave your diamonitirion with me, and I will speak to my superior. Come back later in the day, and I will have an answer."

When I return that afternoon, I absentmindedly begin whistling while climbing the stairs in front of the building. Immediately two guards rush toward me. "Okhi, Okhi, Okhi," they shout, looking disgusted and making zipping gestures across their mouths. Whistling as well as recreational singing are forbidden on Mt. Athos, a rule particularly difficult for a compulsive whistler like myself to remember. As I reenter the small office, the robed official looks up, smiles and hands me the permit without saying a word. At the bottom of the page, next to "4 days," is "+6 days."

Back at Koutloumousiou, Costas suggests that we talk briefly prior to the next service, and I agree. Grabbing two wicker chairs from his room, he pulls them out onto the third-floor gallery and gestures for me to sit down. "I came here almost eight months ago," he begins, "and will remain a novice until the Holy Father determines that I am ready to take the vows of a monk." Costas explains that Holy Father is the term used for an Orthodox abbot and that preparation can take up to three years.

I have been wanting to inquire about the monks' training on Mt. Athos. "Are there prescribed classes that you take for preparation?"

"There are scriptures to read and recommended books, but no formal classes," he explains. "But that can differ from monastery to monastery. However, I must conform to the rules of the community, attend regular church services and maintain a discipline of obedience at all times." Officially, there are seven prayer services a day, referred to as "canonical hours."

In *O Holy Mountain,* M. Basil Pennington, a Trappist monk from

St. Joseph Abbey in the United States, writes,

> For the Orthodox, in the making of a monk there are three elements: the profession, which takes the form of a series of questions and answers in which the candidate declares his intentions; the tonsure, which signifies coming under the authority of the abbot; and receiving the monastic habit, which means taking on a new way of life.

Father Pennington goes on to say that tonsuring once meant shaving the head, but on Mt. Athos today, the act is symbolic: Only four snips of hair are cut off in the shape of a cross.

"In Catholic monastic communities there is some form of regular confession for all members of the community," I say to Costas. "Does this practice exist in Orthodoxy?"

"Oh, yes. We call it *starchestvo*. It's a time set aside to reveal temptations and inner thoughts to the abbot," he replies. "It is done almost daily."

"It becomes part of the regular schedule?"

"In a sense, yes. You see, our days are basically divided up into three activities: prayer, work and rest," says Costas. "We rise at about 6:00 A.M., Byzantine time, which is about six hours after sunset, and pray individually in our cells for an hour."

"So, according to the clock in the outside world you are getting up at 1:30 or 2:00 A.M.?"

"That is right, and after private prayer we go to the katholikon for the liturgy and communion, lasting between two and three hours."

"Do you then start work?"

"No, we return to our cells and sleep for a few hours, then rise again for an additional service before our first meal of the day." I'm only now beginning to fully appreciate the demands of this monastic life as Costas continues outlining their daily schedule. "It's after the meal that we begin working at our assigned tasks for maybe two hours, followed by another period of rest or study."

I inform Costas that I have read most of the book he gave me yesterday and ask if he can recommend any others on Orthodox monastic prayer or their methods of meditational scriptural reading.

Costas thinks for a moment, looking out over the railing. "Do you know the book titled *Way of the Pilgrim?*"

"No, it's not familiar."

"It was written back in the nineteenth century by a Russian Orthodox layman who was searching for a way to pray unceasingly. The book focuses on what we, as Orthodox monks, call the Jesus Prayer," he says, and repeats the prayer, "'Lord Jesus Christ, Son of God, have mercy on me a poor sinner.'"

"So, the prayer is repeated over and over, similar to a mantra?"

"It is similar. It is learning to pray [silently] with each breath. On the inhale you recite to yourself 'Lord Jesus Christ, Son of God,' and on the exhale 'have mercy on me a poor sinner,' until it becomes second nature in your life."

I make a point of noting the book in my journal and writing down the unfamiliar prayer as we continue talking. "Costas, has there been any one thing that you've particularly missed from your former life since becoming a novice?"

The gentle, fair-skinned man answers without hesitation, "I miss my hobby of photography. But I felt it was important to give it up for the monkhood."

"Maybe in the future you will find a way to integrate your photography skills into monastic life," I say without thinking. "You know, taking photos of the other monks or the architecture on the Athos countryside could be a way of sharing your life with others."

"I never thought of that. Maybe that is a possibility." He seems to like the idea.

I spend most of the next day lost on the confusing trails around the peninsula. Some routes are clearly marked in white letters (in Greek, of course) on simple wooden signs, but others force the hiker to guess which way to turn. The heat and humidity only add to my frustration and uncanny ability to make the wrong guess.

Luckily, I meet up with another pilgrim on foot who has a much better sense of direction and a keen sense of humor. His name is Trevor, and he is a middle-aged art teacher from Port Elizabeth, South Africa. We hike together until his journey takes him down toward the coast while mine leads me to Monastery Philotheou, situated on a plateau at the top of a steep, winding, sometimes overgrown path.

Entering through another dark archway, I am hot, my clothes are soaked with perspiration, and I am looking forward to the traditional refreshments. Two guestmasters, one in civilian clothes and the other in monk's robes, bid me welcome, and one records the pertinent information from my permit into the monastery's ledger. Their offer of raki, some chewy candies and a glass of cool water followed by black coffee is gratefully accepted. The server, wearing a shirt and black slacks and looking more Latin American than Greek, introduces himself as Andres. As we talk, his story becomes more and more interesting.

I start with a casual question: "You aren't from Greece, are you?"

"No, I'm originally from Chicago and have been here for only one month," he tells me.

His reply is unexpected. "Are there other novices or monks here from the United States?"

"Oh, yes," he responds. "Not only from the U.S. and Canada, but also from Western Europe."

"Can we talk later?" I ask as he gets up to welcome more pilgrims walking into the monastery.

"Sure, I'll look for you when I have some free time."

Because I spent much of the day wandering, my arrival is quite late, and vespers is about to begin. So a monk quickly shows me to a room for a shower and a change of clothes. Rather than attending the service, I rest and join the community members when they leave the basilica and go to the refectory.

This is a festival day, related to the Orthodox Easter celebration, and a special vegetarian meal has been prepared, complemented by a full-bodied red wine. One of my non-Orthodox tablemates informs me that all of the vegetables come from the monks' garden and the wine from their vineyards. Surprisingly, a contingent of military men in full uniform is seated with the monks in the front of the refectory. Andres tells me later that military personnel come here four or five times a year for meetings, but he doesn't seem to know why. They make me uneasy. This won't be my only encounter with the military on the peninsula. Their presence remains a mystery.

Wandering the divided courtyard after the meal, just prior to compline, I meet another American named Tim Johnson, a professor of religion at a small school in the northeastern United States. He is friendly and eager to share his experiences, and even his clothes reflect his relaxed attitude. He's dressed casually in a plaid sport shirt, khaki pants and penny loafers. "I come here every May to catalogue the monastery's library collection that dates back to the eleventh century," says Tim.

"You must have seen many changes."

"You bet I have," he says. "For example, back in the 1970s, there were three monks, followers of an Athonite hermit named Joseph the Cave Dweller, who requested and were given permission to come to Philotheou to live."

"Back then, this monastery was idiorrhythmic rather than cenobitic, correct?"

"Yes, that's right. You've been doing your research. The monks had their own living spaces, cooked their own meals and owned private property," he pauses a moment, glancing at his watch, then continues his story. "Anyway, these three monks initiated a movement to return this community back to cenobitism."

"Obviously they were successful."

"I'll say. Philotheou is now a hotbed of conservative Orthodoxy and strongly opposed to the international Ecumenical Movement. In fact, this very day they are sending a delegation to visit their Patriarch in Constantinople to propose that Mt. Athos be given the right not to become part of the Ecumenical Movement." In Greece, Istanbul is still referred to as Constantinople.

"I met a man named Andres earlier," I tell Tim, "and he says there are a number of monks here from the United States."

"That's right. There are close to a dozen North Americans, from the U.S. and Canada, who have joined the monastery as a result of annual visits to the States by a former abbot of this monastery."

I'm curious to hear the professor's viewpoint on why there has been a resurgence of interest in monastic life. While I have already asked several monks about it, they, of necessity, view the matter from within their communities.

"Oh, I think it's a combination of things. Young people become disillusioned with urban life, crime, pollution, meaningless jobs; lots of things." His answer strikes me as very much that of an academic. He refers almost clinically to external forces, not mentioning the internal — the "calling" of which monks often speak.

Walking into the katholikon that evening, I notice for the first time a large eye painted in the triangular, glass-covered window. It's just under the roof of the small porch protecting the entranceway. Someone tells me it's the "eye of God," positioned so that it observes whoever enters or exits. The eye is a Christian symbol for both the ever-present God and for the Holy Trinity: Father, Son and Holy Ghost. Continuing on into the dark esonarthex of the basilica, I take a choir stall close to the entrance, near that of an old, bent-over monk who is chanting brokenly, wheezing with every labored breath. I haven't been there long when a younger monk strides in from the nave. He comes straight toward me as if he'd seen me enter, and I immediately think of the watching eye outside.

"Are you of the faith?" he demands in a loud whisper.

He must mean Orthodox. "No, I'm not."

"Then you must sit in the exonarthex," he says, pointing to the doorway and escorting me into the outermost hallway of the basilica. It's a very awkward situation.

Professor Johnson's earlier comment, "hotbed of conservatism," comes to mind as I am settling into the lone choir stall, next to the benches, on the other side of the basilica doors. Now, the rituals of the service are very far away, and I am distracted by my anger and weariness. But gradually there comes the realization that I am just a guest in this house of worship and on this republic of monks, not a citizen with full privileges. Recalling the Jesus Prayer, which Costas taught me at Monastery Koutloumousiou, saves me from my anger. I inhale and silently begin: "Lord Jesus Christ, Son of God"; exhale, "have mercy on me a poor sinner." Repetition of the prayer successfully carries me into a deep meditation that lasts through the end of the service.

Before departing in the morning, I arrange to meet Andres in the visitors reception room, where he reveals that he is one-quarter Chinese and three-quarters Guatemalan, among other things. Andres is anxious to tell his story. "I received my plumber's journeyman card just this last year in Chicago, so my salary increased significantly, but then I was fired," he explains.

"Had you met someone in the Orthodox Church prior to your firing?" I ask the plumber.

"Yes, at work. You see, when I was nineteen I had a spiritual crisis that was very, very difficult for me. At that time I sought advice from an Orthodox man on my job site. He was extremely helpful, introduced me to his family and eventually welcomed me as part of the family. So that's how my interest in the faith began."

"Andres, have you made up your mind whether or not you will stay here and enter the monkhood?"

"No, I'm not clear. I have not made a commitment at this point. But I'm very, very happy to be here. I have never been so content."

~~~~~~~~~~

Midway through my visit to the Holy Mountain, on yet another long hike, I find a well-marked trail that leads me down to the third oldest monastery on the peninsula, located near the beach on a picturesque bay. Because it is easily accessible, Monastery Iviron is frequently filled to capacity with pilgrims. Its five stories, under repair, enclose one of the largest courtyards that I have yet seen on Mt. Athos. An old, extremely tall cypress tree grows to the side of the katholikon, which, like so many on the mountain, is painted a deep, dark red.

I have plans to visit two other monasteries in the same day, so I arrive early to secure a place for the evening. The reception room is empty. Slowly, through the doorway there comes a tall, stoop-shouldered, white-bearded monk, who introduces himself as Kalogeros (Monk) Iakovos, the temporary guestmaster. He reviews my permit with a puzzled look. "Oh, I see you have an extension of six days," Iakovos finally says. "You must be one of the 'special ones.'"

"Well, I don't know about being one of the 'special ones,' but the authorities were kind enough to give me an extension," I reply. He offers no further explanation of his comment but, rather, goes on to tell me something about himself, quickly putting me at ease.

"You know, I have been to the United States many times, from Portland, Maine, to Portland, Oregon," he says slowly, expressing the considerable distance with his long outstretched arms. "I like both of those towns very much." His clear, green eyes hold my attention.

"Me, too. I lived in Portland, Oregon, for a few years and visited Portland, Maine, a few years back.

"Have you been here for many years?" I ask, pulling up a chair and sitting close to the curious old man. I know that some men join the monastery after they retire from their jobs in the outside world.

Monastery Simonos Petra (not in text)

Monastery Iviron

"Have I been here for many years?" he repeats my question. "No. I'm really only the gatekeeper here, filling in for the guestmaster. So I'm not very important; second man from the bottom." He avoids giving me a direct answer.

"Where are you from originally?"

"Where do I come from?" he responds. I wonder if he is mocking me or just kidding around.

"It's not important where I come from or what my profession was," he says emphatically without raising his voice. "What's important is to be aware of what we're doing right now, in the moment."

After a period of silence, I change the subject. "Today I am planning to hike over to Monasteries Stavroniketa and Pantokrator and then return here in time for vespers. Is it possible?"

"Oh, sure, it's possible. Just keep a steady pace." His response renews my sense of confidence.

"I'll tell you what. If you return from your hike before vespers, you can find me in front of the katholikon. If you like, we can sit together during the service. And afterwards I'll take you into the nave and show you some of the frescoes in the domes and on the walls."

I leave right away, and when I return hours later, I find Iakovos sitting alone in the courtyard, waiting. He immediately motions for me to join him. "The service will begin shortly, so why don't we walk on in," he suggests.

"Well, I should clean up first."

"You're fine," he comments, taking my arm. "You can get cleaned up before you go to bed."

Covering the ceiling and interior walls of the glass-enclosed exonarthex of the katholikon are worn and aged frescoes in which I can just barely make out the saints. Red, yellow and blue panes of glass in the hallway windows catch the sun and create pools of color on the rough marble floor. Stepping into the dusky basilica arm in arm, we take seats in adjoining choir stalls and watch while the others file in.

"Today vespers will be a 'low service,' which means there will be less chanting and singing," Iakovos whispers, his breath smelling of garlic. "It is low because today is not a feast day or special church holiday." He sits for a moment in silence then adds, "You know, our Psalter is divided up into twenty-eight sections. We repeat three sections at the liturgy and

Eucharist service in the morning and one every night at this time." Their Psalter is the book of Psalms organized for use in Athonite churches.

By now my eyes have adjusted to the dark, making it possible to identify the oftentimes wrinkled and always bearded faces of the black-robed figures here in the esonarthex. The interior of the katholikon still has a mysterious feel. It is more somehow than just the darkness and the fact that the language is foreign to me. It also has to do with these scores of flickering oil lamps hanging down in strategic positions and the multitude of icons they highlight.

Sitting next to Iakovos, I feel a strong sense of connection and familiarity with the man, something I've not often experienced on the road. I am drawn to him and appreciate the opportunity to simply be in his presence. His distinct smell of wool and sweat reminds me of other people and earlier years.

I cross my legs in the choir stall, and Iakovos gently reminds me of the rules of conduct: "You know, Orthodox monks are peculiar people. They don't want men to cross their legs while in the katholikon." I immediately put both my feet on the floor and sit up straight. He continues, "You might also keep in mind that if you fold your hands, do so in front of you, not behind you."

Soon the officiating priest begins making rounds in the nave with the silver censer. Stopping in front of each individual, he swings the censer sharply and offers a blessing. As the priest enters the esonarthex, Iakovos again guides me, saying, "The priest will be most happy if we stand and bow when he passes by." Happy to have a mentor, I mimic his every gesture.

Casually taking my arm at the conclusion of the service, the old man escorts me into the nave, asking me to sit down for a moment while he gives a brief lecture, in Greek, to a group of laymen. I watch as he interacts easily with the men, joking with them and enjoying their company. I admire his lack of self-consciousness. As he finishes, one of the Greek visitors bows down to kiss Iakovos' hand, a gesture of respect, but the monk abruptly pulls his hand away. It's an uncomfortable moment for them both. After the group leaves, I ask why he refused to allow the man to kiss his hand. "Because I am not worthy," he answers. His reply and my own response to it startle me: Tears begin welling up in my eyes. I have to look away to compose myself.

"Now, Mr. Claassen," Iakovos says, quickly shifting to a lecturing tone, "Let me explain the usual order of the frescoes in an Athonite basilica." Taking a few deep breaths, I focus on what he is saying and follow him to the center of the room; there he directs my attention to the ceiling. "Almost always, you will find the Pantokrator, a painting of Christ the almighty and ruler of all, in the central dome, the center of the universe." A colorful and decorative bust of a longhaired, bearded Christ, holding the scriptures in his left hand and offering a blessing with the fingers of his right, looks down upon us.

Iakovos strokes his long beard for a moment, seeming to gather his thoughts. Then he continues. "You know, in the days of widespread illiteracy, uniformity of images was a way to teach and reinforce the biblical personalities and stories to the peasant monks and laymen." These images on the basilica dome remind me of the Sacro Speco interiors in Subiaco, Italy.

After the lesson on frescoes, I ask if I might be permitted to see the relics of Iviron. The monastery is reported to have many, including the right hand of Basil the Great, one of the major figures in Eastern Orthodox monasticism.

"I'm afraid it is not possible," he answers. "Only those of the faith are permitted to do so." His reply does not come as a surprise, but it is disappointing nevertheless. Relics in the Orthodox tradition are important objects of veneration. Every Athonite monastery has a unique collection of bones, skulls and maybe hands, as well as other physical parts of holy men that have been preserved and are believed to have miraculous powers. Often these special relics are enclosed and sealed in decorated wooden boxes or gem-encrusted metal cases.

Leaving the basilica together and taking a seat in the courtyard, we wait for the refectory to open. Iakovos asks if I've ever heard of Iviron's famous icon "Panaghia Portaitissa," the mother of God. I tell him that it was mentioned by one of the other monks and ask if it is on view.

"Sorry, my friend. The doors to the chapel where it is kept are temporarily locked. So it is not possible to see the icon," he explains. "But I can certainly tell you the story behind it. Do you know the legend of the Virgin Mary landing on the peninsula?"

"Yes, it's familiar. It is said to have occurred in the year A.D. 49."

"That's right. Now to the story of 'Portaitissa.'" He looks away for

Pantokrator in a katholikon dome

a moment as if conjuring it up in his mind, then he begins the tale. "The legend says that there was a woman of high regard in Constantinople who threw the icon into the sea to protect it from being destroyed by the iconoclasts. And it was floating for seventy years before landing on the coast near to Iviron. The monks here knew where to find it because a column of light shone onto it from the heavens.

"Well, the story goes that the monks picked it up and put it into our katholikon with all of the other icons. But on three different occasions, the icon, quite on its own accord, moved out of the basilica to the entrance gates. So that chapel over there," he says, indicating a small, red and white painted domed building in a corner of the courtyard, "was built specifically for the icon." Each monastery on the mountain has particular, unique icons that receive special treatment and are credited with miraculous feats, as are the relics.

When the refectory doors finally open, Iakovos enters with his brothers, and I follow with the other laymen; inside, we divide into Orthodox and non-Orthodox and claim our respective tables. Once the abbot rings his bell, we begin passing around the bowls of food. Today there is a special treat, boiled eggs that have been dyed a dark red. This is the church's color for martyred saints and, during Pentecost, for commemorating the coming of the Holy Ghost.

Roused at 2:30 A.M. by the now-familiar beat of the semantron, I quickly dress, pick up my flashlight and leave the room. No one else is stirring in the guest wing, including my two roommates, and I cross the courtyard and enter the basilica. At this first service of the day, all the Athonite monks raise their collective voices in prayer to the heavens, singing Psalm 150.

> *Praise the Lord in his sanctuary,*
> > *praise him in the firmament of his strength.*
> *Praise him for his mighty deeds,*
> > *praise him for his sovereign majesty.*
> *Praise him with the blast of a trumpet,*
> > *praise him with lyre and harp,*
> *Praise him with timbrel and dance,*
> > *praise him with strings and pipe.*
> *Praise him with sounding cymbals,*

praise him with clanging cymbals.
Let everything that has breath
praise the Lord! Alleluia.

From my choir stall, it's possible to observe more of the movements of the priest, his assistants and their fellow monks up front in the nave than in previous services. At the closing of the service, each monk leaves his stall, walks to the iconostasis and kisses the holy icons. Beginning with the painting of Christ, hanging to the right of the heavenly gate, the monk crosses himself, places a kiss on the glass cover and then moves to the next icon and the next, repeating the gestures of reverence at each painted figure. Returning to the first icon to the left of the gate, the Virgin Mary and Christ child, he repeats the ritual, moving in the opposite direction down the row of icons.

For me, the clearest definition of an Orthodox icon was written by the Greek theologian Nikephoros Theotokis, who lived in the late eighteenth and early nineteenth centuries. Cavarnos quotes him in *Anchored in God:* "The Orthodox do not deify nor worship the holy icons, but through them lift up the mind to the person(s) represented, venerating and kissing them out of their aspiration of love for the prototype."

A few hours later, I look for Iakovos to thank him in person. But even though I delay my departure from Iviron, I can't find him. Tearing a blank page from my journal, I write a short note and leave it taped to the desk in the reception room. A strong sense of his presence will remain with me for months to come.

Today I plan to hike across the peninsula and along the coast to the Russian Monastery Panteleimon. Rather than hiking along the rutted, dusty road, I opt for the pass that cuts right through to the other side of the peninsula. After maneuvering along the winding trail for not more than half an hour, I come upon a chapel. Its walls are painted a bright red and blue, and its dome is gray. Behind the chapel sits a white stuccoed cottage, wisps of smoke escaping from its chimney. The two buildings are enclosed by a whitewashed stone wall. Walking through the light blue wooden gate into the small courtyard, I call out to anyone who might be about.

Out the door of the cottage lumbers a big man who introduces himself as Girosimos. He isn't wearing the usual hat, black robe or leather belt around his waist; rather he is dressed in a white peasant shirt and loose-fitting black pants. The monk's long salt-and-pepper hair is pulled back into a ponytail, and his eyes are mesmerizing. They are extraordinary: an intense, penetrating ice-blue. I resist glancing away and stare directly into them.

"I live here with my 'spiritual father,' Father Maximus," he tells me, explaining that his mentor lived at Iviron for a half century and in this cottage for almost four years. "He's blind now and unable to cook or walk by himself, so I have come from the monastery to stay with him indefinitely."

"Please come into the chapel." He motions for me to enter. Inside stands a miniature altar, and playhouse-sized icons hang from the walls. A line of scented votive candles burn near the base of the altar. Even in this small chapel, Girosimos keeps his voice barely above a whisper as he answers my questions about how the chapel came to be here.

"Father Maximus built it, next to the tree where a miracle once occurred," he says, tightening the band around his long ponytail. He seems out of place in the chapel without the monk's uniform of head-to-foot black.

"And what was the miracle?" I ask as we move outside and sit down on the ground.

"Many years ago," he begins, "there was a traveler on the Holy Mountain who stopped at Iviron Monastery toward the end of the day to ask for some bread. But the gatekeeper turned him down. So the traveler walked away sad, hungry and tired. When he came to that tree over there," says Girosimos, pointing to the gnarled one behind the chapel, "the traveler sat down next to it and fell into a deep sleep." Even outside, his voice is low and gentle, and I move a bit closer to better hear him. "In a dream the Virgin Mary appeared to him, the very same Mary from the famous Iviron icon. She gave him a gold coin and told him to return to Iviron and buy some bread. When the traveler awoke, a gold coin was in his hand, which he took back to the monastery. Well, when the gatekeeper heard his story, he realized what had happened and provided the traveler with food and hospitality."

Girosimos explains that in 1960 Father Maximus built the chapel and used it as his prayer site every night. When he could no longer manage the daily trip from Iviron, the senior monk decided to live here. A weak,

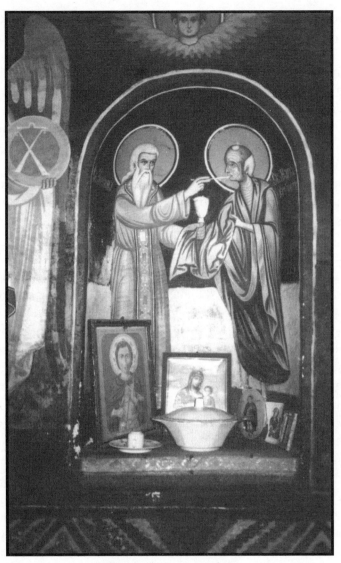

Altar in an exonarthex

pained voice calling out from inside the cottage interrupts our conversation. Through a gauze curtain hanging in the entrance to the cottage, I can just make out the figure of a bearded man sitting up in bed. "He wants something to eat, so I must go," says Girosimos, waving good-bye and hurrying away to care for his spiritual father.

I move on and reach Karyes by midday. There is time to have a simple vegetarian meal and a welcome stein of cold beer at one of the two small cafes in the village. Paying for my meal back in the kitchen, I am taken aback to discover a lone blackrobe, who seems almost to be hiding behind the counter. With a cigarette in one hand and a beer in the other, the stout, disheveled, solitary monk is a most unusual sight. He looks up at me briefly with his watery, bloodshot eyes, and then looks away.

In the late afternoon, I am hiking up a steep, heavily wooded hillside toward the rear of Monastery Panteleimon, tearing through an obscure path long overgrown with weeds and vines. Suddenly, before me is a four-story brick wall with empty window frames, standing alone like a movie set facade. The wall is what remains after a serious fire many years back that destroyed the former guest quarters operating out of an old wing of the monastery. Visitors were welcomed into this once-grand reception space called the "tsars' room," a remnant of old Russia. Beyond the wall are eight green, bulbous "onion" domes, pierced with gold crosses, sitting atop the katholikon, and a scattered assortment of buildings in ill repair. The community has the appearance of a large village rather than a monastery. The entire complex, sitting in a pine grove, overlooks the greenish blue sea.

In the early twentieth century, Panteleimon was the wealthiest and most populated monastery of any on the peninsula and home to more than a thousand monks. After the Russian Revolution of 1917, the money dried up, and new recruits stopped coming. Later, the governing body in Karyes wouldn't permit new Russian converts into the monastery for fear of Communist infiltration.

By now, I've reached the courtyard, and I follow a group of laymen into a dusty old reception room. We take our places on the scratched wooden pews that are aligned with the exposed beams in the ceiling above.

The guestmaster welcomes each visitor into the community by handing him a tiny, green-enameled cross, like a lapel pin. The manner of the monks is lighthearted and welcoming. The guestmaster and his assistants are gregarious, laughing and socializing with us while serving the refreshments.

Nikos and Chris, two young pilgrims from Athens, strike up a conversation with me in English, and we quickly take to one another. The two seem very different. Chris, well muscled and in his early thirties, is a truck driver from Athens. Nikos, his friend from boyhood, wears old-fashioned black glasses with thick rims and works as a banker. Soon they begin conversing with one of the Russian monks who has a cherubic, freckled face and frizzy red hair sprouting from the top of his head. Brimming over with energy and talking nonstop, he offers to show us some of the monastery's prized relics.

"Are there restrictions as to who can go?" I ask Chris, always cognizant of my status.

"He hasn't said anything," Chris replies, "so come on and follow us."

Escorting us across the courtyard, past the katholikon painted an unusual rich terra cotta with blue-and-white trim, the boisterous red-haired Russian leads our group to the third floor of the north wing. The hallways with their sagging floors are dark and look neglected, but the chapel that we enter is spectacular. Sunlight, pouring in through the bare windows on one side, accentuates the iconostasis covered in gold leaf and laden with hanging icons in gilded frames.

My eye is drawn to the collection of relics, enclosed in richly decorated wooden boxes with glass covers, sitting on an ornate, dark wooden table in the back of the large room. In one box is a hand with dried flesh the color of leather, and in others are collections of bones. Many times monks have told me that the sacred relics will always emit a sweet odor, a sign of their holiness. So I pick up each one carefully and smell it, only noticing a peculiar, sweet odor to some. But Nikos and Chris insist that they all emit the holy scent.

Later, during vespers, buoyed by my recent experience viewing the relics, I dare to walk into the nave and take a choir stall between two Orthodox laymen. No one tells me to leave. This will be the only monastery in my Athos experience where I am permitted to worship in the main body of the basilica.

*Katholikon of
Monastery
Panteleimon*

Inner courtyard of Monastery Panteleimon

At the evening meal, I am struck by the size and beauty of their refectory. Rebuilt in the late nineteenth century, it has seating for many hundreds of men, and its interior walls are covered in frescoes. In this expansive dining room, the servers have to practically run to deliver all the plates of potatoes and bowls of cabbage soup in a timely manner. Again, there is a lightness of being, an almost tangible joyfulness here at Mt. Athos' only Russian monastery. In the years since the fall of the Soviet Union, money and young novitiates have begun to trickle back into the monastery, which I'm sure improves the monks' attitudes and sense of well-being. No doubt, cultural differences play a part in my perceptions, as well.

Back out in the courtyard, Chris and Nikos say that this evening there will be an all-night service. It is one of many observed throughout the year. "All-night services on Athos are as frequent and physically demanding as their many 'days of fasting,'" explains Nikos. My new friends decide to go to bed early, but I return to the nave as the marathon worship service begins, marveling at the informality practiced inside the basilica. There are constant whispered, usually brief conversations and uninhibited movement throughout the building.

M. Basil Pennington describes the situation in *O Holy Mountain:*

> The scene in the katholicon ... was seemingly holy chaos. While the priests ... were receiving Communion behind the screen and the cantors were chanting beautiful Communion hymns, some monks were running around pulling down chandeliers or carrying long sticks to put out the dozens of candles lit for the service. Other monks and laypeople were going in many different directions venerating the icons, some were sitting in the stalls conversing, others were settled deeply in their stalls evidently enjoying intimate prayer (or sleep). It is a chaotic scene to Western eyes.

~~~~~~~~~~~~

Two days before departure, my journey leads me to St. Anne's Skete, where monks live in cottages spread out over the lush green mountainside. Each skete shares a common katholikon and remains dependent upon one of the twenty major monasteries. Such an arrangement is not uncommon on the peninsula. Today, I will either climb to the top of the Athos peak or return to the dock to wait for the daily mail ferry, hoping it will sail to the oldest monastery, Megisti Lavra. For the past two days, the ferry's captain has canceled the trip because of choppy and dangerous waters.

Before starting up the mountain, I filled my water bottle in the kitchen and received warnings from the monks there to watch carefully for poisonous snakes. A few minutes into the climb, I happen to pass by a wooden crate full of bones, behind a black wrought-iron gate, upon which sits a sun-bleached skull. It's common practice here for the monks to exhume the bodies of brothers after years of burial, clean and dry their bones and then place them in the charnel house of the community. The bones are sacred relics to the Athonite monks.

Kneeling beside the skull, I carefully copy down the black lettering printed across the forehead. (I'm later able to translate the Greek. It reads, "Christopher Monk, from the kalyva hut, in the year 1986.") After sitting for a long time communing with the relics, my plans suddenly change. Turning back, I trek back down to the dock to wait, once again — but with confidence — for the ferry. There's nothing rational about my decision, just a gut reaction. An hour later the ferry pulls up to the dock. The captain, recognizing me from the days before, flashes a big grin and yells, "Going to Lavra?" He welcomes me aboard.

The Aegean is choppy and the ride adventurous and wet as the boat cuts through the sea around Karoulia, the tip of the Holy Mountain. In these jagged boulders and treacherous drop-offs lived some of the earliest hermit monks on Athos, back in the ninth century. It's the most secluded, least accessible part of the peninsula, where men still live today in small huts and cave dwellings, tucked away but often visible from the sea.

When we arrive at the Lavra dock, laymen and monks join hands in unloading supplies and then carry them up the steep road leading to the monastery gates. The reception room, painted a pale blue, is on the second floor of the vast complex. Built high on a plateau overlooking a harbor, Megisti Lavra was the first monastery constructed in the mid-tenth century under the direction of Kalogeros Athanasius. It was he who composed the original *Typikon,* the constitution for the monastic republic. Providing most of the money, supplies and labor for the construction was his close friend, the Byzantine emperor. Now it is badly in need of repair, and the monks could again use a rich patron.

View of Monastery Dionysiou from the pilgrim's trail
(not in text)

Among the friendly group of pilgrims sharing refreshments is an uncle with his nephew from Athens. Adonis, the nephew, has recently completed his MBA at Indiana University in Bloomington. "My uncle wanted to bring me on a spiritual retreat before entering the world of work," the young man tells me. "He's hoping that it will make a trustworthy businessman out of me." The recent graduate is not making fun of his uncle, just speaking the truth.

"Well, your uncle might just have the right idea."

"Yes, I think so, too," he admits. "That's why I came along."

They invite me to attend vespers with them. However, as they move up to the choir stalls in the nave, I'm directed to my usual place in the esonarthex. But tonight, the service is not foremost in my mind. Instead, my thoughts are about the history of Lavra. This was the physical and organizational model on which all other Athonite monasteries were based. The founder, Athanasius, followed St. Basil's teachings in organizing this cenobitic community. Taking vows of poverty, chastity and obedience, the men here committed themselves to a spiritual life on a then truly isolated mountain.

St. Basil, born in the Cappadocia region of what is now Turkey, was a significant leader in the Christian monastic movement in the fourth century. His teachings helped define community life as "God's will" for the monks; they were not to live as hermits, separate from one another and apart from the world. Rather they were to come together and live in community.

After the evening meal, I begin exploring the huge, overgrown courtyard where old wooden staircases cover sometimes-crumbling stonework, and enclosed porches with broken windows jut out from the walls. Some buildings are in various states of renovation. As it gets dark, I return to the reception area to record my observations. I have just begun writing when in strolls a tall blonde Englishman who introduces himself as Robert Lloyd Parry, a recent graduate of Oxford University with degrees in Greek and Latin. He's a most curious sight in this land of dark, blackrobed men. "I will be here for seven weeks," he tells me in a distinct British accent, "at which time I will visit some of the other monasteries on the mountain and then return home."

I ask him what he's doing at Lavra.

"Well, the monastery advertised at my school for a summer helper.

I applied and got the job. I'm hoping that while I'm here I can discover what my future holds."

We talk about my observations these past ten days and Robert's experiences as a helper here at Megisti Lavra. "Just the short time I've been here," says Robert, "I feel like all the monks' energy goes into hospitality. As you know, this is one of the most frequently visited monasteries on Athos, next to Iviron."

I sympathize with his concerns. When I visit a monastery, I am conscious that I am something of a burden on my hosts, although one they cheerfully accept, and I take care to be as little trouble as possible. I have found myself cleaning up after other guests. "On the long hiking trails I have sometimes filled up small plastic bags with trash — sardine cans, cigarette butts, candy wrappers and soda cans — left by visitors," I tell my acquaintance.

Before retreating to his room, Robert gives me two articles that he's sure I will appreciate, written by an Englishman named Timothy Ware. Also known as Kallistos, a name given him upon his ordination as a priest and monk in the Eastern Orthodox tradition, Ware is a prolific writer on the topics of church and spirituality. After completing my journal writing, I read through Ware's articles with great interest. The first piece, titled "Wolves and Monks: Life on the Holy Mountain Today," was written just prior to the recent renewal movement here.

"On Athos today, as in the past, the monastic life continues to be an inward martyrdom," writes Ware. "With its lengthy services, broken hours of sleep and strict fasting, its physical isolation and lack of twentieth-century comforts, Athos makes heavy demands. It is maximalist in outlook — not a place for the half-hearted." The author's focus is on the interior life of the men making a commitment to remain here. But he also warns of the potential danger of the "two-legged wolves" who come as tourists, not as spiritual pilgrims.

A decade later, in "Athos after Ten Years: The Good News and the Bad," Ware expresses his concern about the increasing pressure visitors are placing on Athos:

> Athos is today facing a crisis in its relationship to the outside world.... There is ... the problem of tourism.... In Eastern and Western monasticism, hospitality has always been understood as an integral part of the monastic vocation: the guest is to be

received as Christ himself. But what if the guest comes in such numbers . . . to disrupt the monk's life of prayer? And what if most of them, Greeks as well as foreigners, come not as pilgrims on a spiritual quest, but as holiday makers moved by idle curiosity.

The "two-legged wolves" have become a major problem. How does a religious tradition over a thousand years old maintain its solitude and spiritual strength, and continue providing hospitality to the multitudes of laymen visiting annually? I take this question back with me to the overcrowded dormitory.

Chapter Four

IN THE BEGINNING

Let us not look back upon the world and fancy we have given up great things. For the whole earth is a very little thing compared with the whole of heaven.

> St. Anthony
> third century

It has taken three-quarters of an hour to ascend the stone-and-wood staircase leading to the top of the barren cliffs of Mt. Kolzom in Egypt's north-central region, known as the Fayyum. Near the top of the stairs, before the narrow mouth of the cave where St. Anthony spent the first half of the fourth century, are close to a dozen pairs of shoes and thongs in disarray. They belong to the people whose faint voices are coming up and out from the darkness.

Removing my shoes and turning on the flashlight I have carried with me for just this purpose, I squeeze through the tight opening in the rock. Immediately the floor begins to descend. After a bit, uneven slabs of rock give way to wooden steps. The farther down I go, the warmer the air and the louder the voices become. Reaching the bottom at last, I find a circular chamber. In the center is a small altar made of bricks and stones and covered with a white cloth on which stand two partially burned white candles. Musty throw rugs have been scattered around the floor as cushions to protect bare feet from sharp stones and pebbles.

Carefully climbing over the arms and legs of the other, noisy, visitors, I find an empty space to squeeze into and begin exploring the cave walls with the high beam of my light. To one side of the altar, near a naturally formed niche, hangs a gold-painted icon of the bearded St. Anthony clutching a black cross in his right hand. On the opposite side, the flashlight beam reveals a slight ledge, a rectangular indentation where the saint is said to have slept. And scribbled over the smoke-darkened surfaces is sophisticated but unreadable graffiti reportedly dating back to the Middle Ages.

Since my arrival, three young people have joined us; thirteen bodies are now wedged into a space barely comfortable for eight. When the chatter reaches a deafening decibel level and the walls begin feeling like they're closing in, I start crawling back toward the stairs, hoping that more people aren't on their way down. There is only enough space for one person to maneuver in either direction.

Upon reaching the mouth of the cave, I drink in the fresh air, welcome the open space and embrace the solitude of the cliffside. Beyond the edge unfolds an extraordinary vista of craggy, multicolored mountains rising from the desert plains. The late afternoon sun is covering the sky with pastels, and shadows cloak the desolate landscape.

"Hello, hello, hello," yells a bushy-haired, dark-skinned teenage boy, emerging from the cave, breaking through the magical spell of this awesome panorama. "My name is Magdi," he says while lacing up his high-top sneakers. "You are from the United States, yes?"

"Yes, and my name is Bill. Tell me, are all of the young people up here in one group?"

"Yes, all of us are members of the same Coptic Sunday school youth group. We are here for a ten-day retreat of work and prayer." Magdi's English is as good as mine, maybe better.

"And what is your group doing right now, working or praying?" I ask jokingly.

"Oh, I forgot," he says, hitting his forehead with his hand and laughing. "We have recreation, too."

As we talk, a friend of his emerges from the belly of the mountain and greets us. He introduces himself as Besem. "Did you see all the writing on the cave walls?" he asks excitedly. "I could not understand any of it." Magdi admits that he could not either.

~~~~~~~~~~

St. Anthony called this cave home for more than forty years. And although he was certainly not the first hermit or anchorite to live in the wilderness, he is still regarded as the "father" of Christian monasticism. Born into a well-to-do religious family of merchants in the middle of the third century, he lost both parents when he was just a teenager and was forced to take control of the family business and responsibility for a younger sister. Within a year of his parents' death, Anthony had decided his future and made some very dramatic moves. That's when his spiritual pilgrimage really began.

According to St. Athanasius — author of Anthony's biography written in the fourth century — the future saint was greatly influenced when hearing the scripture of Matthew 19: 21 read aloud at a local religious service. "If you seek perfection, go, sell your possessions and give to the poor," Jesus says in the reading. "You will then have treasure in heaven. Afterward come back and follow me." Anthony sold the business and all of the family's possessions, giving most of the profits to the poor, except for a sum put aside for his sister, whom he entrusted to a women's convent. He then began the quest of a solitary religious man seeking the grace of God.

In his search for spiritual solitude, Anthony moved to several different wilderness areas, but each time he attracted followers who sought his wisdom. At Mt. Kolzom, his final home, a group of semianchorites organized a community at the base of the mountain, designating him as their spiritual leader. From this foundation, the Christian monastic movement evolved.

~~~~~~~~~~

Magdi, Besem and I are enjoying the silence and the view when their retreat companions begin pouring out of the cave. Spotting me, the young Copts immediately start firing a barrage of questions: "Who are you? Where do you come from? Why are you here? Are you a Christian? Did you like the cave? Are you married? Do you have children? How long will you stay?" Their intense excitement and enthusiasm is overwhelming. I try to answer some of the questions but soon discover that each answer brings forth additional inquiries.

I offer a compromise: "I am staying here for a few days and will be happy to meet with your group at a designated time. Just let me know when." That seems agreeable, and most of them retreat, putting on their footwear and descending the mountain. However, two young men remain behind, introducing themselves as Haytham and Haney, both pharmacology students from Cairo. They are here supervising the Sunday school class. Climbing down together — slowly — we begin talking about their daily retreat schedule, one that I will follow as a guest of St. Anthony's Monastery. As expected, the day begins a few hours before dawn and draws to a close by early evening.

Midway down the wooden stairway we pass a small, gray, domed chapel. "This is used during special times of the year when pilgrims, *abuna* and *anba,* stop for prayer and rest on their way up or down," explains Haney.

"What is an *abuna* or an *anba?*" I ask.

"Oh, sorry," replies Haney. "An *abuna* is a Coptic monk and an *anba* is a church bishop." We stop to try the doors of the chapel, but finding them locked, we continue our descent.

"Haytham, please tell me what the word *Coptic* means to you."

He stops for a moment, then responds to my question. "It means the native people of Egypt."

"Yes, yes," chimes in Haney. "It comes from the Greek word meaning Egyptian, the true Egyptians."

"The word *Coptic* was used originally to describe the language spoken by the native Egyptian population," adds Haytham. My inquiry has triggered a welcome history lesson.

"You see," says Haney, "The Egyptian Christian Church began under the influence of the Apostle St. Mark."

Haytham takes up where Haney leaves off, "He brought his teachings to Alexandria in the year A.D. 63. And so we, as *Copts,* trace our church back to the time of St. Mark."

In the mid-fifth century, during the Christian Council of Chalcedon, the influence of the Egyptian Christian Church, or Coptic Orthodox Church, changed significantly. At the council, the Egyptian Patriarch of Alexandria declared his belief in the Monophysite theory of Christ, that Christ was one person with one nature, a divine nature. That position was in direct opposition to the belief shared by the larger Church, both East and West, that Christ was of two natures, human and divine. The Coptics' theological stance was certainly considered heresy, and as a result they were shunned and separated from the hierarchies both in Rome and Constantinople.

Haney and Haytham continue the history lesson, only stopping long enough to emphasize a particular point. One of them begins a thought, and the other continues it in their dual presentation. They tell me that after the tenth century, due to the influence of the Arabs, the Coptic language was supplanted by Arabic except in the church.

By the time we reach the base of the mountain, the burning orange sun is melting into the desert, and the air has begun to cool. Haytham and Haney say good-bye and amble over to their dormitory. I return to my room. Before showering, I record some of the day's events in my journal.

This morning I caught a dilapidated old bus leaving from the congested transportation park in downtown Cairo near the renowned Egyptian Museum. It was so crowded that many of us stood most all of the way to Suez, the battered city adjacent to the Canal. In Suez, a city practically destroyed during the wars with Israel in 1967 and again in 1973, I caught a second bus traveling a road parallel to the Red Sea which dropped me off near the village of Zefarana.

I knew that Dair Anba Antunius, the monastery of St. Anthony, was about thirty miles inland from my present location, and with a little bit of luck I could hitch a ride to the exit road leading into the monastery. Three Egyptian laborers within sight had the same idea. They huddled together under a nearby bus stop shelter next to the highway leading west into the desert.

"Salam alekum, Dair Anba Antunius?" I said hello and mentioned the name of the monastery. They nodded their heads, so I joined them under the shelter to escape the scorching sun. Within a short time, a diesel truck stopped, and the four of us jumped onto the back of the cargo bin. Less than an hour later, we arrived at an entry road, but there were no signs indicating that it led to the monastery.

"Dair Anba Antunius!" exclaimed the truck driver, although there wasn't anything visible down the road but more desert. My fellow hitchhikers nodded their heads reassuringly, so I hopped out and thanked them, "Shukran." After passing down my backpack, they sped off, disappearing into the desert. Luckily, there were two quarts of water in the pack to keep me wet for at least the remainder of the day, if need be.

According to the map, the trek was six miles in. After hiking probably the first five, I was picked up by a small lorry driven by another laborer and he gave me a lift to the main entrance of the monastery. I was surprised at the size of the dair, the monastery. Otto F. A. Meinardus, in his book Monks and Monasteries of the Egyptian Deserts, *wrote that "the monastery walls enclose an area of eighteen feddans, an Egyptian unit measuring a little more than one acre, of which ten belong to the garden. The walls . . . are ten to twelve meters high and surmounted by a* chemin de ronde *(sentinel walk) between one and two meters wide. The old walls may go back as far as the tenth century, while the new ones were built . . . in*

1854. They . . . are about two kilometers in length." From a distance, the snaking monastery walls had the smooth look of brown stucco or adobe. But upon closer examination, they were constructed of tightly packed stones and mortar.

To one side of the small, arched green entrance doors, and two-thirds of the way up the wall, was an opening, like a porch, with a carved wooden partition halfway covering the front. It housed the pulley and rope once used to lift supplies up into the monastery. Across the road was a group of dormitories built in the shape of a half-moon.

"Excuse me; can I help you?" Turning around, I faced a black-bearded man standing at eye level. "My name is Abuna Thelonius — Monk Thelonius as you would say in your language," he said, looking down at the English guidebook in my hand. "I am the xenodochus, the guestmaster here at St. Antunius."

He was wearing a long black habit and a pair of light blue thongs, and hanging from the man's neck was a large wooden cross inlaid with pearl or ivory. A black cloth hood, like a helmet, covered his head, fit snugly over his ears and tied under his chin. Sewn onto each side of the helmet were six white stars symbolizing one of three things, depending on whom I spoke with later: They were representative of the twelve tribes of Israel; they indicated the stars in heaven and the "angelic" nature of the man wearing them; and/or they symbolized virginity, the celibate monk.

"Come in, come in," Thelonius motioned for me to pass through the entrance of the thick wall. After introducing myself, I requested permission to make a retreat for two days. "Do you have a letter from the office of the Coptic Patriarchate in Cairo?" the abuna inquired.

"Ah, no. To be honest with you, I didn't do the homework to find out if a letter was necessary. I simply wanted to come."

Monk Thelonius, neither smiling with approval nor frowning, said that maybe something could be arranged. "We do have a number of youth groups here on a ten-day work and meditation retreat, but I believe there is room for you at the inn," he said dryly. "I mean one of the dormitories across the road. Wait just a moment." He walked into the nearby gatehouse and returned momentarily. "Did you hitchhike part of the way here?"

"Yes, part of the way. First a bus to Suez, another to Zefarana, then caught a ride with a truck driver."

Coptic monastery in Wadi'n-Natrun

Monk's interior residential cells

"I think you are very lucky," said Thelonius. "We don't get many hitchhikers out here because of the heat and the desert; usually only groups in rented buses or cars coming for the 'work retreats.' You must have been determined." He was curious about my work, but obviously preoccupied with other things.

"Come," he said, walking back out the entrance, "let me show you the dormitory where you can leave your things. Then I have a suggestion as to how you can spend the remainder of the afternoon."

At the dormitory, he introduced the cook and showed me a dorm room where my backpack could be left. Three electric fans hung down from the ceiling, and near the top of two walls was a series of open windows. It was unexpectedly cool inside. Transferring my water bottles to my shoulder bag and slipping it on, I followed the guestmaster back across the dusty road to the monastery. "Supper is between 8:00 and 8:30 tonight," he explained, "so between now and then I suggest you climb up Mt. Kolzom behind the monastery and visit the cave of Anba Antunius, St. Anthony."

He paused a minute as if he'd forgotten to tell me something. "Would you like to meet briefly in the morning to talk?" he asked.

"Yes," was my immediate response.

Glancing at his watch, he said, "Meet me right here at 9:00 in the morning," then hurried off.

I awake hours before dawn to a steady tolling of the bells across the road. Hurrying out into the darkness, I discover a black sky filled with stars that appear almost within reach. It reminds me of another celestial showcase witnessed when visiting a monastery at Valle de Elqui in northern Chile. There, barren mountaintops were speckled with gargantuan international telescopes recording events in the star-filled heavens.

Following the stream of flashlight beams flowing into the monastery, I move with other visitors down a dirt path and under an archway between the tolling bells. The procession continues past an old three-story adobe building in disrepair, probably housing some of the monks' cells. At the end of the path is another domed archway leading to a single entrance into the Church of the Apostles.

Removing our shoes and lining them up with many others already there, we step inside onto soft, red carpeting. The air is heavy with the sweet smell of incense. A thick, smoky haze inside the basilica gives movement a feeling of dreamlike slow motion. Hanging from hooks in the ceiling, providing a soft yellow light, are scores of old oil lamps. There are no conventional windows here to let in fresh air. Built in the fifteenth century, the Church of the Apostles was designed in the traditional rectangular mode, with no exterior symbols or markings to indicate its purpose. It would be hard to spot or identify as a place of worship; it is a relic from the days of persecution.

After adjusting to the lamplight, smoke and incense, I see that the interior, devoid of chairs or pews, is divided into sections by three ornate wooden lattices, each with an opening in the center. The monks direct me to the last one. The front section, behind the iconostasis, is reserved for the clergy, and the entrance is protected by a thick, appliquéd, red velvet curtain. In the second section are a half-dozen prayer lecterns for the officiating monks, who will chant and read scriptures. And the nave, a third section, is designated for those who have been baptized into the Coptic Orthodox faith. In the very back is the *narthex*, a place for those not of the Orthodox faith.

Hanging from all three lattices are smoke-stained icons arranged in an orderly and deliberate fashion; each group of iconic saints is placed in a particular section for a specific reason. Nothing is randomly set in this church.

Yesterday afternoon, when descending from St. Anthony's cave, Haney had described the meaning of Coptic icons, the paintings of Coptic saints that fill their churches. "As far as I know, both the Coptic and Greek Orthodox think of their icons in a similar way," Haney said, stopping for a moment to consult with Haytham in Arabic and then expanding on his comment. "People of my faith don't think of icons as art, the way you Westerners might, but like 'windows' into the spiritual world. They can help the believer achieve a prayerful mind. By meditating on the saints in the icons, I can concentrate on learning to copy their lives."

As a Westerner, the noticeable difference to me is in the style of art. Coptic icons appear to be folk art. There is a sweetness and humility in the disproportionate, simple figures. In contrast, Greek Orthodox icons are more realistic in presentation. Taking my place in the back among a group of mostly attentive teenage boys, I silently witness the unfolding early morning service.

Assistant guestmaster

*Tour guide at
the monastery*

Standing behind the lecterns are six of the abuna dressed in black, and behind them the white-robed novices. As the official service begins, the reading and chanting of scripture is enhanced by the delicate ringing of hand bells, miniature cymbals and triangles. The sounds of the common percussion instruments are easily integrated into the service. Periodically, one of the priests disappears behind the thick velvet curtain where the altar stands, staying out of sight for a while then returning to the choir section.

At times the chanting is harsh, and differs markedly from any liturgical music used within a Catholic or Eastern Orthodox context. In those traditions, the chanting is frequently soothing, almost hypnotic in nature.

This Coptic tradition of chant was transmitted orally for more than a millennium, and only within the last century has the church created liturgical books with musical notations. Although Coptic chant uses melodic formulas as a starting point, improvisation remains an integral and important part of this liturgical music. On the one hand, Coptics' improvisational style of chanting lends an element of surprise and excitement to a service. But on the other, it strikes me as disruptive and not conducive to settling into a meditative state.

This early morning service, the first of seven canonical hours, is focusing on a repetition of the Psalms and Gospel readings. Although Arabic is spoken in most of the liturgy, the Coptic language is sometimes used in the statement of the Nicene Creed, the Lord's Prayer and some of the scriptural readings. Here at Dair Anba Antunius, the entire community of monks gathers for a common prayer twice a day, once in the early morning and again in the late afternoon. The remaining canonical hours may be observed by the monks in their individual cells, assigned workplaces or in various chapels scattered throughout the dair.

It's during the second canonical hour — the Mass and the Eucharist — when Coptic clergy and laymen practice one of three liturgies, the most common being the Liturgy of St. Basil. Although in the early Egyptian Christian Church there were fourteen liturgies, all of which are believed to have been composed by the Apostles as taught to them by Jesus, almost a dozen of them have been destroyed over the years during invasions and plundering of the Coptic churches and monasteries.

Standing and watching these ancient rituals creates both a feeling of reverence for my witness and a sense of frustration at being relegated to the rear of the church. The only time one of the abuna walks to the back is to awaken some of the young boys who have fallen asleep on the floor. So, following the communal prayer, but before the initiation of the Eucharist, I quietly slip out of the church back into the starlit early morning. Enveloped by the aloneness of the desert, I welcome the feeling of being wrapped in a blanket of predawn darkness.

By midmorning, I am ready for company again. Monk Thelonius is sitting with me under a shade tree near one of the stone walls that surrounds a community garden. Thelonius explains that when the monastery doors open to the public, he will have to leave to lead the morning tours. "We never really know how many believers will show up on our doorstep day to day," he tells me. "But our largest numbers tend to be around the special holidays."

"Today I hope to give you an overview of our life here, and then you can ask questions," he says and then waits for a response. I nod my head, and he continues, "Community life here is really made up of a few important elements common to all Christian monastic traditions: Constant worship is one; celebration of the divine liturgy is another; and then there are the personal devotionals." He explains that every abuna is assigned daily to some form of labor, such as working in the garden or maybe assisting in the kitchen or bakery. Or, he might be managing the library or leading the daily tours and participating in the frequent retreat programs.

"How many years have you been living and working at St. Anthony's?" I inquire.

"This is my twelfth year here, and I am certain that I shall remain until my death," Thelonius responds. His calm, contained presentation underscores his statement. I sense in his manner the tremendous distance between the two of us.

"What I want you to know is that there has been a surprising revival of interest in our monastic life since the early 1960s."

This reminds me of the situation on Mt. Athos. "What do you think accounts for this increase in interest?"

"There are really two answers to that question, in my opinion," he says, adjusting the star-studded hood on his head. "First is the continued emphasis on the 'Sunday School Movement' under the leadership of our Patriarch Shenouda III. The movement provides religious education for children unable to attend Coptic schools. And secondly, a program initiated by His Holiness that has created a much stronger relationship between monks and laymen."

I ask him to explain the program.

"A few decades ago, Shenouda began encouraging laymen to visit the monasteries in groups for the purpose of spiritual retreats. In this way, according to our leader, the monasteries could 'produce and give something back to society.'"

On several occasions, either through my reading or in conversations, I have been informed that the "Coptic Church is only as strong as its monasteries." The reason is that all of the clergymen in leadership positions are selected solely from the men in the Coptic monasteries.

Thelonius continues, "The number of monks here is greater than eighty, with the average age range between twenty-five and forty-five. Now the majority of men are academically trained, coming from professional fields, including physicians, architects and pharmacists, as well as tradesman. You know, it wasn't too long ago when the majority of monks were from a rural background with little advanced education, but maybe a trade."

I inquire about the training for Coptic monastic life, and the abuna replies: "Well, there is biblical study, prayer, meditation and, of course, manual labor like you would find in any Christian monastic training program. But what is unique to Coptic training is the requirement to live as a hermit for a period of time, inside or outside the walls of the monastery, and participating in rigorous fasts throughout the year."

When I ask if any of the professed monks live as hermits outside the walls of the dair, he tells me there are a half dozen men currently living as anchorites. Inside the community, each monk has his own separate living cell, but he shares daily meals with his brothers.

"Are there Coptic nuns that live in convents?"

"Ah, that's an interesting question," he says with a slight smile. "I don't often hear that asked by a visitor. Yes, there are five convents that are currently occupied, all near Cairo. There are also women of the Church who have taken holy vows, but choose to reside at home." Father Thelonius checks his watch, appearing surprised at the time. "Excuse me; I didn't realize we had been talking for so long. If you have one more question

I will answer it, and then I must go."

"Well, I am curious about the architectural design and organizational scheme of the first monastic communities here in the Fayyum. They were quite different from what we see today, yes?"

"Yes and no. Early Coptic monks living in the mid-fourth century used the term 'lavra' to describe their first communities." He explains that the lavra consisted of only the most essential buildings, and the monks, or anchorites, lived in groupings of detached cells under the leadership of one recognized spiritual father. At times, the monks would gather for communal worship and a common meal. "Living in one community, or what we call cenobitic monasticism today, only developed later for reasons of discipline, safety and mutual fellowship. Now I really must go." Before rushing off, he suggests that we meet at the same time the next day for a walk around the monastery.

Late in the afternoon, when the heat is not quite so stifling, I meander around the community, visiting chapels, wandering into blooming gardens, getting better acquainted with this village. For that is really what it feels like, a walled-in Egyptian village with narrow streets and two- and three-story brick and adobe buildings. When returning to the dormitory, I happen to cross paths with Haytham.

"I have been hunting for you."

"You have? Why?"

"I have a gift for you," he says, handing me a small piece of folded paper. On the outside is a minute picture of St. Anthony and the Holy Virgin. Inside is a prayer written in Arabic next to a stapled packet of very sweet smelling powder or incense. The smell is pungent.

"What is this, my friend?"

"It's a henot. Herbs and perfume are in the packet." The herbs had been applied to the dead bodies of the Holy Ones, then later collected and distributed among those of the faith.

"Thank you very much. It will travel with me through the remainder of my trip." The henot is a welcome addition to the amulets I carry with me when traveling abroad: an agate from a friend, a smooth black stone picked up on the Oregon coast, my St. Christopher's medal given to me by a fellow traveler, a charm from the "Witches' Market" in La Paz, Bolivia, and a string of red "worry beads" from the Middle East. This odd assortment of items frequently provides a sense of well-being when I am on the road. There are times when simply rubbing the smooth stones, feeling the St. Christopher's medal hanging around my neck, thumbing through the worry beads or clasping the Bolivian charm in my hand helps relieve the tension and anxiety of being a long-term traveler. They are reminders of spiritual guides and friendships and past experiences around the world. They keep me company.

The next morning Father Thelonius and I begin our walk, making the first stop inside the very small, ancient Church of St. Anthony. Here the religious frescoes on the walls and domed ceiling are almost completely covered by centuries' worth of accumulated soot and grime left by burning incense and oil lamps. After exiting the church and proceeding deeper into the dair, the guestmaster stops in front of dual four-story stucco-covered buildings connected by a wooden drawbridge. Their walls are spotted with small openings, like air holes.

"This is the keep, or fortress, built in the sixth century by Emperor Justinian. It provided a place of safety for the monks." Thelonius says that inside are a chapel and a storage area for food, abuna cells and, most important, a deep well that still provides a reliable source of clean water. I knew that the Coptic monasteries in the Scetis, a northwestern area of Egypt, had a history of attacks by nomadic tribesmen, but I did not realize there had been similar problems here.

"The same dangers existed here as in the Scetis?" I ask my guide.

"Oh, yes," says Thelonius. "There have been four major attacks, over time, here at St. Anthony's. In the eighth and ninth centuries we suffered from Bedouin tribal attacks, again in the eleventh century at the hands of the Arabs who were in power, and then later when the disgruntled servants of the monastery revolted and murdered all the monks here. So you see, Mr. Claassen, the desert is not always a place of quiet, peace and solitude."

Circling around the interior of the monastery, we pass the cemetery and the charnel house where, for centuries, the skulls and bones of past abuna have been exhumed, dried and added to the collection. This is a sacred place, a place of holy relics. "So, I understand that you won't be hitchhiking back to Cairo this morning," comments the guestmaster with a grin. He has made arrangements for me to return on an old school bus rented by one of the retreat groups.

"No. Thanks to you, my return will be in a luxurious school bus," I respond in jest.

Before we separate, he strongly encourages me to visit Wadi'n-Natrun, a group of four Coptic monasteries in the desert between Cairo and Alexandria but says I *must* get a permission letter if I want to stay there overnight. "Remember, we are always here," says the guestmaster, "and you are always welcome. May God be with you."

Back in Cairo, my departure date is extended in anticipation of receiving the letter granting permission to make a retreat at Wadi'n-Natrun. For the better part of two days, I attempt to get that permission letter from the secretary to Patriarch Shenouda III, but I am finally forced to admit defeat. The official offers no explanation for his refusal. On my third and final attempt, the office door is closed abruptly in my face.

Despite the discouraging experience at the patriarchate offices, I make two day trips. Catching an early morning public bus and traveling for hours to a drop-off point on the highway, I hitchhike the remainder of the distance on the first visit. On the second trip, the bus driver — quite unexpectedly — takes a few minutes of his time at the drop-off point to arrange a ride for me to the monasteries. His consideration is greatly appreciated. Without the ride, I probably would be hiking hours in the desert during the hottest time of the day.

The Scetis, often referred to as Wadi'n-Natrun, is where Christians fled from the wrath of the Romans back in the fourth century. More than fifty active Coptic monasteries populated this partially cultivated valley at one time, but only four of those communities have survived.

Webster's definitions of the two words, *wadi* and *natrun,* help provide a vivid description of much of the area today. Wadi is "a shallow, sharply defined depression in a desert region of poorly developed drainage." And natrun refers to "a hydrous sodium carbonate . . . occurring mainly in a solution or solid and with other salts." This sodium carbonate, left when riverbeds dry up, was used at one time in Egypt for mummification.

When arriving at the second of the four Coptic monasteries, Dair as-Surian, I feel comfortable, probably because it is midweek and there are few visitors and no buses in sight. The historical name of this monastery comes from a time when the monks here were primarily from Syria.

Abuna David, extending a warm welcome upon my arrival, makes a point of accompanying me throughout the community. The same height as Thelonius and dressed in similar religious garb, David is probably more than a dozen years younger, maybe in his early thirties. The wooden cross around his neck is small, almost unnoticeable, and his eyes are dark and probing. He begins our walk by explaining that, although physically smaller than St. Anthony's, this monastery is home to more than one hundred monks, many of them born and raised in urban Cairo. A small percentage of the men are living in hermit cells in the surrounding desert.

"I have been an abuna for five and a half years now," he says as we stroll through the monastery grounds. "For two and a half years I trained as a novice, then took my vows and was accepted into community. Prior to that I was a student of philosophy at the university in Cairo."

When discussing community life, he explains that each Coptic monastery keeps a somewhat different daily schedule. "Here we have common prayer twice a day and then each of us is responsible for observing the remaining canonical offices independently. And we take our meals alone, only eating in common on special occasions."

"When did monastic history begin here in the Scetis?" I ask David.

"It began with Father Makarious, a disciple of St. Anthony's from the eastern desert, who came here and established the first community of monks."

Because of its accessibility to both Cairo and Alexandria, Dair as-Surian has benefited, in some respects, by newly paved roads, government irrigation projects and now electricity. On the downside, according to David, the monks are no longer guaranteed a quiet and peaceful daily existence.

One of the major structures inside the walls is the familiar keep, a fortress built for the same reasons as the one at St. Anthony's. Here, the marauders were often Berber tribesmen and sometimes Muslim zealots. It has a very intriguing history. This structure, built in the style of a Roman fort, was a gift from Emperor Zeno in the late fifth century. The story goes that when the king discovered that the famous Coptic monk St. Hilary was actually his lost daughter disguised as an abuna, he immediately provided the supplies and manpower for the construction.

Throughout the monastery, smooth, inviting architectural forms and structures blend into one another, giving the appearance of a single, extended unit. Time and again I can see in my mind's eye Georgia O'Keeffe's paintings depicting adobe forms in the New Mexico landscape, or Ansel Adams' black-and-white photographs of the indigenous Taos Pueblo in the same state. The earth tones, gentle curves and rough textures draw a comparison. But for me, the most intriguing structure is not far outside these thick walls, standing alone in the desert.

"It is a semi-anchorite living complex constructed from a sixth-century architectural plan, built by one of our monks," explains David. "It helps create some historical insight." Three separate cells are attached to a common room and a small chapel, all of which are domed and covered with small holes providing for adequate ventilation. Crude stick crosses jut out from the top of most of the domes. Being built halfway under the ground facilitated warmth in the cold evenings and coolness during the heat of the day. Unfortunately, the two entrances are locked.

Walking around it again and again and becoming progressively more excited, I peek through the ventilation holes with the enthusiasm of a child, trying to visualize daily life in the desert during the sixth century. It is "appropriate technology" at its best, where all of the building materials come from the earth, and the design blends easily into the desert environment.

David and I spend our final hour together on a weathered wooden bench just outside the monastery entrance, where he talks about his life as a student and an urban dweller. "I have always had a strong desire to find solitude in the desert," he tells me. "It was not difficult for me to leave the city. Although this community may not provide the degree of solitude I sometimes desire, I have never regretted my decision to become part of this life and this community."

The monk's comments echo the words of Meinardus's book, *Monks and Monasteries of the Egyptian Deserts:*

> The desert has provided, from time to time immemorial, a testing ground for the souls of men and women. Go to the desert for food and drink and you will find a barren waste. Go there to listen to the voice of God and you will receive insight, understanding and wisdom. The desert is silent, apart, different. It conveys a picture, waterless and featureless, yet overwhelming to the senses.

*Architectural design
within the monastery walls*

*Replica of a sixth century monastery
near Dair as-Surian*

Before I leave, David extends an invitation to return when "the weather gets cool." It's so easy for me to forget that there are seasons here in the desert because my visit is during the hottest time of year. He then offers me a few simple gifts, the first of which is a small booklet titled *Dair as-Surian Monastery Saints.* The monk explains that "each Coptic monastery adopts a coterie of saints, from martyrs to monks, that become special teachers to those in the community." St. Nivard's room at the Abbey de la Trappe in France comes to mind. "There are specific reasons for each of these twelve saints to be chosen by our community," he says.

The second gift is another henot displaying a picture of His Holiness Patriarch Shenouda III standing next to a monastic novice. Its perfume is even more pungent than the one given to me at St. Anthony's, now carried in my shoulder bag with the other amulets. I express my appreciation to David, slip the henot into my bag and begin the long trek back to the drop-off point at the highway.

It has truly been a day full of blessings; I am once again feeling thankful for the good fortune of meeting up with my "special guides," be they bus drivers from Cairo or monks from the Egyptian deserts.

Chapter Five

WHIRLING IN ECSTASY

Come, come, whoever you are,
An unbeliever, a fire-worshipper, come.
Our monastery is not of desperation.
Even if you have broken your vows a hundred times,
Come, come again.

Mevlana Jalaluddin Rumi
thirteenth century

In the oppressively muggy heat I cross the Galata Bridge, over the Bosphorus Strait, leaving behind European Istanbul for the Istanbul of Asia. This is my second visit since arriving by train a few days ago. Hiking up a steep, narrow lane, I finally discover Istikal Street. The old stone buildings huddle together on either side of me, housing a hodgepodge of small businesses: Art galleries, bookstores and antique shops are interspersed with grocery stores, butcher shops and the occasional mosque. Around one corner, I'm surprised to see painted women and anxious customers spilling out from a brothel onto the street. Continuing on, I find a brick archway that dominates the block and through it an overgrown courtyard adjacent to a small cemetery.

~~~~~~~~~~

In the early twentieth century the archway was closed and locked by order of Mustafa Kemal Ataturk, the founder and first president of the Turkish Republic, as a means of enforcing the new separation of religion and state. The site, the Sufi Galata Mevlevi Tekkesi, or the Sufi Whirling Dervish Monastery, had been in use for more than six hundred years. But many of the Sufi orders strongly resisted Ataturk's separation policy, and so their brotherhoods were declared illegal, their *tekkes* were closed and their devotees were driven underground. Only years later were some of the worship centers reopened under the supervision of the government, an arrangement that presently remains intact.

The Mevlevis, known in the West as Whirling Dervishes, took their name from Mevlana Jalaluddin Rumi, a thirteenth-century Sufi mystic, theologian and poet who lived in the central Anatolian region of what is now Turkey. Sometimes referred to as Islamic mystics, the Mevlevis, like other Sufi orders, consider the Prophet Muhammad to have been the first unnamed Sufi and the *Quran* to be their primary spiritual guide. Unlike traditional Muslims, the Mevlevis and other Sufi sects integrate mystical practices with dancing, singing and the playing of musical instruments to enhance their worship of Allah. Their belief is that we are all one, all a part of God, and thus, able to communicate directly with the Divine without an intermediary.

In the center of the courtyard sits an empty, dilapidated fountain once used by the Whirling Dervishes for ritual cleansing before worship ceremonies. Near the fountain stands a modest, two-story, wood-frame building called a *tekke,* the central prayer lodge, or the Hall of Celestial Sounds.

When I enter the lodge, a young woman at the door, dressed in black, hands me a program titled "The Sema Ritual" printed in both English and Turkish. Integrating prayers with chanting and whirling, this ritual is rumored to induce a state of ecstasy, allowing for mystical exchanges with Allah, the Creator.

In the center of the tekke, smooth, varnished wood forms an octagon on the floor. A low, decorative metal railing encloses the space where the Whirling Dervishes will enact the Sema Ritual. Above is a second-floor gallery, supported by wooden pillars and extending around three sides of the interior. A wooden lattice covers a section of the gallery once used for women and children. Now that separation is no longer practiced, all observers are permitted to sit behind the iron railing on the first floor.

Directly across the room from the entrance is a niche in the wall, the *mihrab,* indicating the direction of Mecca, which Muslims always face when praying. In the middle of the floor sit wooden chairs arranged in a semicircle around a set of kettledrums and several music stands.

I take a front-row seat next to a middle-aged couple and make a tentative comment to the woman. My eyes are immediately drawn by her red hair and the silk paisley scarf around her neck; the richness of the colors is pleasing. She happens to be fluent in English, and we talk.

Introducing herself as Aishegul, the woman says that many generations of her family have been Sufis and that she frequently attends the Sema Ritual: "This is not only an opportunity to observe, but also a time of worship."

The audience begins to quiet down when the musicians — both male and female — walk in carrying their instruments, take seats and begin tuning up. There are two stages to this ritual: religious choral music with musical accompaniment that is followed by whirling, a kind of Sufi liturgical dance.

"The wooden flutes we call *neys,*" Aishegul whispers, pointing to the instruments. "They symbolize souls longing to be reunited with Allah." Handheld drums and three stringed instruments the size of mandolins complete the musical section.

Attired in black and white, symbolic colors for the Mevlevis, a small coed chorus enters briskly and moves to a place behind the musicians. The service begins immediately with a prayer and a recitation from the *Mesnevi;* a collection of poetry and prayers written by their spiritual master, Mevlana Rumi. It's been aptly described by some as a collection of "sensual love poems to God." Many of the audience members join the chorus and musicians in reciting the famous works quietly and with respect. I feel like a member of a large family witnessing religious practices held dear.

The kettledrummer and one of the ney players offer solos and then lead the chorus into singing a litanic hymn, a composition with very little melodic variation. The music is dirgelike. Reminiscent of some works by the contemporary American composer Philip Glass, it maintains a repetitive continuous middle range of sound. To me, it is melancholic, uneventful and interminable. After completing the droning ritual, the musicians leave the floor — much to my relief — for a brief intermission.

I tell Aishegul that I find the music very dark, and she explains, "It is meant to bring everyone into a meditative state, a calm state of mind." I feel agitated rather than calm. Several people go outside for intermission, but I stay in my seat and continue reading, gathering additional information about the dervishes. The program reveals that prior to the ceremony, each dervish still performs the holy ablutions of the Islamic faith before dressing for the ritual. So, there must be a working fountain on the grounds.

Once the audience returns and settles down, a lone dervish sweeps onto the floor. Perched on his head, sitting high and covering the tops of his ears, is a honey-colored, cone-shaped felt hat, symbolizing a tombstone. Representing a burial shroud, the dervish's long black cloak drapes over his broad shoulders and covers his heavy, white, ankle-length cotton skirt and jacket. To the Mevlevis, white indicates life and rebirth. On his feet is a pair of high-top black leather shoes with laces. He is carrying a fluffy crimson sheepskin called the post, which he reverently places on the opposite side of the floor, directly in front of the mihrab. He exits, and a moment of silence ensues.

Suddenly breaking the silence and bursting through the gates are a dozen solemn-looking dervishes — both men and women — heads bowed, marching single file. Except for their headwear — red, green and white crepe scarves covering their honey-colored hats — the women's dress is identical to the men's. They move to one side by the railing.

Walking out alone and stopping in the center of the hall, their spiritual leader — the sheikh — bows from the waist in the direction of Mecca, then shuffles slowly over to the crimson sheepskin as if in a trance. From the second-floor balcony, a baritone vocalist begins chanting a mournful prayer to the deceased Rumi, and the dervishes respectfully drop to their knees. The steady beat of a drum and lonely wail of a ney accompany the funereal ceremony.

Then, unexpectedly, the dervishes break the mood by slapping the floor in unison, and their leader immediately steps out assertively in front of the post. He bows and begins to slowly circle the ritual space followed by his devotees. His solemn state has altered. Circling the floor three times, each dervish bows to the one behind him/her when passing the crimson skin. Once the sheikh returns to his original position, his followers go back to their side of the floor, and another moment of silence follows.

Quite dramatically, the dervishes again break the silence, tearing off their cloaks, kissing them, then throwing them onto the floor. Their actions represent the shedding of worldly possessions and escape from their tomb — death and resurrection. Inspired by the power of the act, I want to throw off my own figurative black shroud and break free from a self-imposed tomb.

Hypnotic music, wafting down from the gallery, lures each dervish into crossing his or her arms, right hand clasping the left shoulder and left hand clasping the right, then walking single file to the crimson post.

Mevlevi Dervish bows to the crimson sheepskin

Each bows to the sheikh and kisses his right hand; in turn, the spiritual leader kisses the top of each one's hat. Lightly brushing past him, one by one, they slowly begin to whirl, unfolding like butterflies breaking free of cocoons, arms extended with their right palms facing up to the heavens and their left palms down to the earth. A collective sigh rises from the audience as if these symbolic movements are a catharsis for all of us witnessing this rebirth.

They turn counterclockwise, whirling ever faster until the entire floor seems to be spinning. Like Buddhist prayer wheels, they are throwing blessings out to the world as they turn. Their energy, intensity and excitement are contagious; I want to jump the railing and join them.

Longing to participate in their ritual, I am envious of their disciplined physical movement channeled as a means of worship. I once participated in a liturgical dance ritual inside a church sanctuary. It was a joyful time, an incredibly freeing experience of reclaiming a part of Christian history when dance was honored. What better way to honor the Creator than to dance for the Creator.

The *selam,* these extended periods of whirling, are repeated numerous times, with each repetition building on the momentous energy of the previous one. In between, the dervishes stop, again crossing their arms over their chests, file past the sheikh and kiss his hand. Then they spin back out into orbit. Their whirling is a reunion with the cosmic order of things, when the dervish gives full attention to Allah. As they whirl in community with others, they move alone in their relationship with God.

In the fourth and final selam, the sheikh, moving into the center of the whirlers, begins turning clockwise very slowly, step by step, in sharp contrast to the ecstatic speed and direction of those moving around him. His face is again solemn and turned slightly to one side. Abruptly, the wailing of a ney brings all movement to a stop.

Returning to their original places at one side of the floor and almost reluctantly slipping on their black cloaks, the dervishes are necessarily returning to their earthly tombs, but they have experienced a powerful encounter with the mystical. Their flushed faces are glistening with perspiration as they catch their breath, intently listening to the "Bakara Sura, 2/115," a Quranic scripture proclaimed from the gallery above.

Ve lillahil mesriku vel magribu, fe eynema tuvellu fesemme Vechullah. Innelahe, Vasi un Alim . . .

*Female dervish in
the Sema Ritual*

*Whirling dervish in
a meditative state*

...God is in the East and in the West. Wherever you turn, you are faced with God. God fills everything and is everywhere. God is lofty. God is omniscient.

Now the devotees humbly bow, then kiss the floor. They rise up again slowly as their sheikh begins offering a prayer to Rumi, loudly and with pleading, sounding the "Hu"; echoed by all of us in the hall. As "Om" is the Hindu sacred sound of the universe, so "Hu," for the Sufis, is the sound of all the names of Allah in one.

Worship is ending, and the sheikh leads his exhausted followers from the room. Each dervish pauses at the gate to turn and bow to the crimson sheepskin. Despite the heat generated inside the tekke, the audience remains seated and silent, extending the ritual just a while longer. Some people are misty-eyed; others are sitting with their heads bowed; and still others are smiling contentedly. I recognize expressions of my own feeling, one of joyful, cathartic exhaustion.

A dozen years ago, I participated in an extended silent meditation retreat in the densely forested Oregon mountains. At the end, some of us resisted returning to words and instead wandered off into the woods, wanting to hold onto the silence just a while longer. I feel something similar now, and I stay in the building until asked to leave so that the doors may be locked.

Out in the courtyard, a few of the dervishes are lingering. With them stands a woman who appears to be an American, or maybe Canadian; she's speaking English. "Excuse me," I say, walking up behind her, "could you answer a few questions about the Sema Ritual?"

Looking a bit flustered, she answers, "I don't think I am the one to ask, but perhaps you can speak to my friends." She tells me her name is Laura, then introduces me to Farid, her partner, and their friend Ali. Olive-skinned Farid, a dervish novice, has a full black mustache and is impeccably dressed. Ali, clean-shaven, with very angular features, smokes a hand-rolled cigarette with conviction. He is an active dervish in the Mevlevi association.

Laura is casually dressed in a long, full, patterned skirt and white blouse with her brown hair pulled back into a ponytail. There is an unmistakable rural Midwestern look about her. She tells me she is from Minnesota. She has not decided whether to begin the preparations for entering the association, now open to ordaining women. Both men are willing to answer my questions, while Laura offers to translate when necessary.

Because the crimson sheepskin was obviously the focal point of the Sema Ritual, I ask Ali to explain its significance. "Well, I can tell you it is symbolic of a number of things," he replies slowly, with the help of his friends. "It represents Rumi's beloved teacher, Shamsi Tabriz, who taught him the art of whirling and the sacredness of the ritual. It also represents the sun, the center of our universe. And, as you probably know, crimson is the color of a sacred ceremony."

I turn to Farid with another question: "At the beginning of the ceremony, when the dervishes were on their knees, they slapped the floor. What did that represent?"

Farid defers to Ali. "As I understand it, slapping of the floor symbolizes the crushing of the ego, getting rid of the selfhood; also the day of the Last Judgment," he replies, taking a long drag from his homemade cigarette, then releasing the smoke slowly when he speaks.

Momentarily caught up again in what I've just seen, I toss out another question excitedly and ask why the dervishes whirl with one hand pointed upward and the other down at the ground.

"I can explain that," says Farid. "The spreading of the arms really represents the embracing of Allah. The power and blessings of heaven enter through the hand reaching up, and come to the earth through the hand pointing down. The whirler is serving as a vessel or channel for Allah." It seems so obvious after hearing Farid's explanation.

Ali excuses himself to go home, but Laura and Farid say they can stay a while longer. We stand beside the unused ablution fountain while Laura tells me that she has worked as a journalist in the recent past and Farid says that he owns a business here in the city. He enthusiastically recommends a few books for more background information, and he informs me that his Mevlevi association meets almost weekly at another Sufi lodge in a different part of the city.

"Would you be interested in attending one of our gatherings?" he asks, squinting slightly as he watches me.

I respond without hesitation. I would like to attend. "But," I add, "only if the sheikh and the other dervishes have been forewarned and have no objection." Giving me their work numbers, Laura and Farid tell me to call them midweek for confirmation.

Acquiring more books on Sufism and continuing my homework keeps me busy for the few days to come. In Istanbul's Old Book Bazaar, a noted bookshop owner and, later, a university professor welcome my interest in the dervishes and answer a multitude of questions. They willingly share the names of other dervish orders, which also meet regularly in different parts of the city.

~~~~~~~~~~~

Organized brotherhoods of Islamic mystics came to be called Sufis back in the eighth century. Shems Friedlander explains in his book *The Whirling Dervishes*:

> Sufi means awareness in life, awareness on a higher plane than on which we normally live.... Some say the label Sufi (in Arabic, suf means wool) grew from the wool cloaks worn by these holy beings. Others like to think that its origin is from the Greek word sophos which means wisdom.

Each of the brotherhoods recognized a particular spiritual guide as their leader, such as Mevlana Rumi. And from the thirteenth through the early twentieth centuries, the Whirling Dervish tekkes were training lodges, or monasteries, for those dedicated to the teachings of Rumi.

"The ideal of the Muslim spiritual masters," suggests Juan Manuel Lozano in MacMillan's *World Religions*, "is 'solitude in the midst of the multitude' — that is, a state of remaining habitually in the presence of God without being touched by the tummult of one's surroundings. As a means of achieving this state spiritual masters recommend detachment, silence, and interior peace."

In Turkey, a boy who wanted to enter a lodge had to have a "spiritual master" or sponsor from the tekke. Once he was accepted, the teenager was initiated, by the sheikh, in a ceremony designating him a *mureed,* or novice. A mureed was then required to swear allegiance to the sheikh and vow to continue his studies to completion. He was given the choice of approaching his training in one of two ways. He could either participate in an extended monastic retreat, lasting for almost three years, during which time he would reside in the tekke, or he could train during the day, living outside the lodge at night as a commuting novice.

Responsibilities accepted by the novice ranged from performing prayers numerous times a day and working for the upkeep of the lodge to learning the art of whirling or playing a musical instrument and diligently studying the *Mesnevi*. Of course, he had to memorize the mystical practices unique to his particular Sufi order.

Only after the successful completion of training could the mureed choose whether to stay in the tekke or live in the city. If he decided to stay, the young man remained unmarried, was supported by government money given to the tekke and worked as a teacher in his brotherhood. In essence, he accepted a monastic life with his Sufi brothers. On the other hand, if the novice decided to live in the city, he was permitted to marry but could return only once a week to the lodge to participate in the religious services.

This additional information piques my curiosity as to the kind of training a mureed experiences today, especially since the tekkes are now officially under government control.

~~~~~~~~~~

I call Farid and Laura at the agreed-upon time and hear the good news. They tell me to meet them at the Galata Mevlevi Tekkesi and we will all proceed from there to an unspecified meeting place. On the appointed day, the three of us rendezvous near the locked gates of the lodge late in the afternoon and hike down to the Galata Bridge. There we catch a ferry to another neighborhood via the Sea of Marmara.

Prior to the dervish gathering, the couple takes me to their favorite cafe for a snack, but I can eat almost nothing. My persistent stomach problems are aggravated by the excitement of attending another Sema Ritual. "Some of my reading has been about mureed training before the early part of this century, when a young man could decide to become a monk or live in the world," I tell Farid after we've gone through the buffet line and are sitting down at a table. "Those choices no longer exist, correct?"

"Well, they don't exist in Turkey, but I can't speak for other countries," he answers. "There are Sufi orders today in north and northwest Africa, as well as Burma, Afghanistan, India and Pakistan. In fact, there are active Sufi orders in the United States." I discover later that these choices still exist in some of the countries he mentioned.

"So, can you reveal anything about your training here in Istanbul? Or is it confidential?"

"I can tell you that I have been searching many years to find a spiritual practice that feels right," he reveals. "And now I am sure that I have found it. In terms of the training, that can depend upon the individual sheikh and the particular order of dervishes. The books that I have suggested to you give a basic introduction to the training." He will not be more specific.

Turning to Laura, I ask if she plans to enter the association. "I am, of course, excited for Farid that he has found a spiritual home and made a commitment." She looks away for a moment. "However, I need more time to think about it."

After eating, we walk briskly into a nearby residential neighborhood off the main street. Passing through an open gate, we join others who are waiting for the sheikh to arrive. I recognize many of the people from a few days ago.

When the sheikh arrives, we follow him up an outside staircase into a large second-story room, above one of the lodges, that looks like an unfinished loft space. We all remove our shoes before entering. As the chorus and musicians begin rehearsing over on the far side of the room, the rest of us roll out colorful Persian carpets with intricate designs and gather around the sheikh for his weekly talk.

Two of us are visitors. A Turkish radio newsman, recently returned home after years of working in the Netherlands, is making a documentary on the Sufi orders and recording his dialogue with the sheikh. The spiritual teacher apparently has no objections to having his words on tape. A grandfatherly figure with a trimmed mustache and full head of white hair, the sheikh easily fields questions. Although the dialogue is in Turkish, I am comfortable simply observing and receiving the occasional translations from Laura.

After an hour or so, there is a pause and the Sema Ritual begins. It seems less formal in this setting, but it is no less powerful. At one point, Laura directs my attention to one of the youngest whirlers. "I remember him at the lodge," I whisper to her. "He seemed particularly adept at the meditation and whirling."

"That is interesting," she answers, "because the sheikh has identified this young man as possessing certain qualities that make for an exceptional dervish." Some months later, I believe I see this young dervish again, on the cover of *National Geographic*. The issue has a feature on Turkey.

Tonight, upon completion of the fourth selam, everyone is invited to form a single line down the center of the room. We all kneel, sitting on our heels. One of the dervishes turns out the lamps and lights a score of large candles, transforming the space into an intimate, mystical place. After the sheikh speaks briefly, we begin chanting the zikr, the remembrance of God, with a constant repetition of the word Allah. The chanting begins slowly and quietly as we close our eyes. Each time the name of Allah is repeated, we bow to the wooden floor with our palms flat against the smooth, cool surface.

"Allah, Allah, Allah, Allah," we chant in unison. Our chanting begins to pick up speed and volume as the ritual gains intensity; we are moving as one, up and down, up and down, up and down, as if joined in a light trance.

"Allah, Allah, Allah, Allah," we chant over and over and over again.

Abruptly we stop, my voice ceasing a moment after those of the others, and sit in silence. My body tingles from head to toe. Kneeling in the candlelight for what feels like a very long time, we wait for our leader to release us. He finally ends the zikr by wailing a prayer to Allah. Although members of the lodge will remain longer with their sheikh, it's time for me to leave or risk missing the ferry back to the bridge. Laura and Farid escort me to the door, and Laura asks with concern if I'm all right. "I hope the chanting didn't alarm you," she says.

Assuring her that it didn't, I tell Laura it was an honor to worship with them. "The intensity was incredible. There is something so powerful about giving yourself over to the Spirit."

I shake hands with them, say good-bye, and they offer me the Sufi farewell: "May your time be happy." In Sufism, the word *time* is symbolic of the union with Allah.

"May your time be happy, too," I reply, and turning away, start down the long staircase into the night.

Chapter Six

AN ETERNAL FLAME

Buddha is more pleased when you debate the meaning of his sutras than when you merely venerate his words.

Tendai saying
The Marathon Monks of Mt. Hiei

As the JR Local pulls into Eizan Station, I hoist my heavy backpack and my shoulder bag and step off the train when the silver doors slide open. It is beginning to rain, so I stop to retrieve a clear plastic poncho and blue Japanese phrase book from my satchel. I step over to the subway ticket office seeking directions to the Sakamoto cable car.

"Sumimasen ga, Sakamoto cable car?" I say to the uniformed official standing behind the thick pane of glass. He points to one of the three residential streets just beyond the tracks. I thank him, "Arigato-gazaimasu," and covering my head and pack with the poncho, I set out.

Walking through the village of Sakamoto, a suburb of Kyoto and home to both the administrative offices and the academic center of the Tendai Buddhist sect, I pass by tidy rows of small homes and businesses, all with manicured lawns and gardens. By the time I reach the Sakamoto cable car at the base of the mountain, my clothes are soaked despite the poncho. The cable car is unheated. I am still shivering half an hour later when I reach my destination: the summit of famed Hiei-san (Mt. Hiei).

~~~~~~~~~~~

Less than a week earlier, when checking "poste restante" in Tokyo's central post office, I had discovered nearly a dozen letters waiting for me. One was from Koji-rin, the Lay People's Training Academy on Hiei-san, and the others were responses from additional Japanese Buddhist monasteries regarding my requests for permission to visit.

A translator at a nearby office explained that the Tendai Buddhist *ajari,* a saintly master from Koji-rin, had granted me permission to participate in a weekend training session as an introduction to the life of a Tendai monk. From March through November, interested individuals and groups can request a retreat at the academy led by a high-ranking Tendai master. Over a weekend, participants practice the disciplines of *shikan* meditation and *sutra* copying, listen to *dharma* talks given by the master and fulfill assignments of physical labor.

Striking out the following day, I began searching for Kan'ei-ji Temple, which the letter had explained would be located near Ueno Park, the largest recreational area in Tokyo. I was to contact the authorities there. Cutting through the crowded park and around the enclosed zoo, then passing by Tokyo's white, sterile-looking National Museum, I discovered the path leading to the rear of Kan'ei-ji Temple. In contrast to the museum, the temple was made of dark wood that had weathered for centuries. There were hundreds of intricate metal hinges and support pieces. The traditional sweeping roofline emphasized the temple's size and, thus, its importance in this neighborhood of small, economical buildings.

Beside the walkway leading to the temple's entrance were erect stone memorials, including six gray, life-size statues of Buddha and a seventh the size of a child. Each adult statue was dressed in a red cotton cap and bib, and the child's figure was wrapped in a single red piece of cloth. At the base of each sculpture were candles and vases of fresh flowers. I knelt to examine the pieces of stone.

Later, I came to understand that the figures were a representation of Mizuko Jizo, the Japanese Buddhist god of children, who watches over the souls of aborted fetuses. *Mizuko,* or "water baby," is the Japanese word for fetus. The statues, and oftentimes temples, are reportedly sculpted or built to provide for the spiritual and emotional needs of women who have had abortions. However, critics say that these practices exist to exploit women's emotions.

"Excuse me, please," a voice said from behind me. Startled, both by the voice so near and the sound of English, I turned to find two short, slightly built Asian men looking down at me. "Where are you from?" inquired one, who was wearing dark-framed glasses.

"Ohayo gozaimasu." I returned confidently, and then realized I had just wished them good morning, and it was afternoon. "From the United States. And where do the two of you come from?"

Isamo, the man in glasses, was an engineering professor at nearby

Tokyo University and was fluent in English. The second man, Li, was a doctoral student in engineering from Mainland China. They told me they frequently walked to the temple on their afternoon break and invited me to join them for tea at their favorite teahouse, just a few blocks away.

I explained that I first needed to make arrangements for visiting Hiei-san. "My instructions were to speak with the authorities at this temple, but as you can see it is closed. Do you know where I need to go?"

"Yes, I know," answered Isamo. "Follow me — I will translate for you." He walked to the other side of the temple with Li and I trailing behind. "That is the Tendai training monastery," he said, pointing to the plain, unmarked, one-story building just ahead. "We go there."

We stepped into an entryway, and Isamo asked for my "permission" letter and rang the small brass bell attached to the wall. Promptly, a middle-aged monk emerged from behind a dark green curtain, and we all raised our hands, palm to palm, and bowed. The common gesture, known as *gassho,* indicated our gratitude, as well as humility and respect.

My acquaintance spoke with the monk for only a few minutes. They stood facing one another, passing the letter back and forth, until Isamo finally turned to me and said, "You must come back tomorrow afternoon and speak with Mr. Aonuma." We bowed once again, and the monk, after returning the gesture, disappeared behind the curtain. "Now we go for tea," declared the professor.

At the traditional wood-frame teahouse a few blocks away, we first removed our shoes, then the hostess seated us on firm, square pillows placed around a low table sitting on thick, tightly woven tatami mats. For nearly an hour we talked, drank bitter green tea and ate delicate cakes made of clear gelatin filled with sweet plum and apricot preserves. Each cake, wrapped in a green leaf, was served individually and eaten with short wooden sticks.

"Did you know that it was an eighth-century emperor who asked the Tendai Patriarch Saicho to establish a temple on Hiei-san?" asked Isamo as we sat eating the sweets. I had thought that Saicho established the first Hiei-san temple under his own volition.

"No, no," he said, "the emperor wanted the temple built to keep the evil forces away from Kyoto." The man paused and then hesitantly asked, "Do you want to know more?"

拝啓

　私は コーネリアス・クラッセン と申します アメリカ人です。ジャーナリズムの修士課程を
最近卒業 いたしました。　本年七月より日本にまいりますが、それに先だって
貴院へ 体験訪問の 許可を お願いするために 手紙を 書きました。

　大学院を卒業して 以来、文筆活動をしています。 その課題は 仏教
ヒンズー教、キリスト教 における 現代の 僧院生活です。この研究のために
昨年 スペインとエジプトに六ケ月滞在いたしました。 その旅で 私は カトリック、
ギリシャ正教 そして 三世紀に建てられた 世界最初の キリスト教 僧院 - アブラック
を訪れ、各々の僧院に宿泊いたしました。

　本年七月より六ケ月間、日本を起点にインドまで 旅をいたします。そして 仏教及び
ヒンズー教の僧院を訪れ、宿泊させて頂きたいと思っております。

　日本に滞在中に 貴院での 日常生活を是非体験する 機会を与えて下さい
ます様お願い至します。 私は日本語は話せませんが、辞書を持参いたします。

　この手紙が 貴院に届く頃には、私は日本に向う途中のため 下記の住所へ
御返事を下さいます様お願い至します。
　　東京都 中央郵便局留　　Cornelius　Claassen　宛

　御配慮・感謝いたしますと共に、お手数をお掛けしますが 宜しくお願い至します。
　　　　　　　　　　　　　　　　　　　　　　　　　敬具.
　　　1995年　6 月 14 日

　僧院関係各位 の 皆様

　　　　　　　　　Cornelius　Claassen

Request letter to Japanese Buddhist roshi

"Please. Any information you can give me will be helpful."

"It was only after the death of Saicho that the official Tendai sect was established," he said taking a long sip of tea. "And then it grew in numbers and influence to dominate the religious affairs of the time. Do you understand?" the professor asked.

"Yes, yes, please go on. This is most interesting."

"Well, as I said, the Tendai school became very powerful and lost sight of its spiritual foundation," continued Isamo. "And there were warrior monks trained to eliminate religious and governmental opposition to Tendai policies. But in the late sixteenth century the monks were defeated by the laymen, and many of the mountain monasteries were destroyed."

Much of my research about the Tendai had focused on the cultural and spiritual influences of the sect. But I knew nothing of the powerful warrior monks or the period of history to which the professor referred. According to Isamo, all of the major schools of Japanese Buddhism developed either in conjunction with, or sprung from, the Tendai sect. However, it is no longer very influential in Japan.

"It is good that you start your visits with the Tendai," he told me. "They are the foundation." Isamo and Li had shown me an unexpected and generous aspect of Japanese culture. When we parted, we bowed, then shook hands, took time to exchange business cards and thanked each other profusely.

~~~~~~~~~~

Returning the following afternoon to the Tendai monastery for my appointment, I was informed that Mr. Aonuma had canceled our meeting. However, the guestmaster said that it was possible to meet with one of the other monks who spoke English.

I waited briefly in the entryway, and a substitute monk walked in. His head was shaved, and he wore a short, white kimono shirt held together with a cloth belt and loose-fitting, white cotton pants. Thick, traditional socks, with a separation only between the first and second toes, covered his feet. We bowed to one another immediately, and he began speaking softly, in English. His name was Ryoei, a man in his final year of training as a *gyoja,* a Tendai monk. Handing over my letter, I explained the situation, and we sat down on the tatami mat, as if to negotiate. After looking over the letter, Ryoei returned it and then sat silently, waiting for me to begin asking questions.

My initial question was an obvious one. I asked how long he had been in training.

He watched me quietly for a moment, then replied, "I am training twelve year. Six year I study book and six year I practice. I also study priesthood for six month at age fourteen." Now, at the age of thirty-seven, he has almost completed his studies. The gyoja explained that both males and females are eligible to participate in the sixty-day training period for the Tendai priesthood. For the first month, the trainee studies the *sutras*, or Buddhist scriptures, and practices the ceremonial chanting that requires extensive memorization. In the final thirty days, the student focuses on the practical training of performing rites, the fire ceremonies and detailed daily purification rituals. On their last day, the trainees participate in a rigorous mountain pilgrimage, the *kaihogyo,* visiting the major sacred sites on Hiei-san.

In many ways — according to Ryoei — the twelve-year training period for a gyoja, appropriately referred to as a "spiritual athlete," is an extension of the training for priests, except that it is restricted to men. The first half of the training is devoted to academic studies in the Buddhist principles, particular Tendai practices and liberal arts courses, with the remaining six years focused on practical applications of academic work.

It's interesting to me that the Tendai sect strongly encourages physical as well as mental tests. Various levels of demanding physical training are available to a gyoja, ranging from long-term silent and walking meditation or years of running demanding pilgrimage routes daily, to meditating for days without food, drink or sleep. The demands of their training are not to be taken lightly.

"I take father's place when training complete," he revealed. The monk's parents and grandparents reside near Tokyo, where his father is the Tendai priest in the village temple.

"Do you live here all the time?"

"No, no," answered the man. "I here during day from 9:00 to 5:00 and return to wife and child in evening. But many men in community live here." A vow of celibacy is not required in the Tendai sect, and oftentimes the trainees will marry and have children.

Changing the subject, I asked if he could help me make arrangements for a stay on Hiei-san. Rather than answering immediately, he posed some questions to me. While listening to my answers, Ryoei remained still and fully at attention, his dark eyes seldom leaving mine.

During the question-and-answer session, he explained to me the origin of the sect's name: "Tendai Patriarch Saicho study with Chinese master Chih-i on Mt. T'ien-t'ai in Mainland China." Of course, T'ien-t'ai translates to Tendai in Japanese.

Following a series of thoughtful inquiries, mostly about my journey, he abruptly stood. "I make call now and see if possible to stay," he announced, passing back through the green curtains. Fifteen minutes later, he returned. Raising his head and smiling, Ryoei gave me the welcome news, "I call Koji-rin at Hiei-san, and you can go for weekend training." He continued, "You be there Friday at 2:00 P.M., and training finish next day same time. When arrive at gatehouse, ask for Mr. Osumi."

Elated, I thanked the gyoja for his assistance, then began pulling on my boots and preparing to leave. It was then that the Tendai gave me a small manila envelope and said, "This gift for you. Stay healthy on journey."

"Arigato-gozaimasu."

The smiling Tendai replied, "Arigato-gozaimasu."

Once away from the monastery, I opened the envelope and found approximately $320, in yen, carefully wrapped in thin, white rice paper, just enough money to cover transportation costs for the duration of my journey in Japan.

~~~~~~~~~~

Exiting the Sakamoto cable car, I walk back out into the rain. The tiny raised gatehouse that Ryoei mentioned is barely visible through the dense fog. As I get closer to it, I can see an elderly monk peering over the tops of his glasses through the small window. He opens it and looks down at me.

"Konnichiwa," I call up to him, confident that the word means "good afternoon." There's a moment of silence, and I feel my confidence waver. "Claassen to iimasu, Bill Claassen."

"Huh?" he shouts, now staring down with a furrowed brow.

"Bill Claassen — Koji-rin — Mr. Osumi," I shout back. Just then, I lose my grip on my phrase book, and it falls to the wet pavement. Suddenly, the monk makes the connection.

"Oh, oh, oh — Amerikan, Osumi, Koji-rin, oh, oh, oh!" exclaims the old man. He hands me a folded piece of paper and then shuts the window decisively.

Hunching over the paper to protect it from the rain, I carefully unfold it. It's a map, the lines of which have smeared, with words printed in English. There are circles labeled "BUS STOP," two roads and a square box marked "KOJI-RIN," then more words and arrows pointing this way and that; it's frustrating because the damn map is confusing and this potential trainee is running way behind schedule.

"Wait a minute, wait a minute, calm down now," I say to myself out loud. "Take a few deep breaths and relax." Standing in the rain, slowly and spontaneously turning in circles, I begin to appreciate the dark green cloud forest surrounding me, recalling that this holy mountain is a natural wildlife reserve known around the world. And according to a wonderful legend, there is a flame in one of the temples here — the eternal flame — lit by the Tendai Patriarch Saicho more than a thousand years ago.

John Stevens writes in *The Marathon Monks of Mount Hiei* that the mountaintop

> ...offers the seeker every type of religious experience — sacred scholarship, grand ritual, austere meditation, heartfelt repentance, heroic asceticism, mystical flight, miraculous cures, ceaseless devotion, divine joy and nature worship — while promising enlightenment in this very body. Further, it provides the seeker with a splendid environment — stately buildings, sumptuous Buddha Halls, icons of celestial beauty, music from heaven, food and drink seemingly prepared by the gods, magic costumes, spectacular scenery and breathtaking views — to support the seeker in his or her quest.

I stop circling, select a road and hike until I encounter other visitors here for the day. With the assistance of one of the gracious older Japanese men, I find the shuttle bus. I watch out the window, and I see a small wooden sign with neatly painted red letters and an arrow pointing in the direction of Koji-rin, marking my stop.

From there, a winding trail, heavy with the smell of pine needles, leads me into a thickly wooded area and under a corridor linking two

Amida Butsu, the Buddha of Infinite Light and Life

outwardly identical temples: the Hall of Perpetual Practice and the Lotus Hall. I read later that they were built in the seventeenth century and furnished only with Buddha icons, tatami mats and a few pieces of furniture. Both are used constantly for the rigorous ongoing training of the Tendai gyoja to the ways of disciplined meditation.

The Hall of Perpetual Practice is where a trainee observes three months of solitary walking meditation, in which he circles the hall repeating the four words "Hail to Amida Butsu" the entire time. Bathroom breaks are permitted, and the trainee may sit for meals, a brief daily meditation and sleep. He may not lie down. Rigorous training demands as much in the neighboring Lotus Hall where, over the same span of time, a trainee sits for meditation in a chair. Movement is permitted only at mealtimes, during a short period of walking meditation, and when using the bathroom.

Further ahead is a larger, more impressive wooden temple with a solid stone foundation and substantial columns extending across the front. Built in the fourteenth century, Shaka-do Temple is one of the primary buildings on Hiei-san and the oldest structure on the sacred mountain. It has been painted a deep red. It is here that a Buddha icon carved by Saicho is rumored to be kept hidden.

Continuing on the path around and beyond the Shaka-do, I discover a small, traditional Japanese house where a gyoja directs me to the nearby Koji-rin, set back in the forest away from the path. Finally, standing in front of the training center, I glance at my watch: I am almost one hour late. Unexpectedly, the traditional doors slide open to reveal a man, dressed like Ryoei, standing imposingly before me. His hands rest on either hip; his body language radiates impatience.

"Mr. Claassen, you late. Please follow me," he tersely suggests in English. Quickly pulling off my muddy boots and wet socks, I trail behind him down a long, empty corridor, tiptoeing on the polished wooden floor and then up a few steps into a sleeping room. It is spotless and orderly.

"My Tendai name Kakushun," he announces, turning to face me. "This where you sleep." He points to one of six futons rolled up and sitting on the tatami mats. "Please change and come upstair. You hang clothes on hook." Before striding out, he hands me a schedule printed in English.

Friday		
2:00-4:15 *Tour, introductions*		7:00 *Video on Tendai Sect*
4:30 *Shikan (meditation)*		8:00 *Bath, Shikan*
6:00 *Dinner*		9:00 *Lights out*

Saturday		
5:00 *Wake up, wash*		8:00 *Breakfast*
5:15 *Shikan*		9:00 *Sutra copying*
6:30 *Kaihogyo (pilgrimage)*		11:00 *Tendai master talks*
7:00 *Calisthenics*		12:00 *Lunch*
7:30 *Clean training hall*		1:00 *Closing ceremony*

I take off my soaked clothes, carefully hang them up as instructed and scramble into damp ones from my pack. Grabbing my conversation book, I run upstairs to join the others. Sitting in a semicircle around Kakushun and his assistant are almost a dozen Japanese men and women who are all listening intently to something Kakushun is saying.

"Speak Japanese?" asks the assistant.

Flustered and nervous, I try to answer in Japanese, but I stumble. Holding up my damp blue book, I say, "No."

"You need help then?"

"Yes, yes, thank you."

One of the women, Yoshi, volunteers to be a translator and quickly slides over to my side. She has pulled her long black hair into a ponytail, accentuating her fair skin and dark eyes. She, like the other students gathered around Kakushun, is dressed in casual clothes. Yoshi immediately begins translating in a loud whisper as the assistant continues talking. When the lecture ends, all of us shuffle out of the room and down the steps to the front porch where we slip on our shoes and line up. My place is at the end of the line.

We march briskly down the wet path to the Shaka-do, remove our shoes again and enter the temple. The interior is open, blocked only by massive, red wooden columns. The walls are likewise painted red, but the wall-to-wall carpeting is light green. A simple altar, lacquered a gloss black and built into the back wall, is revealed from behind the two sliding doors where burning incense and a single flickering candle sit on the shelves near the lone Buddha icon. Above the altar hangs a large, circular, turquoise metal plate, symbolic of the life, death and rebirth cycle of reincarnation. Though austere, the space is both inviting and comfortable.

Patriarch Saicho once said,

> Even with the best of intentions it is difficult to master the way under unfavorable conditions; living in a quiet place in the bosom of nature is the most conducive for practice. It is better to rely, at first, on the place rather than the mind.

Arranging us in parallel lines facing the altar, Kakushun places Yoshi at my side. Then, while explaining the proper Tendai meditation technique, *shikan,* he moves among us, correcting our posture. I watch the people around me and listen to Yoshi's whispered translation of the instructions. After a moment of silence, the teacher lightly taps a gong, and we begin. This first shikan is scheduled to last one-and-a-quarter hours.

Taking a half-lotus position — putting my right foot onto my left thigh and my left foot under my right thigh, then placing one hand, palm up, on top of the other in my lap — I feel comfortable, momentarily. Glancing briefly at the Buddha before closing my eyes, I shift my focus to the breath moving in and out of my nostrils, as instructed. But midway through the meditation, my nose begins to itch, my right foot tingles and a voice in my mind begins chattering. Trying to ignore the distractions, I begin silently counting my breaths — one, two, three — until it's no longer possible to maintain this position. In my own practice, I seldom sit for longer than forty-five minutes at a time.

Breaking posture and scratching my nose, I quickly alternate the position of my feet. Kakushun is standing directly behind me, but he doesn't say a word. Finally, I hear the welcome sound of the gong bringing this meditation to a close. Rising to our feet in silence, we line up again and shuffle out of the Shaka-do. This time, we march down the path to the dining hall. Last in line, I am able to observe the other trainees. None of them seem unsteady, but I stumble a few times as my legs are regaining feeling.

Inside the refectory, each of us bows to the Buddha sitting on the altar in the front of the room and then finds his or her appropriate spot at the low-set tables. Individualized name cards, carefully printed in Japanese calligraphy, have been placed at each setting, and Yoshi, again, has been assigned to my right side. Together we bow again to the Buddha, sit down on our knees and begin the discipline of *shojin ryori,* or "food for practice."

At each place setting is a circular wooden tray holding an assortment of delicate black lacquered bowls. White rice has been served in the large bowls, with the smaller ones containing miso broth, a square of peanut tofu, cooked seaweed, some steamed vegetables, strong herbal tea and a few unidentifiable items. The colors of the various foods are brilliant: orange and red, purple and green, with each setting arranged to highlight the aesthetic of the items. Everything on the table has a place and a presentation. As Saicho said, "It is better to rely, at first, on the place rather than the mind."

Watching the ajari, using our peripheral vision to track his every move and imitate his movements, our group picks up the sutra books that unfold like accordions and begin chanting in unison. While observing the trainee directly across the table, and listening to Yoshi's chanting, I feebly try to imitate their sounds and actions. In these brief moments, we try to speak as one. After completing the sutras, all of us remove the finely decorated chopsticks from their rice paper covers and commence eating.

"No make noise when you eat," Yoshi whispers without turning her head. "Watch me and finish all food." Paying strict attention, I follow her lead, mindfully lifting each bowl close to my mouth before taking a bite.

Noticing that the other trainees are leaving one pickle in a bowl, I ask Yoshi why.

"To clean bowl; watch and follow," she replies.

Passing the teapot, which has been delivered from the kitchen, down the center of the table at the end of the meal, each of us pours the aromatic liquid into our small bowls. Then, clasping the pickle with our chopsticks, we brush the sides of each lacquered container until our entire setting is clean, after which the pickle is eaten and the tea drunk. There are to be no leftovers. At the conclusion of the meal, the ajari leads us in chanting the sutras and bowing to the Buddha, then assigns us to chores. While the women clear the bowls, the men get down on their hands and knees, crawling along the floor in search of lint, dust or food particles. After completing our tasks, we bow again to the Buddha and return to the training hall, through a fine mist, marching in single file.

By early evening, our group is sitting on the second floor, attentively watching a black-and-white documentary on the history of the Tendai sect. Although I can't understand the language, the visuals are stunning, particularly those that reveal the physical rigors of the Tendai practice. How curious it is to be training in a centuries-old Tendai practice and watching a video.

The narrator, a renowned Tendai ajari, reminds me of Thomas Merton, who inspired me and, in a way, brought me here. It's the Tendai's manner and smile, the man's intensity and bushy eyebrows, that bring Merton to mind. Interestingly, Merton was partially responsible for initiating the international dialogue between Christian and Buddhist monks back in the 1960s that continues today.

Moving closer to Yoshi, I ask where all of these people come from. She doesn't appear to understand, so I ask her again, slowly this time.

"Oh, we work same factory near Kyoto," she answers. "Boss make us come."

"So you didn't come because you wanted to?"

"No, no, we not come on our own," she tells me.

Unfortunately, there is no discussion after the video. Instead, we are given a limited amount of time for bathing — a disciplined ritual, as in every other aspect of Tendai life, where there is even a specific order to washing oneself — before bed. Although in most Japanese Buddhist monasteries a particular deity figure is to be honored before entering the bathing area, he is conspicuously missing here at Koji-rin.

After stepping into the bathhouse, a white-tiled room filled with steam, all of us men quickly strip down to wash. A substantial metal tub brimming with hot water, sits in the middle of the room, and against one wall are small benches with buckets placed next to cold-water spigots. Each of us takes a turn, moving quickly and quietly. Oh, how I want to slip down into the hot water and soak, but there is only time for a brief dip in the steaming tub.

Back in our room, we sit in shikan at the ends of our futons before turning out the lights. Facing one another in three pairs, we move into a proper posture and close our eyes. I am totally relaxed, focused and thankfully — if only temporarily — free from that nearly incessant interior chatter. Initially, my focus is on breathing, then it shifts to repeating the word *Buddha, Buddha, Buddha,* in silence. Tonight's meditation is immensely pleasurable, truly an emptying of my mind. When the gong rings, indicating the completion of half an hour, each of us slips under his heavy cotton comforter and rests his head on the hard, cloth-covered block that serves as a pillow.

Rising quickly to the sound of the meditation gong just before sunrise, we all shuffle back down to the bathroom. Splashing cold water on our faces and brushing our teeth, we begin acting as if we're all in a marathon of sorts. Feeling an unspoken sense of competition, we speedily roll up the futons, get dressed at top speed and run outside to line up alongside the women in the cold morning air. Marching with a purpose to the Shaka-do, we take our prescribed places and prepare for shikan. But at this hour, the temple no longer feels comfortable or inviting. I have discovered a new distraction. An extra layer of clothing would have been helpful.

"Just relax, time go quickly," Yoshi whispers, detecting my mood.

Leading the meditation this morning is the Tendai master grasping the *keisaku,* a warning stick, in his right hand. He says that it is meant to assist the meditator in regaining focus and explains the procedures for requesting its use; however, his instructions are unclear to me. Before we begin, he walks up and down the rows, gently correcting our posture while making helpful suggestions. This is the time to ask for clarification of his instructions, but unfortunately I hold back. When stopping behind me, the master lightly pushes against my lower back, and I immediately straighten. Soon the sound of the gong initiates shikan.

Much to my dismay, it doesn't take long for my left foot to begin going numb. "Just be with the pain and it will pass," I keep thinking to myself. Then the beads of sweat, starting at the back of my neck, begin inching their way down my spine, tickling as they go. There is both a feeling of pain and pleasure, the yin and yang of my meditation. Gaining, losing, then regaining a sense of focus, I try to visualize a pleasurable setting. But unwelcome images begin racing through my mind; I count seconds that become minutes and finally open my eyes just as the ajari walks by with the keisaku in hand. Now, of course, there is regret for not asking my questions earlier.

Deciding my only recourse is to change positions, I listen to my sixth sense. When it feels appropriate, I quickly curl both legs to my left, adjust my posture and let out — very softly — a sigh of relief.

There are no repercussions.

Now, time moves rapidly, and soon the gong ends our shikan. Breaking position, we silently stand. Hobbling out of the Shaka-do, I begin the daily pilgrimage route, the *kaihogyo,* with the others as scheduled. Jogging at an easy pace in the cool mist, we follow our leader up, down and around the mountain trails. By the time we reach the *Jodo-in,* the circulation has returned to my lower extremities.

This is where Saicho, the patriarch, is entombed. No one says a word at this dark, unpretentious temple that sits back from the path. The longer we stand, the more I sense we all appreciate this visit. In the lush, protective, cloud forest, the ancient Tendai traditions briefly envelope us all.

We dash back, on command, to the Shaka-do, then follow Kakushun in a series of rigorous calisthenics. Beginning with jumping jacks and leg lifts, then moving on to sit-ups and push-ups, we slip back into our competitive mode. All of us are in good physical condition and revel in demonstrating our strength to one another. Working out in the oldest temple on Hiei-san seems odd. But, I remind myself that exercise is as important as silent meditation or eating properly or bathing mindfully. These are the teachings of the Tendai.

Cleaning tasks — the daily samu — in the training hall follows; Kakushun shouts out the assignments. Each job must be completed in less than three-quarters of an hour. My assignment is to clean the men's bathroom — toilets, sinks and floor. Handing over the wire brush, a wet mop, a natural sponge and some harsh cleanser, the taskmaster leaves me to my work. It was Chih-i, the Chinese master of Saicho, who suggested "a good preparation for the ultimate meditation was latrine duty for eight hundred consecutive days" writes Stevens in *The Marathon Monks.* My task is completed on time.

After the morning meal, we return to the second floor of the training hall for our introduction to calligraphy, the copying of the sutras. A small desk, an inkpot and a set of practical tools are assigned to each of us, and we are given a page of calligraphy to begin copying onto a large blank piece of rice paper. Copying, I discover, demands tremendous concentration and patience.

Walking by my desk and looking down at my scribbles, the master shakes his head in disapproval and slips the prepared sheet of calligraphy under my nearly blank sheet of paper. He wants me — and only me —

to literally copy over the lines. The heat of humiliation races through me then quickly cools. I remind myself that the master is here to instruct and assist, not to embarrass. The longer we copy, the greater is my interest in the process, even though it's simply tracing the characters. It is with reluctance that I return my tools and desk in preparation for the master's *dharma* talk that is to follow.

The ajari stands before us wearing a thin black robe over his white cotton clothing; his garments distinguish him from the men in training. Around his neck hangs a piece of embossed white silk, like a large amulet, another symbol of status. He begins talking slowly, standing in one place and purposely making eye contact with each one of us kneeling on the floor. As his volume increases, so do the strong, graceful gestures of his hands and arms. Periodically he uses an English word or phrase for my benefit.

Yoshi isn't translating now, but it's obvious that the lecture is focusing on the importance of maintaining respect for Japanese cultural and religious traditions. The speaker's manner is both earnest and passionate, and the trainees are all attentive. Abruptly, he stops, picks up a pair of chopsticks and carries them over to me.

"Hold these like you eating," he commands in English. Taking the sticks confidently, I hold them in the proper position.

"Ah-hah! Ah-hah!" he exclaims, as if to say that the American can hold them properly when many Japanese have forgotten. I am relieved to have finally done something correctly. However, I lose whatever points I have earned after the lecture, when I commit a very serious error.

It happens at lunchtime. Halfway through the meal, I begin feeling nauseated and simply cannot finish the big bowl of rice sitting in front of me. Sweat begins beading on the back of my neck. One more mouthful of rice and lunch will be coming back up. Embarrassed, I don't know what to do. But, after glancing up at the ajari, his assistants and my fellow trainees, the answer comes to me; I will clean all of my small bowls but leave the large dish of rice. By now, of course, the white rice looks as if it has increased tenfold.

Kakushun looks in my direction, trying to catch my attention, but I studiously ignore him. Getting up slowly, he begins moving toward me. I watch him out of the corner of my eye while facing straight ahead. The gyoja kneels directly behind me, breathing down my neck.

"You not finish rice, Mr. Claassen," he whispers. The other trainees immediately cease moving, all of them staring straight ahead.

"My stomach is upset," I whisper back, my heart thumping hard against my chest. "It's not possible for me to eat more."

"Important to finish food," he tells me, emphasizing each word.

"It cannot be done now — I am sorry." My reply is barely audible. I am feeling very small. He sits, waiting, for a long time. Finally, he stands up and returns to his place. Kneeling, he too stares straight ahead.

After chanting, then bowing, clearing the dishes, cleaning the floor, and bowing again, the others shuffle out of the dining room in single file. Staying behind, I trudge into the kitchen with lowered head, bow and begin apologizing to the staff. "Sumimasen, sumimasen, sumimasen." By the time my apologies have been made, all the other trainees have returned to the training hall, and I hurry to join them with some trepidation.

In our final hour together, we are honored to witness the reenactment of the *Goma*. Symbolizing the flame of wisdom that consumes all passions and purifies the world, this fire ceremony is a most important ritual within the Tendai tradition. Standing tall at the altar with his two assistants, the ajari — now dressed in a multicolored ceremonial robe — leads the intricate and dramatic ritual, beginning with the ringing of bells and the throwing of confetti, then continuing with aggressive chanting and, in closing, the burning of Japanese anise. All three Tendais perform their roles superbly and bring our brief training to a dramatic close.

Gathering outside in the midafternoon to say our good-byes, we stand while the master offers us a lengthy blessing, after which we bow and thank him and his assistants. I talk briefly with Kakushun, express my gratitude for his help and again apologize for the incident at lunchtime, then turn to leave.

"Mr. Claassen," he says, and I turn around to find him grinning, "be careful in future how much rice you put in bowl." I bow to him and then start down the path. I'm the last one in line.

Chapter Seven

ONE SINGLE DROP

To try to make the whole world truthful would be like trying to cover the whole world with soft leather.... That is impossible, of course. However, if on our own two feet we wear a pair of soft leather shoes, then it is the same as if the whole world were covered with soft leather.

> Bodhisattva's teachings,
> interpreted by Ekai Kawaguchi Roshi,
> twentieth century

"Do you have any questions?" asks Mitra. "Would you like to walk through it one more time just to make sure you understand everything?"

"No, no more questions," I say. "The instructions are clear. Your careful attention to the details has been very helpful."

Mitra is a stickler for details, an apt quality in the monk responsible for training newcomers to the Rinzai Zen Buddhist monastery of Sogenji, Japan. She must prepare us for the "bowing-in" ceremony, a welcoming ritual.

Standing about five feet, five inches tall and wearing dark slacks and a wraparound shirt, the female monk looks fairly ordinary. Or she would but for her shaven head, which highlights her fine bone structure and marks her as a Buddhist monk. Her hair is traditionally cut every fifth day by a fellow trainee.

Mitra (the name was given to her by the *roshi* at another Buddhist monastery) was born into a military family and moved from base to base in the United States when she was growing up. As a young adult, she married a man in the diplomatic corps, whom she has since divorced. Now she is finally putting down roots. "I'm currently in the process of building a zendo outside of Santa Fe, New Mexico," she tells me. "It will be a training center for those interested in Zen Buddhist practice."

We had met earlier that day to schedule a training session here in the *zendo,* the official meditation hall. All of the monks gather here to practice *zazen,* their form of daily meditation, but at night it becomes the men's sleeping quarters.

Now, waiting in the back of the zendo for the early evening ceremony to begin, I appreciate the beauty and simplicity of the building's soft wooden interior. Measuring approximately forty feet wide by seventy feet long, it is sparsely furnished. Along both sides are extended platforms that stand waist high and are covered with thick tatami mats. The smell of dried straw mixes with the smoke from burning incense that rises in swirls toward the cathedral ceiling and fills the hall. Just inside the front entrance sits a dark lacquered altar, dedicated to the Buddhist guardian of wisdom, to which a devotee will respectfully bow before entering.

A bell signals the beginning of the ceremony, and Buddhist monks of both sexes, all with shaven heads and dressed in lightweight black robes, float into the zendo, taking their designated places on one of the two platforms. They adjust their *zafus,* round sitting cushions, and whatever else the monks use to support their meditation posture. Once settled, each individual looks straight ahead as if frozen in time.

Mitra nods her head, giving me permission to proceed. I place my palms one on top of the other against my solar plexus and begin walking mindfully down one side of the hall, breathing deeply, conscious of each step. When I reach the *jikijitsu,* the elder monk responsible for supervising the others during meditation, I face him and bow deeply from the waist, as Mitra has instructed me. Then moving to his side, I bow a second time, placing my hands on the platform. Turning to face the stern-looking jikijitsu once again, I bow a third time.

Next, I walk slowly to the back of the zendo and repeat the ritual with Mitra. When I've completed it, she indicates that I am to take my place on the single platform, in the outside hallway reserved for visitors. Climbing up and settling into a half-lotus position, I wait for a second bell, then begin counting my breaths, one to ten, over and over as instructed. Participating in this rite of passage has eased me into an extremely focused zazen session that will last an hour and a half.

~~~~~~~~~~~

Earlier in the afternoon, when wandering the neighborhood on the outskirts of Okayama, Japan, I had discovered the magnificent three-hundred-year-old *sammon,* the "mountain gate" leading into Sogenji. Standing several stories high and constructed of thick, dark wooden pillars and heavy beams, the traditional entrance gate is a symbolic passageway between the secular and the sacred worlds.

A wide stone walkway led through the gate and up to a white, stuccoed *hondo,* the primary temple in a Buddhist monastery. Even taller than the mountain gate, with a multitiered, sweeping roofline, it had thick wooden doors and six bell-shaped windows decorating the facade, three on either side. The doors to the hondo were wide open, but the view inside was blocked by a folding latticework screen. Off to my left was another traditional structure, a small, dark wooden building where sacred texts and historical writings unique to the community are kept behind locked doors. It is known as the "scripture house."

With no one in sight, I returned to the sammon for a closer inspection of the architectural detail. But as I was removing my backpack, a slender young woman quietly appeared from behind one of the neatly trimmed hedges and approached, not speaking until she was directly in front of me. "Can I help you?" she asked. I detected an Irish lilt to her voice. She was dressed in blue work clothes with rubber thongs on her feet, and her dark, curly hair framed a very fair complexion.

I told her I had made arrangements to practice zazen here for a few days and handed her a postcard and letter signed "Chi-san." (The Japanese word *san,* when attached to a proper name, indicates a social title: Mr., Mrs., Miss or Ms.) My contact could either be male or female. "My train from Kyoto arrived in downtown Okayama this morning, and the public bus dropped me off here in the neighborhood not long ago," I told her.

"Oh, yes, Chi-san is the guestmaster here at Sogenji, along with her many other responsibilities," she said, glancing over the notes then standing quietly for a moment as if figuring out the appropriate next step. "Excuse me, I have forgotten to give you my name. I'm Beth." The woman was still using her birth name, indicating that she was relatively new to the community.

Before coming to Japan I had had numerous conversations with an acquaintance from my hometown who had studied and practiced zazen with the *roshi* here at Sogenji. He had explained that a student receives a new name from the master only after several years of intensive study: "The name you are given is what you are to become, what you grow into."

Sammon gate at Sogenji

Beth began walking, and I followed. "I think it would be best to take you to the guesthouse, and then we'll return and introduce you to our teacher, Shodo Harada Roshi, or hojo-san as we usually call him," she said. *Hojo-san* is the word for the head priest of a temple or monastery. The term is commonly used in place of the title *roshi* that refers primarily to a Zen master.

The two of us sauntered around well-manicured hedges, then down a dirt road that led past a barn, storage bins and craft studios until we came upon a rough stone path leading up a hill. Along the way Beth informed me she was an artist — a painter to be exact — and that she came from Dublin, Ireland. She had a sister living in Japan, and her mother had once studied at Catholic University in Washington, D.C.

At the top of the hill was a new guesthouse. The hallway still smelled of new lumber and fresh varnish. To one side was a round wooden deck that looked out over Sogenji and the sprawling city of Okayama, a southwestern coastal urban center on Japan's main island. While I was talking with Beth in the kitchen, the French supervising monk, Doi-san, joined us. He led us down the hallway, explaining the layout, and I hurriedly adjusted to the shift from an Irish to a French accent.

"Here, this will be your room," he said in English, opening a door midway down. It was tiny, with barely enough space for a single futon on the floor and a chair, on top of which sat a miniature fan. "As you know, this is the hot season, so you might want to keep both the window and door open and the fan going," suggested Doi-san.

"Oh, by the way," he added, "one other guest will be staying in the house this week. His name is Peter, a Belgian priest living with his religious order here in Japan and working as a missionary. He makes frequent visits to Sogenji to work on his zazen practice, and he's a good man." I was not surprised to hear of a Catholic missionary finding strength and solace in a retreat to a Rinzai Zen monastery. It made perfect sense.

I dropped off my backpack, splashed some cold water on my face and neck and followed Beth back down to the hondo, where we left our shoes near the front steps before entering. Inside there were spacious ceremonial halls and altars simply decorated with candles, polished Buddha icons and colorful flowers, the perfume of which infused the air. Wide wooden planks on the floor shone as if recently polished, the result of centuries of scrubbing by Sogenji monks using nothing but water.

We found Shodo Harada Roshi, hojo-san, also dressed in blue cotton work clothes, behind the hondo giving instructions in archery. His attentive student, a blonde young man named Tiel, was an American, from the state of Vermont. Beth had told me that taking lessons in archery or Japanese or practicing a musical instrument or "throwing pots" were regarded as noble ways of deepening the Zen practice. At least one afternoon a week is always set aside for those various disciplines.

Hojo-san spared us only a quick glance, seemingly annoyed at the interruption, when Beth introduced me. Holding the palms of my hands together just beneath my chin, I bowed my head respectfully. The master responded with a few bitten-off words. He looked much younger than his fifty years. The skin on his face and arms was taut and his body lean and exercised. (One of the monks informed me the next day that the "roshi is fifteen years out of his awakening," meaning that Shodo Harada had acquired "enlightenment" fifteen years ago and was now regarded as a master and qualified teacher of the Rinzai Zen practice.) Because he obviously did not have time to talk, Beth and I continued on around the temple complex.

"The roshi leaves tomorrow to participate in a memorial service for the victims of the atom bomb explosion in Hiroshima. He is preoccupied with his departure," she explained, almost apologetically, just as Mitra joined us and introduced herself.

"The bell you will hear later in the afternoon is the supper call," said Beth and then excused herself and wandered off, leaving me with the trainer.

"Mitra, I thought that Buddhist monks couldn't eat after noontime?"

"Well, technically that is correct," she replied. "So we call the late meal 'evening medicine' and finish the leftovers from lunch." Bending the rules a bit, for the good of the community, appealed to me. "By the way," said Mitra, "you should know that there are three places in the community where you are always to observe silence: the kitchen, the zendo and the bathhouse."

That evening, before taking my place at the long narrow table, I watched as everyone retrieved their eating utensils. Each set was neatly wrapped in a gray napkin, and inside were five plain wooden bowls in graduated sizes, a set of chopsticks and a neatly folded, white cloth napkin. The collection of people hovering around the table had the look of a

United Nations committee. Beth had said earlier that there were almost a dozen nationalities currently practicing at Sogenji, including a few Japanese monks.

At the head of the table, on his own bench, sat hojo-san with his training monk, the jikijitsu, and first assistant flanking him. Occupation of other seats was always determined by longevity in the monastery. Almost immediately after everyone was seated, hojo-san began leading us in the chanting of three sutras. Written in Sanskrit and literally meaning "a thread on which jewels are strung," the sutras are selected Buddhist scriptures that vary slightly according to the mealtime. I soon realized that at Sogenji, a sutra was recited in a loud, forceful voice, quite a contrast to my recent experience on Mt. Hiei.

Large bowls of evening medicine were quickly pushed down the table, following the chanting, without concern for the color or arrangement of food groups. Each monk eagerly selected items ranging from vegetables and brown rice to potatoes and herb-covered tofu. I made a point of taking only as much as I was certain I could finish, heeding the recent warning from Kakushun, the Tendai gyoja on Mt. Hiei. A wooden scoop was passed down the table, following the food, into which each of us put a few grains of cooked rice as an offering to the gakki, or "hungry spirits"; those who have died and not yet realized Buddhahood.

After the meal, Chi-san, a big-boned woman with a contagious grin and seemingly boundless energy, approached me and introduced herself. "Would you like to meet late tomorrow morning for tea?" she asked, and I gratefully accepted. "That will give us some time to get acquainted. We'll talk in the morning."

On my way back to the guesthouse, I met another female monk — this one with a heavy German accent and burning red cheeks — named Zui-san. "If I can answer any questions, please let me know," she offered, smiling and walking alongside me.

I immediately asked about the mixed group I'd seen at mealtime. "I'm curious why there are so many internationals studying and living here." Zui-san explained that since the roshi arrived at Sogenji in the early 1980s, more and more internationals had been coming to the temple for training, but she offered no explanation as to exactly why.

As we passed by the barn and a parking garage, she pointed to the overgrown field beyond, toward a wooden frame that looked like a pole barn. "That is my project over there," she said proudly. An architect, Zui-san had used logs that she cut locally and cleaned herself, along with some two-by-fours, to build the frame.

"Are you working towards completion?" I asked.

"Not necessarily. This is an assignment given to me by the roshi. It's a problem to solve."

"So you're working on it by yourself?"

"Yes, I am. I work on it week to week."

Checking my watch, I discovered that time had gotten away from me. Excusing myself, I ran up the hill to retrieve a pair of glasses from my room. Mitra would be waiting in the zendo to give me instructions for the "bowing-in" ritual.

~~~~~~~~~~

By the time the ceremony and zazen are completed it is dark, and I wearily return to the guesthouse to do some reading on the history of Sogenji. Meanwhile, the others have found private places to meditate, a nightly practice they call *yaza.* "It can last anywhere from one hour to the whole night," one of the monks tells me.

Using a pillow to prop myself up on the frameless futon, with the miniature fan blowing hot air on my chest, I read that more than three hundred years ago the feudal lords of the Ikeda Clan financed construction of the Sogenji temple complex that later became the major Rinzai Zen training center in Japan. Today, that clan is honored by the monks in special services throughout the year.

Shodo Harada Roshi, hojo-san, in his book *Morning Dew Drops of the Mind,* writes that "about two hundred years ago Sogenji became a dojo (training monastery) . . . and people came to train here from all over Japan." But there was also a period of time when Sogenji fell into disrepair, and the number of trainees was reduced to three caretakers. However, in the early 1980s, as Zui-san had told me earlier, Shodo Harada came to Sogenji at the direction of his master with the responsibility to "protect the temple and be its caretaker."

I am intrigued to discover in one of my reference books that a Japanese monk who trained at Sogenji later officially introduced Buddhism to the United States. He did so during the World Parliament of Religions held in Chicago in the late 1800s. He attended the conference with an assistant and translator, D. J. Suzuki, known to students of Zen Buddhism as a renowned teacher and the author of *The Training of the Zen Buddhist Monk*.

The wake-up bell tolls very, very early the next morning, and within five minutes, the three of us inhabiting the guesthouse are out and stumbling down the uneven path and over to the temple. I remember to leave my shoes near the kitchen entrance and then follow the others streaming into the central hall of the hondo. Inside, my eyes are drawn by the thick beams of the ceiling and the cypress pillars supporting them.

Lining up on either side of the altar, in the warm glow of candlelight and the intoxicating smell of incense, we make certain that our lines are straight and the spaces between us are equal. Someone directs me to the end of one line, where I take a place on the tatami among the more than two dozen men and women. Following the signal, the high-pitched ring of a brass bell, we bow and sit down, waiting in anticipation for the roshi. A nearby monk thoughtfully hands me a book of the sutras.

Just then, the hojo-san, wearing a lightweight white robe, enters the hall. He marches between our two lines, bows once to the altar and sits down facing the devotees. He begins by leading us in the opening sutra, the Heart Sutra, considered the ultimate Buddhist statement on the nature of wisdom.

Zui-san, the German architect, is to my right, straddling the *mokugyo* drum — a round, hollow wooden instrument carved in the shape of a fish. Using a cloth-covered mallet, she begins to drum, setting the muffled pulsebeat that we will dutifully follow while chanting. This is *not* the antiphonal, soothing sound of Gregorian chant, but a forceful, low-pitched, almost guttural repetition with tremendous resonance. Among the voices, that of Zui-san can be clearly distinguished.

Years ago, when I was training as an actor, my voice and Shakespeare coach worked tirelessly to help me discover my center, that place where the voice is born. "Let your voice come from your groin," he would say. "That is your center. That's where your strength comes from." Zui-san has, without question, found her center of strength and power. She is emitting the lowest, deepest human sound I have ever heard. It is astounding, almost otherworldly, as though all the spirit voices of past Sogenji monks are joining to speak through her.

As the chanting builds in intensity, it becomes louder, and the drumming faster. Zuisan increases the rhythm steadily, and I feel a rush of excitement and ecstatic feeling, as with the dervishes in Istanbul when we moved in unison, repeating the *zikr* of "Allah, Allah, Allah." Maintaining the power of the chant here in the hondo, we recite three specific groups of sutras before ending by declaring the four basic vows assertively and with conviction.

> *Sentient beings are numberless,*
> *I vow to liberate them.*
>
> *Desires are inexhaustible,*
> *I vow to put an end to them.*
>
> *The Dharmas are boundless,*
> *I vow to master them.*
>
> *The Buddha's Way is unsurpassable,*
> *I vow to become it.*

In his book *Thank You and Ok! A Zen American Failure in Japan,* author David Chadwick surmises that in this particular hondo "under the floor, in the center of the room, rests a rowboat-sized earthen bowl that resonates the voices, drum and bells like the body of a guitar." If this is true, it certainly helps explain the forceful vibrating of the floor and the tremendous power of the chant.

After the ceremony in the central hall, we quickly shift to another altar, near the kitchen, built into one of the interior walls. Every morning, these Zen Buddhist monks come here to recognize and pay their respects to those who built, maintained and continue to support the work of Sogenji. The ritual honors the past and present extended family members of this Rinzai training monastery.

Later, slipping on our thongs and scurrying, disoriented by the darkness, over to the zendo, we all claim our designated places and begin chanting the Heart Sutra again, until the piercing snap of two wooden clappers silences us and the roshi dramatically exits the zendo. I don't know what is next on the morning schedule, so it seems appropriate to settle into my meditation and begin counting my breaths, starting over again each time I reach ten. Soon, a bell rings, and everyone, except me, excitedly jumps down from their platform, and all hell breaks loose. Slipping on their thongs, they enthusiastically scramble out of the zendo, yelling and shrieking. Held motionless by mild shock, I sit amazed by the events of the last few hours.

I regain my focus and continue to sit solo zazen for nearly half an hour, then leave the empty meditation hall. I return to the guesthouse in delightful confusion. Where, I wonder, does all this disorder fit into such a disciplined and ordered way of life? A fews hours later a monk answers my question. She says that the trainees rushed out of the zendo to line up for their daily private meetings with the roshi, the time when each person receives guidance on his or her meditation practice. "The meeting can last from one minute to twenty minutes," she explains. "The scrambling out of the zendo and running to the roshi demonstrates one's enthusiasm for improving one's practice."

During the interview the practitioner can discuss, for example, her sense of progress in the beginning exercise, which she must master before she can move on to the others. This exercise, a particular method of counting the breaths from one to ten, over and over again, is designed to deepen the state of meditation. Once the roshi acknowledges that achievement, the practitioner begins working on a series of additional exercises, hundreds of them, called *koans.*

Philip Kapleau, in *The Three Pillars of Zen,* defines a *koan:*

> ...a formulation, in baffling language, pointing to ultimate truth. Koans cannot be solved by recourse to logical reasoning, but only by awakening a deeper level of the mind beyond the discursive intellect. Koans are constructed from the questions of disciples of old together with the responses of their masters, from portions of the masters' sermons or discourses, from lines of the sutras, and from other teachings.

There are approximately eighteen hundred koans; to become a Zen master, all must be solved, a task that usually takes at least a dozen years.

Two koans are well known in the West: "What is the sound of one hand clapping?" and "Does a dog have a Buddha nature?" A third good example is summarized in Eshin Nishimura's work *Unsui: A Diary of Zen Monastic Life:*

> Zen Master Hsiang-yen once said, "Suppose a man climbed a tree and held onto a branch not with his hands and feet, but with his mouth biting a branch. If a person should come along and

ask him the meaning of Bodhidharma's coming from the West (the essence of Zen), how should he answer? If he does not answer, he will betray the man's trust, but if he does answer, he will lose his own life."

After breakfast and cleanup, I report to Hi-san, the jikijitsu who comes from India, for my daily task assignment. He is the man to whom I bowed three times in last night's ceremony. A few of us will be working together, picking weeds, trimming the hedges and raking leaves because a group of visitors is arriving in the afternoon for a tour of Sogenji. Everything must be tidy and in order.

"I understand you will be going to India in a few months," says Hi-san as we head over to the barn to get tools.

"Yes, that's right; for at least three months."

"Before you go, I must tell you about the Buddhist, Hindu and Jain religious caves north of Bombay and give you some information about Dr. B. R. Ambedkar, the leader of the 'Movement of Untouchables.'"

"I have read of the caves, but Dr. Ambedkar is unfamiliar to me. Who is he?"

"It's not surprising that you have not heard of him, but he was a very special man. He was responsible for writing the constitution of India. Come by my room later this afternoon and we'll talk," he says. I am eager to continue the conversation, and I agree to join him later in the day.

By midmorning, the Indian monk has released me from work duty to have tea with Chi-san in a small "welcoming room" inside the hondo. Chi-san, whose appropriate name means "Big Wisdom," and an assistant named Sho-san, a Jewish Englishman, sit patiently waiting. After welcoming me, they invite me to join them on the floor for conversation and offer me a bitter green tea covered with a light froth. I think a taste for this tea must be acquired (and I haven't yet).

Chi-san, others have told me, is always super-enthusiastic about whatever task she pursues; she runs on "high energy octane," to quote one of the other monks. Sho-san, her counterbalance, tends to be quiet and soft-spoken. Both of them are curious about my journey and particularly interested in my stay on Mt. Athos.

"I suppose you have read *The Way of the Pilgrim*?" inquires Sho-san, enthusiasm a subtle undertone in his voice.

Scripture house

Sogenji hondo

"Yes, I have. The book was recommended to me by one of the guestmasters on the Holy Mountain."

"You know, the Jesus Prayer has helped me get through some of the difficult work in my Zen practice," admits Sho-san. "It's so clear and simple." Asking if we can meet briefly tomorrow morning to discuss how to make arrangements for a stay on Mt. Athos, he reveals that he is seriously considering a spiritual pilgrimage there. "I feel that I need more time to myself for my practice," he says. "Maybe a stay at Mt. Athos would be a good idea."

I assure him I would be happy to meet with him.

"I know of the prayer myself," interjects Chi-san, her characteristic energy bubbling over into speech. "I have not used it in my Zen practice, but have drawn on resources from other religious traditions that have been very, very helpful." Chi-san, when in her mid-20s, came to Japan to throw pots, to study the art of working with clay under a recognized master. In and out of Japan for twenty years now, she continues her practice at Sogenji and has a simple work studio here to throw pots.

"Recently a group of us were in Washington State looking for land on which to build a Sogenji extension, and we met some Eastern Orthodox monks living in the area," explains Chi-san. "A monk from Mt. Athos visits them every year."

"Has some land been purchased?"

"Yes," answers Big Wisdom. "We put a down payment on a section of land on Widby Island, where presently there are already a few sitting Zen groups. But we don't know when we'll actually begin building."

Shifting topics from the state of Washington to daily life at Sogenji, I ask, "Do the monks here still practice morning alms-gathering in the neighborhood?"

Sho-san answers in his quiet way, "Yes, the practice is called *takuhatsu.* And we go out in the community maybe a half-dozen times each month. Some people give us food and others give money."

"Although we are no longer solely dependent on this practice," adds Chi-san, "it is still vitally important to maintain the relationship between the monks and our neighbors. It's that idea of interdependence."

"As you may know," interjects Sho-san, "we place nine offerings on the altar every day to honor our priests, founders and lay supporters. So we are always conscious of the relationship with our extended community outside of Sogenji." We continue our intense discussion for an hour and a half, covering religious traditions, the growing Buddhist practice in the West and our own spiritual development. The two monks also talk of the vows, including celibacy.

Another member of the community, Jo-san, a tall, lithe dancer from Seattle, joins us briefly near the end of our conversation. "I have studied *Butoh* with an instructor from Kyoto, and that was really my introduction to Japan," Jo-san tells us. "The discipline of dance has helped me tremendously in my Zen practice." *Butoh* is a contemporary form of dance often incorporating extremely slow movements through isolating different parts of the body. It demands mindfulness with every motion. This art form, or movement, is really an alternate state of meditation.

While sitting in zazen with the rest of the community that afternoon, I invite my first encounter with the "warning stick," not quite knowing what to expect. We meditate for nearly three hours, alternating from sitting to walking, then back to sitting meditation. After the initial period of walking meditation, when I return to the platform and fold into a half-lotus position, my lower back begins to ache. Only a slight annoyance at first, it gradually becomes more bothersome, causing me to lose concentration. I begin sweating.

Soon after, Hi-san begins treading up and down the outside hallway carrying a long, narrow, flat piece of wood: the *keisaku*. As he approaches I bow to him, indicating a need for the stick, and he bows in return as I pull down my left shoulder with my right hand. Whack! Whack! His keisaku comes down with a sting that is sharp but short-lived. After pulling down my right shoulder for another two "whacks," we again bow to each other, and Hi-san returns to the interior hall. The sting has diverted my mind from my lower back to my shoulders; the pain dissolves momentarily, making it possible to return to counting breaths until the end of the session.

Later, my visit with Hi-san in his cluttered room — given to the jikijitsu because of his position as supervising monk — is delightful and informative. Our discussion is more political than religious or spiritual. "You know, members of my family were considered 'Untouchables,'" explains the pensive monk. "It was only upon the encouragement of Dr. Ambedkar, through his influential political movement, that my family, along with tens of thousands of other 'Untouchables,' broke out of their class repression and converted to Buddhism."

What he is saying intrigues me. Not only did Dr. Ambedkar successfully encourage a significant number of conversions in India, but, as Hi-san pointed out, he was also the man primarily responsible for forming India's constitution. Before departing, I promise to visit the famous Buddhist, Hindu and Jain ceremonial caves in Ajanta and Ellora, India, and to seek out literature on Dr. Ambedkar, whom Hi-san considers India's unsung hero.

The evenings and following mornings pass by quickly as I progressively feel more comfortable with the daily rhythm of Sogenji. A mere stay of a few days has awakened my awareness not only of Rinzai Zen practice, but also to the broad range of people drawn to it.

After lunch on my final day, Zui-san offers me a ride to the train station, which I gratefully accept. While I am loading my backpack into the trunk of the community car, Big Wisdom jogs up and hands me a black book with a textured cover that is decorated with a symbolic gray circle. "It's a collection of essays written by Shodo Harada Roshi, and we want you to have them," she says. "Good luck on your journey."

Sitting in the waiting room at the station, I begin reading the roshi's first essay, titled "Sogen's One Drop of Water." Based on a relationship between a master and his student, the essay truly encapsulates the meaning of mindfulness in Rinzai Zen practice.

It seems that the master was ready to take a bath in the Sogenji bathhouse, but the water was too hot. So he ordered the student to fetch a pail of cold water to cool down the bath. One bucket of cold water didn't suffice, so the student made many trips back and forth until the master said the temperature was fine. Having been told this, the student took what little water was left in the bucket and threw it out nearby. Seeing him doing this, the master yelled at him, calling him thoughtless and saying that the small portion of water could have been put on the garden's trees or flowers especially because it was the dry season. "Why do you begrudge such a small effort as that?" said the master. "In even one drop of water, no matter how tiny a drop, the water's great value doesn't change at all! If you can't understand this value of *one single drop* of water, no matter how hard you train, you'll never become someone who can give life to that training."

153

Chapter Eight

NOTHING IS PERMANENT

When the invaluable work has been done
the result is the comparable one.
The deeds done well fly high as a rocket
so they change the order of this planet.
Whoever endures and has tolerance
shall undertake the works of excellence.
The mountain cannot cease to be steep,
put life at risk, but the faith remains deep.
Those with integrity on Earth shall pardon sins.
Oh, this world of ours — prolonging still.

Ajahn Chamroon Panchand
Wat Tham Krabok

Even before I round the corner of the administration building, I hear a booming voice announcing, "There are 300 bhikkhu here, and 150 of us are former addicts. If you are an addict and decide to participate in this program, you have one try and only one try." The voice belongs to a lanky, broad-shouldered African-American man dressed in the brown robes of a Thai *bhikkhu,* or monk. He is addressing a group of Europeans who are visiting Wat Tham Krabok, a monastery whose name literally means "Opium-Pipe Cave Monastic Center."

"Oh, hello there," the speaker says to me, looking up from the group. "Please have a seat while I finish with these folks." I nod to the monk, then, looking around, I spot some empty wooden tables at the makeshift refreshment stand. I'm still adjusting to the heat and humidity in this part of the world, and a soda seems very inviting. I buy a cold drink and take a seat at one of the wobbly tables.

There is a swirl of activity in the center of this *wat.* A steady stream of laymen and women, children and other brown-robed bhikkhu scurry past as I wait, and two mangy dogs and a tailless cat play tag beneath my table. Behind me, young Thai men and women wearing pink drawstring pants and loose-fitting cotton overshirts but no shoes are milling about in a fenced recreational area between two-story whitewashed concrete dormitories. Another administration building sits to my left, and past it I can see a concrete *sala*: an open-sided assembly hall where the community chants and meditates daily. Beyond the sala is a small Buddhist temple near the visitors' dormitory and a primitive herbal sauna used for treatment purposes. At the far end of the wat are the vocational training facilities.

"Now, how can I help you?" says the black man, approaching and pulling out the chair opposite mine. He startles me, and I swiftly turn my attention away from my surroundings. "My name is Gordon; what's yours?"

After giving him my name and expressing an interest in the work here, I ask Gordon about securing permission to return in a few weeks for a three-day stay. "Some months ago I sent a letter written in Thai to your ajahn, making a similar request, but never received a reply," I explain. He nods his head. "My bus trip from Bangkok today was made with the hope of meeting him in person."

Bhikkhu Gordon takes a moment to respond: "I can answer some of your questions about the program. But you will have to talk to Supin, one of our *mae-chii* — a Buddhist nun — about making a three-day retreat." Surprisingly, the bhikkhu then begins gearing up to deliver his lecture to me. "You know, there are 300 bhikkhu here, and 150 of us are former addicts...."

He must have given this speech thousands of times. I wonder how difficult it is for him to maintain an interest, a sense of excitement and enthusiasm about such a routine chore. In the outside world, people often simply tolerate their daily routines without seeking meaning in them. But here, just going through the motions is contradictory to the very way of life. Recently, when I was talking with both a Christian and a Buddhist monk, they addressed the issue, telling me that one of the most difficult things in monastic life, regardless of the religious tradition, is to accept the routine, to embrace the sameness of things, day in and day out.

"Basically, what we have here is a detoxification center for people with addictions." Gordon pauses for emphasis and then begins listing the addictive substances, ticking them off on the fingers of his left hand, "opium, heroin, crack, ice and alcohol."

I jump in with a question: "It's my understanding that your treatment includes ingesting an herbal drink and taking daily eucalyptus saunas?"

"That's right. The first five days are the hardest," he says. "Of course, that's aside from staying off the addiction for the rest of your life. During those first five days, each participant ingests an emetic herbal mixture once a day." He says that it causes vomiting which allows the body to rid itself of the drug. Daily herbal saunas help sweat out the poisons. The bhikkhu knows of what he speaks. A program brochure reveals that Gordon, originally from New York, is a former drug addict and was a mercenary in Southeast Asia. I suspect he was in Vietnam with U.S. forces and just never went home.

"Following the initial days of detoxification, we continue treatment combining *dhamma* talks — Buddha's teachings — with meditation as well as herbal saunas and counseling."

"And how long does the program last?"

"Participants are usually here for about a month," he says. "Some of them stay longer and take vows as a bhikkhu or mae-chii, but most return to their communities." Gordon excuses himself to get a cold soda.

When he returns, I say, "You mentioned dhamma talks and meditation as part of the treatment. Is there any other religious or spiritual component to the program?"

"Yes," he replies. "Before beginning the treatment, the addict must take a vow to their God that they will successfully complete the program and stay clean. If they don't have a God, they must take a vow to that." And he is not kidding.

"Is that a strong enough motivation for most participants?"

"It certainly is for Thais because Buddhism is such an integral part of their culture," answers the monk, taking a long sip of soda.

When I ask if a person is permitted to return for another treatment if they slip back into addiction, the bhikkhu answers emphatically: "No, they are not permitted to come back. There isn't a second chance here." Later, I discover this is not always the case. Gordon asks me the time. When I tell him, he says he can give me a few more minutes, but then he's scheduled to talk with a student group from Bangkok.

"Is Wat Tham Krabok considered to be a 'forest monastery?' Is the life of a bhikkhu here focused on meditation?"

"Well, let me put it this way. We are a forest monastery in that the bhikkhu here make and maintain their own robes," explains the black man. "We eat only one meal a day, and usually do not use modern forms of transportation. Also, every year just before *Pansa* — the three-month retreat during the rainy season — we go on *tudong.*"

I say I'm not familiar with the word *tudong,* so the bhikkhu offers a working definition. "More or less it's wandering in the forests for a period of three weeks, solely dependent upon the goodness of villagers for food and our well-being. It's a powerful reminder of our transient state as bhikkhu."

"Well, then how are you different from the bhikkhu in a typical forest monastery?"

"We're different because our work is focused on curing addiction, rather than solely on our meditation practice. And some of our bhikkhu work with AIDS (Acquired Immune Deficiency Syndrome) patients in the nearby town of Lopburi. We also do our own construction work here rather than having neighboring villagers do it, as is the tradition." Gordon finishes his soda and leaves for a moment to return the bottle. He sits back down, but lightly. He is poised to leave again. "Let me say this. Within traditional monastic life we're considered rebels." He savors the word *rebels.* "We take vows, do our meditation and focus on our addiction work. And if a bhikkhu or mae-chii remains here for five years, he or she then takes vows to stay here permanently."

Just as he stops speaking, a mae-chii joins us at the table. Thin, with a shaven head and wearing wire-rimmed glasses, she looks to be in her mid-thirties. Her clothing is simple: a long white cotton skirt, a fitted blouse with a rounded neckline, and on the woman's feet is a pair of rubber thongs.

"Just in time. Let me introduce you to Bill from America," Gordon says. Standing up and putting the palms of my hands together, with fingertips touching my forehead, I bow my head in respect.

"I happy to meet you," replies the mae-chii, whose name is Supin. Gordon explains my interest in receiving permission from the ajahn to return for a few days. The bhikkhu leaves and Supin takes his place, explaining that she will be happy to assist. "Let see," she says, "maybe first thing you do watch demonstration. Then we go visit Hmong village and talk to ajahn. I try to make meeting."

She indicates that we should walk and escorts me to the locked gates of the fence I'd noticed earlier. Supin briefly talks to the monks standing guard there. They permit me to enter the yard of the detox

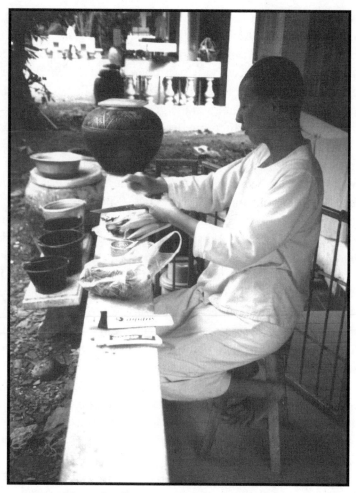

Mae-chii Supin preparing vegetables

center and motion for me to take a seat at a nearby picnic table to watch a demonstration. Across the table sits a dark-skinned young woman with big, brown eyes and thick, coarse black hair, busily writing in her notebook. Looking up and extending her hand, she introduces herself.

"My name is Hagit, and I'm from Israel." Shaking hands with the woman, I introduce myself as well. "I work with drug addiction in my own country and that's my reason for coming here, to get ideas," she explains. As we talk, rowdy schoolchildren begin gathering outside the fence, peering in out of curiosity. Adult supervisors are trying to keep them in line. "I have never seen anything like this before," says Hagit. "Have you?"

The demonstration is still a puzzle to me, too, but its purpose becomes vividly clear within a few minutes. The young people dressed in pink noisily form into rows facing the visiting children. In front of each row sits a water-filled bucket next to a small pail and a plastic bowl. The person at the head of each line kneels as two monks pass by and receives a tall glass of dark brown liquid to drink, which he or she promptly swallows in one long gulp.

"That's the herbal mixture," Hagit whispers. "That gets the poisons out of their bodies."

The others in line begin to chant, then sing, then chant again as the supervising bhikkhu help each kneeler drink several bowls of water in quick succession until the drinkers begin vomiting. The liquid comes shooting out of their mouths with a tremendous force, and the vomiting continues until the addicts' stomachs are empty, and their bodies shake with dry heaves. Their fellow addicts stand near, providing physical support. Beginning to gag, I look away for a moment, but Hagit continues watching intently, taking notes. The schoolchildren groan, fascinated with the events taking place before them.

This apparent exorcism continues until all the kneelers are thoroughly exhausted, making it clear to me why this phase of treatment is limited to five days. At the end of the demonstration, the head bhikkhu begins lecturing to the children, and Supin beckons to Hagit and me from outside the fence.

"Now we go to Hmong village, yes?" says the mae-chii, looking at both of us inquiringly. Nodding our heads in agreement, we leave the enclosure and begin following her. She moves rapidly around an open-air botanical laboratory, then sweeps past a carpenter's shop and a group of small, white stucco cottages where the mae-chii live, but the two of us manage to keep up. After slogging across an open, muddy field, we finally enter one of the Hmong villages.

"This one of four settlement," explains Supin.

"Aren't the Hmong a Laotian mountain tribe?" I ask.

"Yes, they are."

"Why are they here?"

"Some year ago, Hmong tribe member come for treatment of opium addiction," she replies, "and then family member start coming and stay on temple ground. Now it out of control." Because opium has been an integral part of Hmong traditional rituals for many, many years, addiction is a problem among their people. Living conditions in this settlement are not good. Open sewers are not unusual, and water for cooking and drinking must be hauled in plastic containers from distant pumps.

According to *New York Times* reporter Seth Mydons in his March 3, 1997, article "Nomads of Laos," the settlers here are "the last wandering group of refugees from the Indochina War." These are the people "that the Central Intelligence Agency recruited in the 1960s to fight America's 'secret war in Laos.'" Mydons explains that in 1975 the Hmong tribespeople began fleeing across the Mekong River from Laos into Thailand. During the war, these people were promised safety by the American military, but many of them were left behind when the Americans withdrew, "leaving the Hmong to flee the Communist victors in the greatest upheaval their culture has known."

Supin leads us deeper into the settlement to a workshop where some men are beating out metal knives with simple hand tools. "This way they make money," she tells us. "Also, men work in rock quarry and peanut field nearby. Sometime other farm work, too." Hagit and the mae-chii meander into an adjacent shop, where workers are crafting jewelry with a lightweight metal and polished black stones they've gathered from Thailand's beaches. After haggling over prices, with Supin translating, as if in a Jerusalem market of the Old City, Hagit finally buys a few items.

We continue through the village until we reach a jagged hillside. From there, we can look out over the three other settlements; they're not a pretty sight. They remind me of the scores of shantytowns I've seen over the years. I turn to Supin to comment: "There have to be thousands and thousands of Hmong living here. The problems must be overwhelming."

"Yes, thousand and thousand," she responds, shaking her head. "We just take day by day."

Hagit has made arrangements for a ride into town that will leave soon, so we must quickly return to the center of the wat. Once she's gone, I ask Supin if we can now meet with the ajahn. "As Gordon explained, I am scheduled to make a silent, ten-day meditation retreat at Soan Mokh, a wat in the south. Afterwards, my hope is to return here for three days."

"I speak with him earlier. Maybe he ready now," she says, removing her thongs. She leaves me and goes into the main administration building. Returning shortly, she reports that our meeting is in half an hour and then says she's going to run some errands. I decide to wait on the porch and sit down to write in my journal.

Upon her return, we both slip off our footwear and enter the building to meet the ajahn. Inside, I am startled by the feel of air-conditioning and begin sweating even more profusely than before, until my T-shirt and khakis are sticking to my skin. The contrast with the temperature outside only emphasizes how stifling the heat and humidity can be in the Thai countryside. Sitting at the head of a long conference table is Ajahn Chamroon Panchand, the abbot of this wat. After he motions his assistant out, we bow and take seats on one side of the table; Supin has offered to translate.

Ajahn Panchand is a healthy looking man in his sixties with short gray hair. If he were wearing a suit rather than the robe, he could easily pass for a Thai businessman. Earlier, Hagit had told me that Panchand held an important position with the Bangkok Police Department before coming here, a most unusual background for an abbot of a Thai monastery. Supin and I remain silent, as is the tradition, waiting for the ajahn to speak first.

"Wat Tham Krabok start in 1953 by mae-chii," he begins, and Supin softly translates. "Her name Mae-Chii Mien, and she die of cancer at age forty-eight." For a woman to establish a wat in Thailand is very unusual; I've not heard of it happening elsewhere in this country and believe this wat must be an anomaly. However, I have been told that there are mae-chii who have chosen to live in their own communities separate from the bhikkhu and the confines of the wat enclosure. I have seen a photograph of Mien and noticed that she wore the brown robe of the bhikkhu rather than the white habit of the mae-chii. "After she die, I become administrator here."

He offers no further details about Mien, but before we leave, the ajahn poses three questions and asks me to meditate on them. He speaks very slowly so that Supin will not miss a thing. They sound like Thai Buddhist versions of Japanese Rinzai Zen koans:

"Number one: It more difficult to follow elephant or get elephant to follow you?" This is puzzling: I look from the ajahn to Supin and back, trying to pick up some hint from either the words or his expression.

"Number two: You want to walk short, happy road or long, never-end road?"

"Number three: You try to meditate for month and get nowhere. Finally, one day you say, 'If nothing happen this day, then I swear I quit.' So you start to meditate and you successful. But scorpion come to you and take bite out of flesh, but it not hurt. Now, what you do — quit meditation or keep meditation and scorpion slowly eat all flesh away?"

When he finishes, I glance over at Supin, who shrugs her shoulders and looks away. Returning my gaze to Ajahn Panchand, I find he is staring right through me, never blinking an eye. We remain silent for what feels like a very long time until Panchand begins speaking to Supin. "He say you come back for three day after meditation retreat," she reports. "And I be guide when you come back."

Standing up, we bow and I thank him for seeing me, then we exit slowly, walking backward. It is late, and the highway is a mile away. Once I reach it, I will have to flag down a bus to take me to Bangkok tonight. I hurriedly express my gratitude to Supin for her help, leave the wat and jog away down the narrow dirt road.

~~~~~~~~~~

When I return a few weeks later to the community of Wat Tham Krabok, I feel at ease. During my ten-day silent retreat in the south, I've learned a good deal more about daily life in the wat, and possibly about myself. Also, my meditation skills have improved. Supin, happy to see me, escorts me to a stark room on the second floor of the visitors' dormitory, where a few dusty bedrolls and altars sit on the concrete floor. No one else is staying in the room, Supin says; it will be mine alone. Having brought food for the night in my backpack so that I won't have to go back out, I arrange to meet her in front of the refreshment stand tomorrow morning.

162

Our first day together actually begins over at the mae-chii complex, cutting down a line of dead banana plants. While we work, Supin talks about her life. "I come here fourteen year ago and thought of leaving ten time, maybe more." She tells me there are thirty mae-chii at Wat Tham Krabok, and each has made a lifelong commitment to this addiction work. There are six times as many monks, but she says that they will only stay on maybe a year each and then leave.

I ask about designated times for her daily meditation. "My meditation alone in early morning and with other people when I work," she answers. I think it must be difficult for her to schedule solo time given all of her apparent responsibilities on this 350-acre compound.

We load the wheelbarrow with plant cuttings, which are oozing sap that leaves stains on our clothes. Supin keeps talking during the long, tedious walk to the community dump. "My family, they Chinese and live in Bangkok. They have shampoo business, but I not have interest in that."

I'm eager to find out more about her personal history here at the wat. "Who was responsible for your ordination?" I ask.

"I did my ordination and take eight precept. You know most hard thing for me? Hard thing to cut my hair. I first tell ajahn I be mae-chii for fifteen day only. Then for one year and then for one and half year, and then I just stay. Before I cut hair, I go to Bangkok often but now no go at all."

Eight Precepts

1. Abstain from taking life
2. Abstain from stealing
3. Abstain from any sexual activity
4. Abstain from lying
5. Abstain from drinking alcohol
6. Abstain from eating after midday
7. Abstain from dance, song, music and perfumes
8. Abstain from sleeping on a soft bed

After emptying the cuttings at the dump, we return for one more load. When we've dealt with those, Supin leads me over to a construction site of the new *vihara,* a central temple that will hold the wat relics and the Buddha icons. The traditionally styled temple is grand, its walls and roof are made of concrete, which will be painted later with colorful

*Buddha at
Wat Tham Krabok*

Community vihara

depictions of Buddhist deities and legends. Each corner of the sweeping roofline is decorated with a *chofa,* otherwise known as a "sky tassel," that looks like the elongated neck of a bird. To one side of the vihara is a construction crane holding mae-chii and bhikkhu together, high in the air, in a deep steel scoop.

"Do they always work together?"

"Oh, yes. Here at Wat Tham Krabok we share labor." She hollers up to her cohorts; looking down, they wave and shout back. It's unusual behavior in a wat.

Squatting in front of the unfinished temple, beside two shiny, black statues of Buddha, are a few of the bhikkhu on break. Supin begins chatting with them and introduces me. "How long this take to build?" one asks me. Shrugging my shoulders, I guess two and a half years. "Only one year and eight month," he announces with pride. "No architect, no engineer, just good head and strong arm," says another, flexing his biceps and laughing, then returning to work.

"Why did the founder, Mae-chii Mien, wear the robes of a bhikkhu rather than the white habit of a mae-chii?" I ask Supin as we begin walking back to the center of the community.

"Oh, you notice!" Supin appears pleased at my question. "She gain respect that man get because of skill and knowledge."

The words *mae-chii* literally mean "mother priest." At ordination, they take only the eight precepts as Supin had said, while the bhikkhu take over two hundred, and generally they receive less respect than the male monks. It is evident that the disparity disturbs Supin. She's a very bright and energetic person with many duties, so this state of affairs must be difficult for her.

Passing through the botanical laboratory on our way back, we stop for a moment. On top of sturdy wooden tables are a wide variety of plant samples, some growing in soil and others in jars of water; the area is cluttered but organized. "This work of Bhikkhu Yantra, ajahn brother," says Supin. "He start project with AIDS patient. But he stop work because problem with state government." She says that the two brothers seldom talk to one another. While this is an unusual situation in such a community, I am not really surprised. It's my understanding that both men are headstrong and independent.

At the refreshment stand, we find two busloads full of excited schoolchildren waiting anxiously for another daily demonstration. Supin will be busy for the rest of the afternoon and evening with her responsibilities. "You like sit meditation with me in morning?" she asks before departing.

"Yes, very much. Where and when should we meet?" Pointing to the small Buddhist temple near the visitors' dormitory, she says to meet her there the next day before dawn.

That evening, once it's dark, I covertly slip into the nearby herbal sauna. Empty but still steaming, it smells heavily of eucalyptus. Emerging, I have a bucket-shower just outside and sleepily return to my room. I'm in heaven or, more appropriately, *nibanna*. But my sense of well-being doesn't last. Barking dogs and music from radios keep me up most of the night. The sound of dogs is not surprising, but the rock-and-roll is totally unexpected. I remember what Gordon said: "We are considered to be rebels."

After a fitful sleep, I wake just before dawn and go down to meet Supin. Wearing a white cotton scarf over her head as a symbol of respect for the Buddha, she has brought candles, some matches, a handful of flower petals and a book of Buddhist sutras. After lighting the candles and spreading out the petals in a circle, we both sit down and curl into the half-lotus position, and she begins determinedly chanting. Meditating beside Supin, I am struck by how self-contained she appears, alone in community. When she stands, I stand, and we begin a walking meditation, but in opposite directions. Starting with the heel, then moving slowly to the ball of the foot, and finally to the toes; each step is taken with care and mindfulness. Our rhythms easily coincide. Ending the meditation within an hour, we bow respectfully in front of the Buddha, then to one another and silently part ways.

Most of the morning Supin will be busy with the Hmong, but she graciously invites me to her cottage for the day's meal. We prepare the food together. Sitting out on her spotless, green-tiled front porch, we clean and slice vegetables, which she carries inside to steam on a two-burner hot plate. She returns almost immediately and makes an announcement. "You know, I go to Australia soon, for one month," she says proudly. "I ask by Australian Thai Buddhist temple to come and give instruction. Do you think good idea?" I'm flattered that she's interested in my opinion. We've only known each other for a few days, yet we've formed a strong bond.

"Sure, you should go. What a great opportunity."

"I think so, too," she says, grinning and peeling some fruit. "I need speak English or use translator?"

"Well, in my opinion, you should speak in your native tongue. There are concepts you can explain in Thai that might be difficult for you to communicate in English. And the students will appreciate hearing your language; it will give a more authentic tone to your teachings." And I add, "Besides, if the translator makes any major errors you can make the necessary changes because of your English skills."

She goes back into the cottage to collect everything. After several minutes, she brings out a few pots and ceramic dishes on a round tray plus a thermos of boiled drinking water. She arranges the pots and dishes between us and places the thermos within reach on the floor. "Please sit down," she says. "I serve you little everything, and you decide food you like." There are egg noodles, white rice with spicy steamed vegetables, an omelet and a mild vegetable broth. She serves me and then herself.

I ask if I may say the blessing, and when she nods approval, I tell her that this prayer was used at meals every day during my retreat down at Wat Soan Mokh. It was the only time we spoke during the ten days.

> *With wise reflection I eat this food,*
> *not for play, not for intoxication,*
> *Not for fattening, not for beautification,*
> *only to maintain this body,*
> *To stay alive and healthy,*
> *to support the spiritual life.*
> *Thus, I let go of unpleasant feelings*
> *and do not stir up new ones.*
> *Thereby the process of life goes on,*
> *blameless, at ease and in peace.*

After we've started eating, Supin asks if she may tell me about a family problem, and I encourage her.

"I have nephew here in addiction program, and he run away yesterday," she says with a quiver in her voice. "I worry, but not contact his mother."

"Do you think he might hurt himself?"

"No, not think so. But has bad drug problem for few year and try two other program," she hesitates, "he make vow to Buddha to stay here, finish program, but he break vow. Not good for him or family." We finish our meal, and while I wash the plates and pans with rainwater from a nearby barrel, Supin brings out a pot of tea and slices of fresh fruit. We sit quietly, offering one another the gift of companionship.

On the way back to the administration building, we unexpectedly run into Supin's sister and nephew. He is listless and uncommunicative, but his mother talks for both of them. The four of us backtrack to Supin's cottage, where she tells them to stay for the time being. "I hope they let him back into program," she whispers to me. "If they do, he begin all over again." (And, in fact, that's exactly what happens.)

Passing through the botanical laboratory, we notice the ajahn's brother, Bhikkhu Yantra, mixing different colored liquids in a tall glass container, and he motions for us to join him. He asks, in Thai, if we would like to talk about meditation and Buddhism, and we readily accept his invitation.

The bhikkhu sits on one of the tables as we pull up two wooden stools. It is a gesture of respect to choose a seat that is lower than his. Breaking a small, leafy branch off an overhanging tree limb, Yantra holds it up for all of us to see. "This is person who start meditation practice," he says. "The thing we cling to get in way of enlightenment." Suddenly, he strips all the leaves from the branch. He shows us what is left. "And this is person who get enlightenment. All they cling to disappear, and they free."

The world's many religions are the focus of his second demonstration. Picking up another branch from the ground, he draws two large concentric circles in the dirt, and inside them he draws radiating lines, like spokes on a wheel. "All religion come from same place," declares Yantra. "So you Christian, I Buddhist, she Hindu. No matter — all come from same place, yes?" he asks me.

I agree. Since he seems to have finished with the lesson, I ask about his work with AIDS patients, and he tells me it has ended. His expression and tone convey his irritation with the topic. Supin again explains that there were disagreements with government officials regarding the work. "But monk from Krabok still work with AIDS patient in Lopburi," she adds.

"Do you want test for HIV (Human Immune Deficiency Virus)?" he asks me, bringing his round, expressive face close to mine. "I show you how to do it." His question catches me off guard. Telling him that I have tested negative before doesn't deter him. He asks repeatedly until I agree. Obviously, Yantra hasn't completely withdrawn from the work. The bhikkhu gives me a small glass tube and tells me to go to the nearby outhouse and fill the vial halfway. I do as instructed, and when I return, he moves over to three tall glass containers. Two of them are filled with a clear, pale green liquid, but the third container has a milky, coagulated substance suspended in it. Seemingly fascinated with what is transpiring, Supin clearly wants me to take the test.

"What's in the glass containers?" I ask. He ignores my question, and Supin says that he will never reveal his secrets.

"Woman come yesterday for test," he tells me. "I pour her urine into that container and white cloud form. She test positive for HIV." My guess is that the diagnosis is not uncommon in this treatment community. Listening to him talk about this questionable method of testing makes me feel anxious and uncomfortable. Maybe I should ask for the test tube back. But it's too late; he has begun pouring the urine into one of the containers, and we all watch as it mixes ever so slowly with the green liquid. Much to my relief, no milky formation appears, and the bhikkhu declares me HIV free.

Now, there is still something more he wants to show us, so we follow him over to another table. On it is a glass tube filled with colored rocks and a murky, yellowish liquid. Yantra says it's rain water. "It pure; it clean," he assures us. "I drink glass every fifteen day," says the bhikkhu. "Good for eye and stomach and liver." According to the medicine man, the rocks contain different minerals that are healthy for the body. "Like big vitamin. Want to try?"

Supin and I look at one another. It feels like he's daring us to trust him. We shrug our shoulders and agree to accept his offer. The bhikkhu pours two full glasses of the liquid and hands one to each of us. I take a deep breath and drink most of mine down in one swallow, trying to avoid the smell and taste of the liquid. It does not taste like rainwater. Supin wisely takes it in measured gulps, grimacing all the way. Almost immediately a wave of nausea sweeps over me, and I excuse myself and scramble back to the outhouse, reaching it just in time. When I return, there's no mention of what has just happened. The bhikkhu has teased and challenged us, but I sense that he is grateful for our willingness to trust his authority.

Before we leave, I ask if I may take a few photos. He agrees, but the shutter on my camera begins malfunctioning, and the film won't advance. Unfortunately, my other camera is back in Bangkok being repaired. I explain that taking more photographs is impossible after all; the camera isn't working properly. As we leave, the bhikkhu tells us to drop by in the morning before my departure for the capitol because he has something to give me.

Our regular visit to the ajahn is late today. He has only a few minutes to spend with us. Supin receives instructions for the remainder of the day, and to me he poses yet another Thai "koan": "Two boy play ball on side of fence, and ball fall in you yard. They told many time not play close to fence. You keep ball or give back?" he asks, then he hurries away to a meeting with local villagers.

There's an opportunity that evening to talk with one of the European monks living on the top floor of my dormitory — Bhikkhu Peter from Switzerland. His arms are decorated with full, bluish tattoos, and his dark green eyes strike me as unusually soulful. Earlier in the day I had seen him working on a rock pile, using a hammer to break up stones so that the pieces could be used for local construction projects, and asked if I could visit him later. Peter reveals that his addiction is to heroin and that he has tried several detox programs in Europe but always slipped back into using the drug.

I ask why he chose the regimen at Wat Tham Krabok, and he tells me that some Swiss friends had gone through this program and recommended it. "It's outside of my culture, so I'm less likely to slide back into my old ways," he says, hope plain in his voice.

"When did you ordain as a bhikkhu?"

"After I finished my time in detox, I worked for a few months as a lay volunteer and then ordained as a monk."

"So you obviously think the program works?"

"Well, so far it has for me," says Peter, playing with a furry black puppy who's tumbling around on his bedroll. He tells me the puppy was given to him by another bhikkhu "for companionship and responsibility. I think it was a good idea." I agree with him, say goodnight and return to my own room.

When Supin and I find each other in the morning, she reminds me

Swiss Bhikkhu Peter at his daily work assignment

that the ajahn's brother wants us to return to the botanical laboratory. We go straight over, and Yantra greets us with a broad smile. He saunters over to his one-room, wooden hermitage and returns with an expensive camera and twenty rolls of film in hand. Supin translates as he presents them to me. "I know you camera break, so this for you. I wait to give good home."

Choking from a combination of laughter and tears, I put my hands together and, bowing, thank him repeatedly, "Khawp khun, khawp khun, khawp khun." I resist the temptation to give him a bear hug, realizing that it would be inappropriate, contrary to tradition and offensive to him. As it is, he seems a bit embarrassed by my show of emotion. He dismisses us, saying there's work to be done, we all bow, and he hurries away. Supin and I move in the direction of her cottage.

As soon as I'm sure we can't be overheard, I ask her where the camera and film came from. I know they must be expensive. She says, "He give to you as gift. It please him to help you. Please no ask question like, where come from or price. Accept gift."

We've reached her home, and I sit down on the porch to fiddle with my new camera. Not wanting to offend her, I acknowledge that my questions were rude. No more is said about the gifts. We have a cup of tea and some sweet biscuits then return to the administration building where Supin has an appointment with two of the Hmong tribesmen.

I walk back to the refreshment stand for a soda and find a ragtag trio of Europeans, two of them with green, blue and bleached blond hair, sitting at one of the tables. I introduce myself to the two men — who are from Switzerland — and the woman — who is Thai-German and a citizen of Deutschland. All have gone through the treatment program once and are back for a second chance. They are addicted to heroin.

In heavily accented tones, the woman, who is serving as a sort of spokesperson for the group, says, "When we finished the first time, we went back to Bangkok and started shooting up again." She relays the information nonchalantly, as if it were an accident.

"Gordon told me that people only get one chance to go through the program."

"In most cases that is true, but we have managed to get back into the program." In that moment, I can't help thinking that it is a waste of everyone's time and effort if the three have no spiritual motivation to stay clean. I am reminded of Gordon's comment that the Thai addicts have an advantage. They have grown up in a culture steeped in Buddhism, so they are more likely to honor vows made to Buddha, which are accorded great importance in Thailand.

Prior to my afternoon departure, Supin arranges for us to meet with Ajahn Panchand one last time in his cramped and cluttered office away from the administration building. He is sitting at his desk as we enter, bow and kneel on the floor. Behind him is a large black-and-white photograph of five Thai women. Four of them are attired in traditional tribal dress, but the one in the middle wears a monk's robes. Mae-chii Mien, founder of Wat Tham Krabok, must have been a remarkable woman.

"It good idea for you to come," the ajahn tells me. "You wish return and work in community, you welcome." Pausing, he writes something in Thai on a piece of paper, folds the sheet and hands it to me. "You return to Bangkok, someone translate, but not now." Supin and I stand up to go, but Ajahn Panchand motions for us to wait. He has one more story for me.

"You meditate on what I say." He pauses. "Understand?"

"Yes," I reply, nodding my head.

So he begins, "One day boss call you into office and say you do good job and praise you. Two day later he call you to office, say you no good, fire you and tell you go away." The ajahn asks if I understand so far, and I say yes. He continues, "So, I tell you what to do after fire." He glances at Supin for a moment and then returns his gaze to me. "You breathe deep, say okay and go," he says. "It matter of self-confidence. *That* your work for now — self-confidence." Remaining silent, I bow and leave with Supin. His final message has struck home. I turn it over in my mind as I leave and feel the weight of it. I know I will meditate long on this task.

Outside, we spot a group of adults crowding together in the nearby open-air sala, here for the alcoholics' day-treatment program. Each participant has just taken vows to conquer his or her addiction and then knelt at a table to sign a scroll of paper restating the vow. The managing bhikkhu will give the scrolls out as reminders of what has just transpired. Behind him on the back wall is another large black-and-white photograph. From it, Mien, dressed in her monk's robes, looks out over the crowd and keeps an eye on her community.

The next day, the manager at my Bangkok hostel translates the ajahn's note for me. The elderly gentleman, having heard of the respected Ajahn Panchand, is pleased to assist me. Reading the message slowly, he emphasizes each word of this final bit of advice: "First, remember when you give, you receive one hundred-fold back. Second, nothing is permanent. Finally, important you do daily meditation, one hour, until like walking and breathing for you. This will clear path and give self-confidence you must have."

Chapter Nine

MAKING OF MERIT

The things of this world are merely conventions of our own making. Having established them, we get lost in them and refuse to let go, giving rise to clinging to personal views and opinions.

Ajahn Chah
twentieth century

By the time my bus arrives in the Thai city of Ubon Ratchathani, near the Laotian border, it is nightfall, and the streets are practically deserted. I see only a frail old woman, a soup vendor, who watches as the bus empties. She's probably hoping for a few more customers before closing shop. I walk over to her cart and greet her, "Sawat-dii krup," then ask her about the soup, "Kaeng jeut?" The vendor nods, indicating that it contains vegetables and pork. She motions for me to sit down at one of the weathered card tables she's put out for customers and promptly serves me. I eat quickly, drink the water in my plastic bottle and pay for my meal. She thanks me, "Khawp khun," and begins folding up her tables.

From my table, I spied a flickering hotel sign in the distance, and after dinner, I start down the unpaved street toward it. All the businesses between the vendor and the hotel are closed, and the street is dark. I cautiously enter the stark lobby through a torn screen door and am greeted by a blaring television set that dims and brightens to the rhythm of the light bulb above the sign outside. Behind the counter, asleep on an ancient blue sofa, is the night clerk.

"Sawat-dii, Sawat-dii," Raising my voice above the noise from the television, I try to wake the young man. He sits up quickly, looking startled and confused. He remains there for a minute, rubbing his eyes, and just stares at me; he might be thinking that this foreigner is a carryover from the dream world. "Mii hawng mai?" I ask.

"Krup," yes, a room is available, he answers, getting up and grabbing a numbered key from under the counter and handing it over. At the top of the steep concrete steps, I find the room. It's lit by a single bulb hanging from the ceiling. Glancing around, I see an open window covered with a screen and a rusted bed frame with a musty, bare mattress. There's an attached bathroom, and I step inside and turn the tap. The water is cold, but it runs. It is what I had hoped for. Back downstairs I agree with the clerk on a price in *bhat,* the Thai currency.

The next morning, after only a few hours of fitful sleep, I leave the hotel and wander down to the center of town. I am seeking directions to the Buddhist "forest monastery" Wat Pah Nanachat, and when I spot a confident-looking policeman, I approach him.

"Yaak ja pai, Wat Pah Nanachat Beung Wai. Rot meh neung?" Stringing together words pulled from the dictionary, I hope I'm making sense.

"Oh, you want bus number one," he answers in English, surprising me. "You get number one on corner at end of street. Just walk straight ahead. But bus only go to market. There you get *songthaew* to Wat Pah Nanachat." *Songthaew* literally means "two rows" and usually refers to a small pickup truck with benches on either side in the back.

In less than half an hour, the bus arrives at the corner, as promised, and I climb on board. "Yaak ja pai, Wat Pah Nanachat?" The driver doesn't answer my question, but after we cross a bridge, he motions for me to get off and points to a truck across the street. "Songthaew — Wat Pah Nanachat," he says.

"Wat Pah Nanachat?" The unshaven, shirtless driver looks up at me impatiently and responds with something incomprehensible. When I repeat my question, he motions for me to climb into the bed of the truck, where a score of apprehensive women and children are already crowded together on the benches, clutching baskets filled with produce.

They pretend disinterest but dart furtive glances at me as we begin the hot and bumpy ride. I catch the word *farang,* meaning foreigner, in their murmured conversations. Soon the novelty of my appearance on their songthaew wears off, and everyone sits quietly, looking out at the passing countryside, until the truck pulls up to a rural stop. "Wat Pah Nanachat!" my fellow travelers yell, pointing to a small wooden sign.

> ## Wat Pah Nanachat
> ### Bung Wai International Forest Monastery

I jump off and go around to pay the driver, then begin trekking down the dirt road. The reddish brown soil underfoot reminds me of the clay of southern Oklahoma. I scoop up a handful; even the feel of it is familiar. Ahead in the distance, beyond the glimmering green rice fields, is a dense forest. Barely visible through the trees is the outline of a high, gray stucco wall. I continue on the road until I reach an open gate. Once through, I find the temperature noticeably cooler. The canopy above is so thick that it separates sky from earth, and sunlight can barely penetrate the shadows.

Passing by a cluster of simple, square brick buildings that appear deserted, I continue down the shaded road to a two-story structure where the ground floor is completely open. At one end is a kitchen with a row of rectangular folding tables arranged along one side. A tall, slightly stooped man with a round face is standing by the black cast-iron stove. The shaven-headed bhikkhu, dressed in his yellowish brown robes, looks up and greets me, "Sawat-dii."

"Sawat-dii; phom cheu Bill Claassen," I reply. Moving closer to him, I notice that his eyebrows are missing; perhaps they've been shaved off as well.

"Oh, Mr. Claassen, welcome; we've been expecting you. There's clean water in that silver container over there on the table if you'd like some. And please leave your boots **outside**." Good grief — my boots are still on! I'm shocked to have forgotten that in traditional Thai culture, one never wears shoes inside a dwelling. I take them off immediately and place them outside the posts marking the spot where walls would usually appear, then I begin refilling my plastic bottle with the boiled water. "My name is Patrick," he says, walking over to me carrying a bright red coffee cup.

Automatically extending my hand to shake his, I hesitate, then quickly pull back. In Thai Buddhism a layperson is forbidden to touch a bhikkhu. He smiles at my reaction and motions for me to sit down on one of the wooden folding chairs pulled up to the table.

Patrick tells me that he has lived at Wat Pah Nanachat for almost a year but has been a practicing Buddhist for close to twenty years. His home is the Netherlands. "At this wat, it can take a few years to be ordained a bhikkhu," he explains. "The first stage, which you will be interested in, is living in the community as a layman when you must wear a loose-fitting white shirt and pants. If you don't have the proper clothes, we have some in the closet upstairs."

I ask if a visiting layman is expected to take vows.

"You must follow five [of the] precepts and abstain from taking life, human and otherwise; from stealing; from improper sexual conduct; from lying; and from intoxicants." Patrick continues, "And if you decide to stay longer than four days, you must also shave your head." Hair is considered a distraction here, as it is in all Buddhist monasteries.

It occurs to me that the next level of training might be when the eyebrows disappear. "The second stage is what we call a *pahkow*," he says. "It's a Thai word for one who takes the eight precepts and is also assigned a private living space." According to Patrick, it is a relatively new development in Thailand to ordain men using this title. "At one time only a woman could become a pahkow, but there is no longer an official order of nuns, or mae-chii, in Thailand, so the community of men has incorporated the position into its training."

"What are the additional precepts taken by a pahkow?" I ask.

Patrick takes a sip of water from his cup before answering my question. He does not hurry but seems mindful of the impact of each word and gesture. His speech is measured. "The third precept changes in that you must refrain from *any* sexual activity, for example, masturbation. And the additional three include not eating after midday or participating in dance, music or song, as well as not sleeping in a bed. Oh yes, I forgot to say that a pahkow is given white robes to wear and an alms bowl to carry."

I mention that the difference between a pahkow and a novice, the third stage, still eludes me. The bhikkhu differentiates between the two. "A novice agrees to the additional precepts of celibacy and of refraining from touching gold and silver. He cannot handle money."

Patrick grew up in the Catholic Church and equates the precepts with the Ten Commandments. He might also compare the *Vinaya*, rules of training and discipline for the bhikkhu written by the Buddha's intimate devotees, to *The Rule of St. Benedict* in Christian monastic life. "When a man is finally ordained, he accepts 227 precepts; they are collectively called the *Patimokkha*," he says, looking at me directly. "It's quite a responsibility to be ordained as a bhikkhu."

I want to ask Patrick questions about his life and how he was drawn to this place, but first I check to be sure he has time to spend with me. I've not noticed anyone else around, and I know he may have responsibilities to meet.

"No, no," he says, assuring me that he is free. "Most everyone else is visiting our central wat and won't return until late this evening. We have more time to talk."

"Why did you decide to come here? What was it here at Wat Pah Nanachat that was so special?"

Patrick considers the question. "I came here because of the community, because I knew about the teachings of the master, Ajahn Chah, who was responsible for building this international wat." He pauses and says, "You know, this wat was established in the mid-seventies to facilitate the study and practice of Thai Buddhist monastic life for Westerners." He then asks me a question: "Your last name is Dutch, isn't it?"

"Yes, as a matter of fact my full name is Cornelius William Claassen."

"Interesting. In my country, Cornelius Claassen is a very formal name. We usually shorten Cornelius to Cor or Cornel." He says he'll call me Cornel from now on.

Then, even though he's just told me he has time to talk, he abruptly gets up and asks me to follow him to a blackboard standing in the center of the open room. Written on it is the day's schedule. "Check it daily," Patrick tells me as he leads me upstairs to the second level, which is one large room. Looking between the exposed beams of the ceiling, I can see the tin roof. On the wooden planks of the floor are bedrolls, over which stand triangular metal frames with mosquito netting attached. Open windows along three sides provide cross-ventilation, and on the fourth wall is a large painting of the Tibetan Buddhist Wheel of Samsara, beautifully done in saturated primary colors. A Sanskrit word *samsara* refers to the endless cycle of birth, death and rebirth or reincarnation. I'm surprised to see it here, although the wheel does somehow seem appropriate in a dormitory for newcomers.

"In the center of the wheel, the pig, rooster and snake are symbols of ignorance, desire and hatred," says Patrick, pointing to each of the animals. "And as you can see, they're chasing each other around and around in an endless cycle." He pauses, then laughs and adds, "That ought to give you something to meditate on."

In his book *What the Buddha Never Taught*, Tim Ward offers a vivid description of this Tibetan Samsara Wheel to the reader:

All living beings are continually reborn in the six realms which were shown as radiating outward from the center circle of the wheel. In each realm there was suffering. The hell beings suffered physical torment; the hungry ghosts of the spirit realm, with their thin throats and huge bellies, were incapable of gratifying their cravings of thirst and hunger. In the animal realm, beasts suffered from fear and ignorance. Amongst the various activities of the human realm, there was poverty, cruelty and pain…. The entire wheel…was clasped in the yellow teeth and claws of a red-eyed demon.

The powerful images in the Samsara can easily compete with any in the Christian frescoes at Monastero di Sacro Speco in Subiaco, Italy, or those in the painted icons on Mt. Athos. They were all created to teach — or rather convince — those who were unable to read to accept the "one true path."

Before leaving me to settle in, Patrick says that some of the men will meet downstairs in an hour for a sweet drink, and he reminds me again to check the schedule board daily. The routine here is somewhat similar to that of Christian monasteries in the West or Zen Buddhist temples in Japan. The bhikkhu meet for meditation and chanting twice daily, which is in addition to each man's individual practice, and live a celibate and cenobitic life that includes designated periods for daily labor.

Daily Schedule			
3:00 A.M.	*Wake-up bell*	3:00 P.M.	*Daily Chores*
3:30	*Chant/Meditation*	4:30	*Sweet Drink*
5:00	*Clean Sala*	7:00	*Chant/Meditation*
Dawn	*Bindabhat*	9:30	*Solo Time*
8:00	*Meal*		

Before the afternoon refreshment, I decide to wander over to the main *sala,* a one-story building that serves as the temple at this wat. Inside, a substantial, multileveled altar — with two Buddhas covered in goldleaf — is displayed at one end. The figures, one placed in front of the other, are in the same pose: one hand in the lap and the other resting on a knee, fingers bent and pointing down toward the ground. The posture recalls Buddha's sitting beneath a banyan tree for half a dozen years, seeking enlightenment. Although Mara, the Buddhist equivalent to Satan, tempted the master in many ways, the legend states that Buddha held fast, remaining grounded to the earth, as symbolized by the icon's fingers pointing downward.

On either side of the statues of Buddha kneel two devotees sculpted in bronze, each with his hands together, palm to palm, raised and touching his forehead in the posture of *wai,* the Thai Buddhist gesture of respect. And strewn among the figures are vases overflowing with fragrant purple, orange and yellow flowers.

An unexpected element in the temple catches my attention. It's a human skeleton enclosed in a glass case that dangles precariously just above the ground. Moving closer, I kneel to look at the framed black-and-white photograph of a young, smiling Thai woman, which is propped up in front of the skeleton's toes.

I later discover that during her lifetime she had been a frequent visitor to the wat but had developed cancer and committed suicide by shooting herself in the head. The hole made by the bullet is evident in her skull. In Thai Buddhism, a person who commits suicide cannot be cremated, so she was buried instead. Many months later, her husband agreed to have her bones exhumed, cleaned and placed in the glass case. She now hangs as a macabre reminder of the similarity of human beings: We are all nothing more than a collection of bones.

I turn away from the case and see that along the far wall is a raised platform, about chair level, where the bhikkhu take their one meal of the day. Their sitting order is determined by the amount of time spent living at the wat, not by their degree of spiritual development.

When a bell rings, I leave the temple and walk over to join the four men gathered in the kitchen: Two of them are pahkow and two are bhikkhu (one is Canadian and the others are European). Patrick has prepared an herbal drink for us and passes the teapot around, followed by a bowl of chocolate mints; sugar is a helpful source of energy for the remainder of the day, he tells me. Because candy is not regarded as food, the bhikkhu are not violating a precept by eating it. One of the pahkow repeats what Patrick had said earlier, which is that most of the bhikkhu are at Wat Pah Pong, the "motherhouse" to this monastery. That is where their spiritual master, Ajahn Chah, once lived and taught before his death in the early 1990s.

When the men begin drifting away, the Canadian Bhikkhu Panasaro volunteers to show me around the grounds. I had noticed him earlier because he sat in a chair rather than on the floor. He explains, "My knees aren't any good anymore — too much sitting meditation."

Following him along paths leading ever deeper into the forest, I soon realize I will need to find landmarks to avoid getting lost in this maze. When we arrive at his *kuti,* the Canadian asks me to wait, then he climbs up the steps and goes through the door. His *kuti* — a one-room dwelling about eight feet by twelve with an open front porch, a tin roof and windows on three sides — is like a hermit's dwelling except that it's built on wooden stilts. To prevent the scorpions, lizards and snakes from climbing in, uninvited, a tarlike substance encircles each of the pillars midway down. On the ground beside Panasaro's steps sits a covered barrel of water that he can use for washing clothes or bathing.

"Today is unusual," says the Canadian, descending the steps. "Our evening chanting and meditation will be done individually. But we will be meeting in the recently constructed sala early tomorrow morning." It strikes me as unusual for a wat to have two salas. We walk together over to the new open-sided sala, where I decide to stay and meditate by myself on the mat-covered concrete floor. I sit down in front of the lone Buddha icon. Electric ceiling fans keep the air moving and the ever-annoying mosquitoes at bay. "You can join us for chanting and meditation in the morning or sleep in," the bhikkhu says before leaving the sala. "But if you sleep in, you will need to be up in time to start chores and preparation for the meal."

When the bell rings before dawn, I sit straight up and immediately bang my head on the frame holding the mosquito netting. Then, feeling somewhat disoriented, I drop back onto my bedroll, thankful to have more time for sleep. A few hours later, I am sweeping the red soil paths surrounding the kitchen at the central sala with a long rake made from tree branches. A village volunteer has gladly demonstrated the proper way to swing it from side to side, using very broad strokes.

Now the kitchen is buzzing with activity as laypeople, both men and women, sort out the prepared food gathered during *bindabhat* — the monks' morning ritual of collecting alms from the supportive neighboring villages — and cook other items they've brought with them. Bowls made

*Kuti at
Wat Pah Nanachat*

Bhikkhu on bindabhat rounds

of white enamel and aluminum trays are being filled to overflowing with food and lined up atop the long wooden tables.

I join the volunteers carrying these heaping trays, and we walk single file into the sala, where the bhikkhu are getting settled on their platform. Each monk has a wicker stand for his alms bowl, next to his teapot, eating utensils and scrap bowl. Following sutra chanting, the food is passed from bhikkhu to bhikkhu, with each dish presented first to the ajahn. What remains at the end of the platform is carried back into the kitchen where short-term visitors take their meal with the other layworkers.

The selection is amazingly varied, beginning with two kinds of rice — "sticky" white and a darker variety — then continuing with Thai curries and soups, each portion individually enclosed in a tiny plastic bag and sealed at the top with a rubber band. Next is a selection of dried and cooked fish, hard-boiled eggs and barbecued chicken wings, which is followed by watermelon and other colorful native fruits. Homemade cakes and cartons of sweetened juices make up the last course.

Back in the kitchen, a villager in the crowd hands me a cup and bowl and makes sure the new layman receives his share and a place on the floor. While sitting on the straw mat and eating with the locals, I watch a brigade of black ants, marching in our direction, determined to get their fair share as well. One of the villagers beside me gets up and *gently* sweeps them away, reflecting in the gesture an awareness of the precept "refrain from taking life, human or otherwise."

Once the meal and cleanup have been completed and my tasks are finished, I reenter the sala for the purpose of introducing myself to the assistant ajahn, who is also the guestmaster. The man bears a striking physical resemblance to Mahatma Gandhi. He is very thin and has a prominent nose, upon which sit a pair of small, round glasses. I bow, then kneel on the floor in front of the bhikkhu and wait for him to begin talking. Repeating some of what Patrick told me yesterday afternoon, Bhikkhu Sangwaro briefly discusses the wat, then suggests that we meet in the afternoon for further orientation. He says he will send someone to find me at the appropriate time.

A few hours later, following a refreshingly cold shower in one of the communal bathrooms, I return to the kitchen, where I meet a novice from Tulsa, Oklahoma, named Vincent, who happens to be a college student on leave. "My mother is Thai and my father is American," he tells me. "I am here for my mother's benefit, although I wanted to come anyway. By taking the training and ordination I am gaining merits for both my mother and grandmother."

I ask if he will go back to Tulsa once he has been ordained.

"Yes, I will disrobe and then return to the States," he admits.

Thai Buddhists believe that good deeds earn merits that are helpful in both the present and the future life. So, sons become ordained, some villagers give food to the bhikkhu during bindabhat and others volunteer in the kitchen as part of their religious practice to gain merits for themselves and family members.

Vincent says that it is possible for Thai boys to be ordained in a matter of days so that they may earn necessary merits for their families. During the *Pansa,* the three-month monsoon retreat, Thai men can be excused from their jobs or schools to take their training. Now, as in the past, nearly all Thai males are ordained either for the sake of tradition or merit-making, but most men don't seriously consider taking on the permanent life of a bhikkhu.

As expected, a white-robed pahkow tracks me down in the afternoon and tells me Bhikkhu Sangwaro awaits me in the *bhote,* the ordination hall. The small, triangular building is made of marble and glass and looks very much like a postmodern Christian chapel, minus the altar and pews. Flowers bloom both inside and outside the bhote, protected by thick panes of glass. When I arrive, Sangwaro is already in place. I bow, then kneel before him. The bhikkhu begins to speak about himself, informing me that he is in his early thirties, although he appears older to me, and that he grew up in Austria, where his family still lives.

Because I've heard some of the villagers call him Ajahn, rather than Bhikkhu Sangwaro, I ask him to define the word *ajahn.* "The word *ajahn* officially means teacher," he informs me. "But in this part of the country, the northeast, it is used loosely. If you are ordained, the villagers will call you ajahn, but not your fellow bhikkhu." Sangwaro pauses, then adds, "I was ordained eleven years ago."

"And the official ajahn or abbot, how long ago was he ordained?"

"The abbot, Ajahn Jayasaro, was ordained almost twenty years ago. By the way, he is in his late thirties and a native of England."

A friend had told me that Thai monks are expected to live in a number of different branch monasteries during their lifetime, and I ask

Sangwaro how many he's lived in since his ordination.

"I guess you know that stability, or permanently staying in one wat, is not one of our precepts or vows. Many Christian monks do honor that vow, however. I have lived in five branch wats — a Catholic monk would call them daughterhouses — sometimes for up to three months." Sangwaro's use of Christian/Buddhist comparisons help me to integrate new information with what is old knowledge. He seems to be a natural teacher.

"Is the abbot a strong authority figure in all of the branch monasteries?"

"The abbot is not as strong a figure as in Christian monasticism, where he has the unquestionably strong, central role. Here, we do things much more democratically and discuss the issues. On one hand, the abbot is still the primary authority. On the other, the abbot will now bring up issues and try to reach a consensus with the other bhikkhu rather than simply making a rule without consultation." Sangwaro stands to adjust his robe then sits back down.

His explanation of the evolution of leadership roles leads me to question whether the traditions of authority in Thai culture influence monastic life. He sees a strong connection: "Oh, yes. In Thailand, the people are very conscious of seniority. They call a big person *pu yai* and a small person *pu noi*. Among siblings, for example, the eldest and youngest clearly define the line of authority, duty and responsibility. Traditionally, if you disagree you don't say anything. All of this carries over into monastic life in Thailand."

I know that monastic life here has also been much shaped by Ajahn Chah, Sangwaro's former spiritual leader at Wat Pah Nanachat. I've read about him, and I am curious to hear the impressions of someone who knew him personally.

When I ask about Chah, the bhikkhu takes a moment to respond. Finally, he addresses my question in terms of Chah's role: "He was an unquestioned authority because no one doubted his skill in dealing with practical issues or his deep spiritual wisdom. But there is nobody that has filled his place since his death."

"Was it Ajahn Chah who initiated the building of this wat?"

"Two things really came together here. More than twenty years ago there was an increasing number of Westerners interested in living and studying with Ajahn Chah. At the same time, there were a number of

Westerners at Wat Pah Pong, the central wat, and increasing problems." Again, the guestmaster pauses for a moment, pushing his glasses further up on his nose. "A major problem was communication because most internationals didn't speak Thai, and because they couldn't understand Thai, there wasn't any formal instruction. So Ajahn Chah thought it would be a good idea if Westerners had a branch wat nearby. That way, we could still consult with the Ajahn when necessary."

"How did this branch wat actually get established here?"

"Well, the land that we are on used to be the cremation grounds for some neighboring villages. And cremation grounds are traditional places for bhikkhu to live. So, during a certain time of the year, nearby villagers invited us to bring our large umbrellas covered with mosquito nets and spend a few days on the cremation grounds of their forest. It was then that the villagers decided they would like to have a wat right here," explains the guestmaster. He says that when Ajahn Chah gave his permission and selected one of his longtime Western bhikkhu to serve as the new abbot, the villagers then became responsible for building the wat. "Presently, a dozen of us are internationals, and the remaining few are Thai, all living on approximately one hundred acres."

Knowing the bhikkhu's custom of gathering food from local residents, I inquire whether the villagers who invited the Westerners also took on the responsibility for feeding them.

"Oh yes. Every morning we go on bindabhat to the neighboring villages," says Sangwaro. "It's the traditional way, since the time of the Buddha, for bhikkhu to gather their daily sustenance."

"Do most bhikkhu in forest wats depend on the ritual of bindabhat for their food?"

"Yes. Here in northeast Thailand, most wats also have a kitchen similar to ours. So some villagers will come here and cook items in addition to what has been collected in the daily rounds, and others will also leave money in the kitchen to be used for buying perishables. A few of the lay volunteers are responsible for buying food in the market."

It sounds as though the villagers are always volunteering their time. But as Sangwaro explains, "Basically what they are doing is part of their daily routine, their life. For example, both men who manage the food and the kitchen are by no means wealthy, but they have quite a bit of land and can get by. So they come to the wat every morning. They are almost semimonastic themselves." He says there is also a core group of women that come in every day soon after sunrise to cook, and then take home what food is left over.

"What exactly is their primary motivation?"

"Their religion, of course," responds the guestmaster. "It's how they perceive themselves growing in the dhamma — the doctrine and teachings of the Buddha — toward greater happiness. They are also making merit."

I tell him I'm not sure what he means by "making merit," and he elaborates, "The concept of merit is that whatever we do, or the intention of our deeds, determines the consequences of those deeds. Therefore, working for the bhikkhu is a positive act and will effect them in a positive way now and in their next life." He leans down closer to me, as if to confide something: "You see, in Thai Buddhist philosophy there is no such thing as an accident or coincidence. However, only the Buddha can see the connections. So basically, much of Buddhist training is about purifying one's actions in body, speech and mind."

"So all of the villagers work in the wat primarily to better their spiritual life?"

"Yes, they're taking care of bhikkhu, who are upholding the highest principles and practices of Buddhism. They're supporting a source of goodness in the world and thereby supporting both their religion and the bhikkhu."

Recognizing a pattern familiar from my experience of other monastic traditions, I comment on the apparently beneficial system of interdependence between the bhikkhu and the villagers, and Sangwaro explains the system's origin and purpose. "The Buddha established this 'give and take' relationship. This type of monastic life is designed to prevent the bhikkhu from going too far off into his mental spaces. Remember, enlightenment is not just some sort of 'outer space' state of mind. It happens within this physical body as well. So bindabhat reminds bhikkhu of how others live. It's sensory input — a daily test — a reminder of our dependence on one another, or rather the interdependence among ourselves."

My next question is automatic. "When you went on bindabhat this morning, what were you thinking?"

"Well, usually on the alms rounds our basic practice is mindfulness. I try to let my mind wander around the act of walking and appreciation for the food. Because we're doing it every day, it is easy to let it become a routine. And this, as in all monastic traditions, is the great hindrance — getting used to things."

That seems a natural place to conclude our discussion, and after leaving the bhote, I meander over to the kitchen to fetch a coffee cup, anticipating the upcoming late-afternoon sweets. They are to be served at the abbot's kuti, according to the blackboard, where a screened-in room has been built on the ground floor.

I hurry over. Leaving my boots outside the screen door, I step inside, and kneeling, I bow the traditional three times in the direction of the abbot then take my place in the back of the room. The bhikkhu sit in the front row; behind them are the novices, then the pahkows and finally lay visitors. Appreciative silence greets the thick hot chocolate and mints. I find the snack extraordinarily satisfying, especially as I'm just becoming accustomed to eating only one meal a day. Once everyone has been served, the abbot begins talking of his recent experiences visiting Wat Pah Pong, the central monastery.

Soon after sunset, we move down to the new sala, the one built deeper into the forest, for evening chanting. In the first hour, a few of us alternate sitting with walking meditation. I am glad to see others switch back and forth; I frequently find that the combination enhances my concentration. But at the end of the hour, all of us join in chanting at an even pace, paying homage to the three refuges — the Buddha, the Dhamma and the Sangha, the community of Buddhist monks.

Paying Homage to the Buddha
Namo Tassa Bhagavato
Homage to the Exalted One, the Arahant,
Arahato Samma Sambuddhasa
the One Perfectly Enlightened by Himself.

Chant for the Three Refuges
Buddham saranam, gacchami
I go to the Buddha for refuge.
Dhammam saranam gacchami
I go to the Dhamma for refuge.
Sangham saranam gacchami
I go to the Sangha for refuge.

189

After the chanting, individuals drift out along various paths to their kuti. Their flashlight beams, spied through the trees, seem to flick on and off like dancing fireflies. I quickly realize that all the flashlights are moving away from me, and I am forced to turn my attention to the task of finding my way back to the kitchen. The dirt paths are hard to see, and the intersections are confusing, but I finally locate the building. Relieved, I go quickly to the stairs and up to the second floor. Once under the mosquito netting that protects my bedroll, I fall asleep with ease.

But in the middle of the night, an irritating scratching sound awakens me. It seems to be coming from the floor near my bed. Carefully reaching out from under the net, I grab the flashlight and flick it on. Caught in the beam is a plump, scaly, green iguana that looks much longer than my arm. We are facing each other. Fortunately, he is as startled as I am, and he scrambles away across the floor, up the wall and out through a window. He climbs to the roof, and I track his progress across it by the sounds he makes; his claws screeching over the tin remind me of nails on a blackboard.

My heart is thumping hard. The bhikkhu had said to expect nighttime visitors, but they hadn't told me what size the visitors would be. I jump up and thoroughly check the room for any other scaly intruders. For the rest of the night, I am rattled by visions of the iguana returning with his extended family. I envision waking to find my bedroll surrounded by lizards. I'm wide-awake when the ringing bell calls me back to the sala hours before dawn.

After meditation and chanting, I prepare to join half a dozen bhikkhu on their daily bindabhat route. I agree to keep silent and remain a proper distance behind the pahkow, the last man in their group. Bhikkhu Sangwaro, in his bare feet, confidently leads his fellow monks along dirt paths and over railroad tracks, across gravel roads and through fallow fields, inspiring them to mindfully participate in this ritual as it has been practiced for thousands of years. Even wearing boots, it's an effort for me to keep up with his brisk pace.

The villagers wait outside their cottages, kneeling on the roadside, patiently holding up their food offerings. As the bhikkhu approach with open alms bowls hanging from their shoulders, the devotees quickly transfer food from their containers into those of the bhikkhu. The relationship between the two groups is clearly defined: The villagers and the bhikkhu neither make eye contact nor speak to one another during the

Receiving alms

*Traditional gesture
is offered
by a villager*

transaction. As Sangwaro had told me, offerings benefit not solely the individual, but everyone. Once the bhikkhu pass by, each villager raises the offering bowl to his or her forehead, then stands and returns home. The process will be repeated in exactly the same way almost every day of the year, except when the bhikkhu are on tudong.

During the afternoon work session, one of the bhikkhu introduces me to an unfamiliar member of the community named Stephen, a very thin Thai in his early fifties with prominent dark circles under his eyes. We are assigned to do chores together. A divorced father of grown children, Stephen has a unique relationship with the wat. He first came here as a lay volunteer, then he stayed on as a pahkow but decided not to pursue ordination because of the strict daily routine. The man is an unrepentant heavy smoker and enjoys the freedom of coming and going as he pleases. However, he was assigned a kuti and has become a full-time helpmate to the bhikkhu. He has many skills that are put to use here at Wat Pah Nanachat.

Talking while loading up wood from a newly cut tree, Stephen explains that we're to move and stack it where the bhikkhu dye and wash their robes. "They use chip from trunk of jackfruit tree for dye," my work partner explains. "You see slightly different color; sometime more brown, sometime less." He says that once a bhikkhu has been ordained, he is responsible for sewing, dyeing and maintaining his robes; it is a very old tradition.

I ask if the robes are the only things a bhikkhu can actually own. "Oh, no," replies Stephen. "Alms bowl belong to them, and needle and thread. Also razor and water filter, cloth belt, flint and steel, mosquito net, his kettle, one towel, umbrella and toothbrush." It's peculiar — when he lists the items out loud, their number seems greater, as though the bhikkhu are men of many worldly possessions, when really they own only the most basic necessities.

We return to the site of the felled tree. While we're loading more of the logs onto the wheelbarrows, I tell him about my interview with Bhikkhu Sangwaro the day before. "Stephen, it's clear to me what responsibilities the surrounding villagers have to the bhikkhu, but it's unclear as to what specific services the bhikkhu offer in return."

"First, bhikkhu give spiritual advice in Buddhist tradition," he replies without hesitation. "Next, they make ceremony rite and ritual, like house blessing, dedication, funeral and cremation. And finally, bhikkhu provide way for devotee make merit."

I tell him I think that the give-and-take relationship is similar to that in other monastic traditions, but since Stephen isn't familiar with those traditions, he says he can't give an opinion.

"You shave head and eyebrow?" he asks curiously.

"If I stayed longer than four days it would be necessary; otherwise Ajahn Sangwaro said it wasn't required."

Unloading the second load, I question Stephen about the "all-night meditations" now held in the new sala. I have heard some of the bhikkhu talking about them. "Time for all-night meeting set by place of moon — full moon, half moon, no moon," he explains. "On special night, called *wun phra,* bhikkhu confess error to other bhikkhu. They choose partner and confess."

I ask if the abbot has a role in the confessions.

"Ajahn only come in if confession serious — if bhikkhu break important precept." I think that serving as both confessor and confessee must bind the men to each other and to the community.

At nightfall, I again go to the new sala to join in group meditation and chanting. I appreciate the openness of this wat to different techniques. In a forest monastery, the bhikkhu is often encouraged to discover what is appropriate and workable for him alone, within the Thai Buddhist framework. This is my last night at Wat Pah Nanachat, and I remain in the sala long after the chanting has ended and most of the others have disappeared into the darkness.

The only sound is the hum of the ceiling fans, and slowly the quiet enters my mind. A memory from the last few days surfaces, and as I focus on it, the faint chattering of my inner voice stops at last. Sitting in the calm space, I imagine a smiling Bhikkhu Patrick saying, "Cornel, during your stay here, remember the words of a Buddhist sage, 'Do not speak unless you can improve upon the silence.'"

Chapter Ten

WEARING THE SKY

Be non-violent for thy own sake. The good of your own soul requires you to be non-violent. It is no obligation or charity towards anybody.

Lord Mahavira
sixth century B.C.E.

Atop barren Vindhyagiri Hill sits an ancient stone temple, and within the temple's courtyard stands a colossal tenth-century sculpture of Lord Bahubali. Today, my first glimpse of this immense statue is through the windows of a rickety old bus, and even from a distance it again appears impossibly huge. Sculpted from a single piece of granite, the nude male is shown in a symbolic yogic stance, where the body appears to be under complete control. The carved leafy vines that climb his legs and twine around his arms remind the devotee of the lord's ability to maintain this posture indefinitely in his quest for nirvana. He epitomizes the Jain ideal.

According to the *Agamas,* Jain scriptures, Bahubali was the son of the first prophet. The Jains have more than twenty prophets, known as the *Tirthankaras,* who are recognized as spiritual guides on the true path to salvation. Mahavira is the last and most revered of these leaders. His popular teachings were not transcribed until hundreds of years after his death.

When I arrive at the courtyard, once I am able to turn my attention from the statue, I notice a few long-limbed, gray-bearded old men wearing only white cotton loincloths called *dhotis.* They are sitting to one side of the statue, in the shade of the columned temple porch that extends around three sides of the inner court. The men are preparing to sound their long brass horns, which are used to announce the beginning of the daily early morning ritual.

At the base of the statue stands a group of priests; the tallest is wrapped in a lemon-colored, lightweight robe, while the other two are attired in white cotton robes. In the Jain religion they are known as *pujaris*. With them this morning is their apprentice, an enthusiastic and energetic teenage boy also dressed in white.

When the musicians begin blowing their horns, the pujaris face Lord Bahubali. Standing at his enormously long feet, ancient symbols of humility, they gaze up at his face (nearly sixty feet away) and raise high above their heads offerings of burning, pungent incense in Aladdin's lamps. The smoke curls upward, and as it begins to dissipate, the men begin chanting in the ancient Indian language of Prakrit. They may be repeating the words of a tenth-century Jain hymn, the Gommatesa-Thudi (verses 2, 5 and 6 below), which was first performed at the dedication of the Bahubali statue more than a thousand years ago. Meaning good and handsome, as well as benefactor, the word *Gommatesa* is synonymous with Lord Bahubali.

> *His person clothed with purity, cheeks clear like water,*
> *His graceful ears swinging close into the shoulders,*
> *And His mighty arms resembling the trunk of King-tusker.*
> *Before that Lord Gommatesa ever I kneel!*
>
> *His comely neck surpassing the divine conch,*
> *His lofty shoulders wide like the Himalayas,*
> *And His shapely waist so steady and spectacular,*
> *Before that Lord Gommatesa ever I kneel!...*
>
> *Unfettered by possessions all — money and mansion,*
> *Equipped with equanimity quelling pride and greed,*
> *And fasting far for a full twelve months,*
> *Before that Lord Gommatesa ever I kneel!*

Next, libations are offered to Lord Bahubali. One of the pujaris accompanies a petite middle-aged Indian woman, dressed in an exquisite light blue sari decorated with pink and white blossoms, to the right foot of the statue. Together they pour holy water from a glistening silver pitcher. We all watch as the water spreads over the rough granite surface and runs in streamlets down between the toes. Scores of devotees sit cross-legged in the courtyard; some chant, while others silently read from small, red vinyl-covered books of the Agamas. Grasping their prayer beads, many of them slowly finger their way through the more than one hundred beads, over and over again. Moving among the worshippers, I think back to an event from my own spiritual life that helps me better appreciate the purification ceremony unfolding before me.

~~~~~~~~~~

More than a decade ago I was living in an intentional Christian-based community that would begin and end each day with a worship period. At one point, we decided to incorporate the act of foot-washing into our evening service. Some of our members had grown up practicing the ritual in their faith communities. We understood that within a Christian context, the intimate and sacred act was derived from Christ washing his disciples' feet. Among other things, the ceremony symbolized not only humility but the ideal of willing service. The experience remains vivid in my memory.

I was paired off with an Episcopal priest who was almost twice my age. But he was as agile and physically fit as I. Richard, the lanky and gregarious clergyman, wore a full-length beard, giving him the look of Father Time. Having voluntarily gone to Japan immediately after the United States' bombing of Hiroshima and Nagasaki near the end of World War II, he had spent most of his adult life ministering there. Washing the man's feet, gently and with great care, was certainly an act of humility and willing service for me. In my own way, I was honoring a wise elder and God's creation.

~~~~~~~~~~

At the base of the large statue, another pujari makes a second offering to Lord Bahubali, this time at the left foot. The priest pours coconut milk from a brass pitcher onto each of the toes, the longest of which is four feet. The white liquid coats and highlights each of the carved toenails. Now the eager devotees stand and begin to form a line in front of the yellow-robed pujari. Lifting their heads in prayer to the lord, they start forward. As the line moves past the priest, he offers a blessing and gently touches the palm of his right hand to each person's forehead.

The final ritual libation, offered by the third pujari, is a mixture of sandalwood paste in water. The thick, syrupy liquid runs slowly over the granite of the left foot before disappearing into a small channel in the statue's base. When the last pitcher is empty, the trumpeters begin blowing their horns again, and the worshippers step forth with offerings of coconuts, fruit and coins. Sitting in front of Bahubali, the young apprentice respectfully adorns the right foot with fragrant magnolia petals that, from

Lord Bahubali within the Jain temple walls

Jain temple on Vindhyagiri Hill

197

where I stand, look like popcorn.

Barefoot, I join the chanting devotees as they walk around the temple offering prayers to the miniature Tirthankara icons, images of Jain saints appropriately placed in chapels near Bahubali. Then we all proceed single file out of the courtyard, through another outer enclosure and down the over six hundred sun-baked steps that lead to the village of Shravana Belgola, the "town of monks and white lake."

This area was settled in the third century B.C.E. by Jains fleeing famine in the north. Now recognized as one of the oldest and certainly most dramatic of the group's worship sites, it is one of the most sacred of Jain pilgrimage destinations in all of India.

Just beyond the village and across the dusty road is another hill, Chandragiri, smaller than its sister, but no less important in the history and development of Jain monasticism. In the tenth century, a major Jain *math,* or monastery complex, was built there. Although no longer in use, the temples still stand. Even before the math's construction, Chandragiri had been a sacred place. According to S. Settar in his book *Inviting Death*, which explores Jain monastic history, the mesa was better known as Sepulchral Hill or the Mountain of Meditation-unto-Death. It was the final destination for senior Jain ascetics who chose to end their lives in a religiously sanctioned manner. Death came gradually as the individual refused first food and then drink in the ritual called *sallekhana*. Jain ascetics believed that such a death would release them from worldly bondage, including the cycle of rebirth in reincarnation.

A few days ago, during my initial visit to Shravana Belgola, I spent hours exploring Chandragiri Hill. Arriving in the village mid-morning, I chose to hike the smaller mesa first.

Leaving my shoes at the base of the sight, I began hiking up the designated path but soon left the path and began scaling the rough, odd-shaped boulders, precariously perched on the hillside, until I reached the summit. I had expected to relive the excitement and enthusiasm experienced when exploring the monastic architectural model in the Egyptian desert. Instead, I was overcome with a feeling of reverence. There was no one else there.

Slowly moving through the stone archway and into the ancient math, I weaved my way around and through the half dozen *batsi*, the Jain temples. Some of the carved stone structures were layered, like wedding cakes, while others were plain with smooth unadorned exteriors. Inside their pillared, dark and dank-smelling interiors were hundreds of sculpted human figures. Some of them stood independently, while others were skillfully etched into the thick stone walls. They were prominent in a number of the sacred temples. While running my hands over scores of those smooth, polished icons, most posed in a full lotus meditative posture, I was keenly aware that many of them symbolized Jain ascetics who had chosen to "invite death."

~~~~~~~~~~~

Reaching the bottom of the steps, I reclaim my shoes at the gate and begin strolling through Shravana Belgola toward the functioning Jain math that I had visited a few days before. At that time, I had asked to make a retreat here but was told that it was not possible. Here, men who aspire either to become Jain scholars or to join one of the religion's two major monastic orders live and study. I approach the reception area, wedged between the two-story math and its primary deity-embellished temple of worship. Seeking out the familiar receptionist, I again request an appointment with the *acharya,* or abbot. For a second time, I am told he is out of the village on business. However, today the reticent, barefoot man offers an alternative.

"Would you care to meet with Mr. Ashok Kumar, a well-respected Jain scholar and editor of our bimonthly newsletter, *Karnataka Fortnightly?*" inquires the young man at the reception desk. Karnataka is the southwestern Indian state where Shravana Belgola is located and "home to twenty thousand Jain households," he explains. I gratefully accept the offer, and the man immediately telephones Mr. Kumar, who agrees to meet with me in his home on the outskirts of Belgola.

Within an hour, I am standing at the side door of Mr. Kumar's tidy sand-colored house, which is surrounded by hedges, blooming flower gardens and shade trees. The trees provide a welcome respite from the day's oppressive heat. Ashok, a dark, handsome man in his late fifties, has a neatly trimmed black mustache and wears traditional white robes. He welcomes me into his sparsely furnished living room. The red tile floor feels cool beneath my feet. As we take chairs on either side of a dining table, his teenage son walks in, shyly introduces himself, serves each of us a cool fruit drink and departs quietly.

"So, I understand you are an aspiring writer from the United States interested in the life a Jain muni," Ashok begins. Synonymous with the English term *monk, muni* is a Sanskrit word.

I tell him that my most recent academic work has been in journalism and that I'm currently working on an independent project focused on monastic life around the world.

"For many years, I worked in the post office, but always wanted to be a journalist," he admits. "So, upon my retirement, I applied for the job of editor and photographer for the *Karnataka Fortnightly*." His work is now strictly on a volunteer basis. I understand that Ashok is part of an extended family of the local Jain math. His relationship to their monastery may be similar to that of an oblate in a Christian monastery. The retired postal worker is highly respected and permitted to speak on the monks' behalf.

Cool and comfortable for the first time that day, I feel at ease. His soft, low voice and calm demeanor encourage me to talk, and I tell him about witnessing the early morning service, the ritual on top of Vindhyagiri Hill. He's obviously pleased.

"Did you realize that the daily ritual of libations is symbolic of a still greater ceremony occurring here every twelve years?" he asks. "The last event took place in 1993, so the next will be in 2005." I tell him that I've seen mention of it in a reference book, but no details were given. "Well, as you might imagine, Shravana Belgola becomes a Mecca for thousands of Jain laymen and monks who wish to witness the event," says Ashok. "You see, scaffolding is built behind Lord Bahubali up to the top of his head. Then, at designated times during the ritual, five symbolic liquids — sugar cane, sandalwood paste, and reddish cumin, all mixed separately with water, then coconut milk and ghee — are poured out, one at a time, over the head and shoulders of the statue." He shows me color postcards of the event, revealing a Bahubali covered from head to foot in shades of yellow, red and white.

Ashok begins talking about the Jain religion, explaining that his fellow devotees believe that the universe was never created and will never come to an end; it is simply eternal. And he highly recommends reading Sanya Doshi's book *Homage to Shravana Belgola*, because "it is a well-written summary of Jainism."

"The path of virtue is the path of self-realization and from there to moksha," explains Doshi in his introduction. *Moksha* and enlightenment

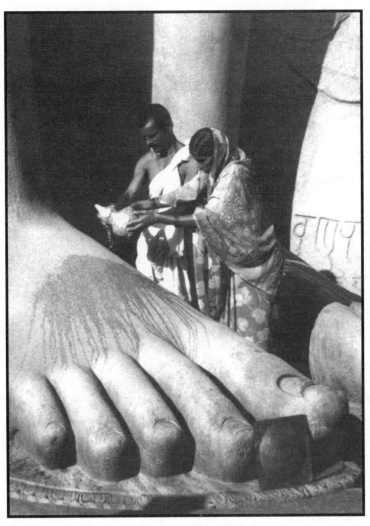

Pouring a libation

are one and the same. "The way to moksha is through the practice of the Three Jewels: Right Faith, Right Knowledge and Right Conduct." He goes on, "The Jain religion emphasizes that individually a man is born, individually he dies and with individual effort he can free himself; there is no God or Supreme Being that can lift him to salvation."

To achieve salvation, the ascetic devotee has vowed to practice five particular disciplines: nonviolence, speaking the truth, refraining from stealing, abstaining from sexual pleasures and shunning worldly wealth. These disciplines, the "five great vows," are the foundation of daily life for every Jain muni. Ashok tells me that there are two primary sects of Jain monastic orders. "The split creating the major sects occurred at the end of the first century," he explains. "Their disagreements were primarily over the issues of nudity and ownership of personal property."

Those in the Digambara sect, the oldest order of Jain ascetics, take on nakedness when they are ordained as muni. Members of the Shvetambara order, a group that split off from the Digambra at the end of the first century, wear clothes. "They believe that the heart can be naked, but not the body," and they own a number of personal items. A third order, a splinter group from the Shvetambara, opposes the use of icons and temples altogether. That order's devotees are best known to the general public for wearing strips of cloth across their mouths to prevent the breathing in of living organisms.

"Any caste member in the Indian society can ordain as a Jain monk," Ashok tells me. He explains that this village and the local math here are affiliated with the Digambara sect.

I ask him to briefly outline the stages of training that one follows in order to become a muni. Although he is a layperson, he is also a Jain scholar. "There are four," he says, fetching a pencil and piece of paper. "It is easier to keep track if I write as we talk. Now, during the first stage, the novice will wear two pieces of white cloth, and is allowed two meals and two drinks per day as he begins his training."

"So some of the men at the math today were in the novice stage? And possibly one of the men assisting with the ritual on top of the hill?" I ask.

"Probably so, yes," answers Ashok. "Some of the men at the math will go on to become muni, and others will become teachers and scholars. Now, in the second stage, the man will be permitted to wear only two pieces of saffron-colored cloth: a dhoti and a pullover that hangs down to the knees. He will only eat one meal a day and is allowed one drink and no more." Each stage of the demanding and rigorous training is designed, layer by layer, to assist the man in gradually disassociating from the material needs and familial connections of life. Pausing a minute, Ashok sips his fruit juice.

"It is in the third stage that the man wears only a dhoti, and begins carrying a whisk broom made of peacock feathers, which we call a *pitchi*. The pitchi is used to gently brush away any living organism in the path of the muni."

"The final stage for a Digambara is when he no longer wears any clothing; he is dressed in the sky. That is the meaning of the word *Digambara*: sky-clad." Each stage brings the man closer to being released from the cycle of reincarnation. That is his goal. Then his spirit can finally experience its own nature in eternal stillness.

I ask my host what novices study during their training.

"There are many things to learn," replies Ashok, "but their primary studies are the Jain rituals and the scriptural texts written in Sanskrit and Pali." He says that many of the men must first learn the two languages, which is quite demanding. It can take many years. "It's their teacher, the *acharya*, who finally determines when the muni ordination can take place." He picks up his drink and finishes the last of the liquid then puts the glass aside. "It's really a matter of finally achieving a state of completely controlling the body and the desires."

When I inquire as to where a muni lives, Ashok says that except for a few months out of the year, June through September, when he is required to live in dormitories built by the Jain laymen, the muni is on pilgrimage and stays where he can.

I know that many Hindu monks travel alone, and I ask if that is true for Jain muni on pilgrimage. "The monks must always travel in groups, which might be anywhere from five men to twenty or more. There are also Jain nuns who will often travel with the men. You haven't asked me about the nuns," comments the editor.

"That's because I didn't know that they existed. Are the women on an equal footing with the men?"

"No. It is the Digambara belief that a woman must be reborn a man, become a monk and then finally achieve moksha."

"So the highest ranking Digambara Jain nun is considered of lower spiritual status than the most recent, inexperienced male novice?"

"That is right." He realizes that his response is difficult for me to understand and allows me a moment to consider it. I move on to another topic. I know that Jain ascetics are strict vegetarians and are not permitted to cook or handle fire. Their strict views on nonviolence prohibit their plowing the earth or harvesting crops. They will not kill an insect or rip a plant from the soil, and so I ask how they sustain themselves. "It is the Jain layman's responsibility to both cook for and feed the muni his one meal of the day," explains Ashok. "This act of feeding, which the muni must always take in the palms of his hands while standing up, is regarded as a way for a devotee to make merit. It is good karma."

Stopping our conversation briefly, he asks his son to bring us two more drinks. Then he asks if I would like to see some of his photographs. Along with the drinks, his son brings out two shoeboxes filled with black-and-white photographs, many of which have been used as illustrations in the *Karnataka Fortnightly*. "Take what you'd like," Ashok encourages me. "I have no use for them anymore." Carefully sifting through the collection, I select almost a dozen photos.

The first one is a shot of six nude Indian men of various heights standing at attention on a low wooden platform. The wall behind them is covered with a painting of Lord Bahubali. Each man has his water pot beside him and his pitchi in one hand. "This is the final initiation ritual of these men who are now officially muni of the Digambara sect," explains my host. "You notice their role model, Bahubali, in the background."

In the left corner of the photograph is a kneeling woman covered in white robes. They even cover her hair. A water pot sits at her side, as well, and she clutches the pitchi in her right hand. I ask about her.

He glances at the photo again. "Her name is Arijika, or mother. She is a highly regarded nun in the Digambara sect." Her presence and participation are obviously important at this rite of passage for the newly ordained muni.

I remark on the varied ages of the men. One individual appears to be significantly older than the others. Ashok tells me that a man can enter the novitiate anytime between the ages of fifteen to sixty.

Also noticing that all the men are bald, I ask if removing hair is an aspect of the ordination, as it is in the Buddhist tradition. He reveals that each initiate plucks the hair from the top of his own head, a ritual based on a practice of their revered Tirthankara Mahavira. It is a symbolic act, demonstrating the monk's determination to meet the severe demands of the ascetic life, and is repeated whenever necessary for the rest of his life.

Three additional photographs portray a group of senior Digambara muni seated on platforms at a public ceremony. The men are emaciated. Their skin is taut; their cheeks are sunken, and their bones seem to protrude. I am reminded of the *sallekhana* ritual, historically sanctioned by the religion only after a muni has lived the demanding ascetic life for at least a dozen years. But I forget to ask Ashok about the men's status. (I continue to wonder if they were in the final stages of sallekhana.)

In still another photo is a symbol I have seen repeatedly in the Belgola village: the *svastika* — a traditional Hindu symbol of good fortune, now tainted in many Western minds by the Nazis' adoption and reversal of it. The symbol is always topped by three dots, above which is a half-moon. I ask its meaning, but my host sidesteps the question, saying that if I had a better grasp of Jain philosophy, he would be happy to provide an answer.

Some months later, I discover from a textbook on world religion that the three dots represent the Three Jewels of the Jain religion. The half-moon symbolizes moksha. And the four arms of the svastika express the four states of birth in their cosmology: those born as insects, plants or animals; as humans; as spirits of gods; or as demons. Nothing about that information seemed shocking, but in retrospect I appreciate why Ashok was reluctant to launch into discussion on such topics. I was a visitor with a beginner's mind.

It is getting late, near the time to catch a bus back to my headquarters a few hours away. After carefully wrapping the photographs and inserting them between the pages of my journal, I follow Ashok back to the side porch, where we say farewell.

Insisting that I make an appointment with the revered leader of the Digambara sect, Ashok gives me detailed information as to where the man can be found. "Our spiritual leader is now living at the Kundakunda Bharati Foundation, a Jain research center in New Delhi, and his name is Acharya Vidyanandji. He has a daily schedule, so you must arrive early in the morning to make an appointment," Ashok says. "The acharya and his assistants can give you more thorough answers to your questions than I. You have to see him."

A few months later, I arrive in Kundakunda Bharati, early in the morning, as instructed. I pause on the well-kept front lawn to scribble down last-minute questions before approaching the front door. The foundation's three-story brick building looks like a contemporary apartment house and is located in a quiet, residential neighborhood on the outskirts of New Delhi. Close by is a small, domed Jain temple freshly painted bright red, green and blue. Just past the entranceway is a white marble altar laden with polished gold and bronze Bahubali icons. Next to it, a landscaped flower garden with a rectangular meditation area occupies the side yard.

A man of medium height dressed in layman's clothes answers the door and introduces himself as Neil. I ask to meet with his leader, Acharya Vidyanandji, and mention that Ashok Kumar of Shravana Belgola had strongly encouraged scheduling an appointment in person. Leaving me standing on the porch for a moment, he goes to check the daily schedule and speak with the acharya, who agrees to a meeting in half an hour. Neil then leads me up a flight of stairs and into a sparsely furnished living room that apparently serves as a waiting room. Along the way, my escort informs me that he is an electrical engineer, but that at present he works as a volunteer for the spiritual leader. He says that he will be serving as my translator during the interview and then leaves me to wait.

Neil returns at the time set for the interview and guides me to another flight of stairs. We climb the steps, walk down a long, unlit hallway and emerge into a room that must have been a bedroom. My attention is caught immediately by a very surprising sight. Built in the center of the space is a thatch hut about six feet high and nine feet long. I assume that this humble abode must satisfy residential requirements for the extremely regimented and austere life of a Jain muni.

Sitting cross-legged inside is the much-respected acharya. Sky-clad, his folded hands draped over his round, protruding belly, the spiritual leader looks quite imposing. His only obvious concession to modern life is his glasses. I bow, then sit down on the cold marble floor and realize that I am very close, facing him directly. This unexpected arrangement is a bit intimidating, and I feel even more nervous about troubling this nationally known spiritual teacher with my simple questions.

My feeling is reinforced about a quarter of an hour into our discussion when the acharya, looking disgruntled, mumbles something to Neil, then

Jain symbol

Sri Vidyanandji, the Digambara spiritual leader

steps out of the hut and walks away without looking back. "The acharya thinks that it will be more beneficial for all if you speak with his assistant, Maharaj," says the volunteer diplomatically. "He will be here momentarily."

Maharaj, a young man of slight build, casually walks in, also sky-clad, and takes the acharya's place inside the straw hut. In contrast to Vidyanandji, this muni is very thin and bony. His generous smile immediately puts me at ease; Neil appears more comfortable as well. Noting the whisker stubble on his face and the almost equally short hair on his head, I initially ask Maharaj to clarify the significance of the ascetic ritual of hair removal. Ashok Kumar's comments about hair plucking are on my mind.

"Pulling hair out of the head and beard demonstrates a progression of stages that a Digambara muni has successfully achieved," he answers. "You might call it a 'rite of passage.'"

"And you will continue to do this throughout your life?"

"Yes, every five or six months. When it is necessary."

I tell Maharaj of my meeting with Ashok Kumar in Shravana Belgola and how he described, in detail, the two major Jain monastic sects. "Because you are a member of the Digambara, can you tell me what that means to you personally?"

He thinks for a moment and replies simply, "The sky is my clothing. The universe is my direction."

When the muni turns on a high-wattage light bulb inside the hut, for a moment my attention is caught by the incongruity of electricity in such a deliberately simple dwelling, but then I notice that the man's entire body is shivering. There is a morning chill in the air. I comment on the cold, thinking that he must be bothered by it.

But he insists that he is not cold, even while he continues to shake uncontrollably. "I am always working on what we call sense control. That is, controlling my sense of touch, taste, smell, sound and sight. I may appear cold, but that is not the case." His reply is sincere and makes me think of the concept of "mind over matter."

Much to my relief, he shows no inclination to cut short our interview, so I move on to another topic: "Do you still maintain emotional attachments to other people, like family members or friends?" I inquire.

Maharaj explains that he has no contact with his birth family or old friends. His primary relationship, as a muni, is to the acharya. "Now the whole world is made up of my brothers and sisters, mothers and fathers."

Without prompting, he begins talking about the relationship between Jainism and Christianity. "Jesus studied with the Jains in India," he tells me earnestly, as if such a statement is commonly accepted. "And what he learned was later the basis for Christ's teachings." It is interesting to note that Jainism is historically recognized as beginning with the teachings of the most recent Tirthankara in the fifth century B.C.E., with written records available as early as the third century B.C.E.

I steer our conversation back to his life and the daily schedule of a Jain ascetic. At my request, he outlines his daily regimen in detail.

Maharaj's Daily Schedule	
5:00 - 6 :00 A.M.	*Review the prior day*
6:00 - 10 :00	*Teach classes and worship privately*
10:00 - 11 :00	*Eat one meal of the day*
11:00 - 12 :00 P.M.	*Discuss spiritual issues with devotees*
12:00 - 1 :00	*Meditate*
1:00 - 6 :00	*Study and teach at local schools*
6:00 - 7 :00	*Meditate*
7:00 - 11 :00	*Additional studies*

Maharaj concludes the interview by drawing my attention to one of the most unique aspects of his religion: "Remember that Jainism is the only religion in the world where monastic practice came before the organization of a lay community of devotees." Having passed along something for me to consider, the muni nods at me, carefully steps from the hut and leaves the room.

Neil, anxious to talk more, invites me to join him for tea down in the basement kitchen, and I accept the opportunity to get better acquainted. He surprises me with the addresses of Jain study centers, both in the United States and Canada, and encourages me to contact them for more information. It never occurred to me that there were practicing Jains in North America, and I question him about how widespread the religion has become.

"I would estimate that there are eight thousand muni and nuns in India and maybe nine million devotees in the world," he tells me. When we finish in the kitchen, Neil escorts me out to the front yard, where the acharya is sitting on a raised brick platform, meditating with half a dozen devotees, men and women. The man looks in our direction briefly and perhaps smiles slightly.

Before I can ask, Neil says, "Every day he sets aside time for this meditation with Jain visitors. Then he answers questions and gives spiritual advice afterwards." Sri Vidyanandji's position as the spiritual leader is unquestionable.

I am ready to leave, but the engineer's role here has begun to intrigue me, and I ask, "Neil, how long do you think you'll remain here working for the acharya?"

"Maybe a year," he replies. "And maybe longer. It's the most important work I have ever done in *this lifetime*, and I am content."

Chapter Eleven

BOWING TO CREATION

He who while fully anxious about his body, desires to realize the self, prepares to cross a river on the back of a crocodile mistaking it for a piece of wood.

Sri Shankara
eighth century

Before entering the enclosed verandah of the ashram, I peel off my sweaty T-shirt, as instructed by the two guards at the door. I step into the oblong, pale blue room wearing only my khaki shorts. Under my feet is a smooth marble floor, and in the air is the sweet smell of incense; I can see the smoke rising from silver trays placed in the corners of the room.

Milling about are groups of Brahmin families, members of the "priestly class," one of the four social castes established in ancient Hindu society and still recognized in certain segments of contemporary India. The women wear colorful traditional saris, with a section of the patterned cloth drawn up to cover their heads, while the men stand bare-chested in white cotton wraps that reach from waist to ankle. Each man also displays the white "sacred thread," a symbol of the Brahmin caste, draped from his left shoulder across his chest to the right side of his waist.

We have all come to receive the blessing of Sri Bharati Tirtha, the thirty-sixth spiritual leader here at the Shankara Math. Situated in the southwestern Indian village of Sringeri, not far inland from the Arabian Sea, this Orthodox Hindu monastery was established in the eighth century by the revered Hindu spiritual leader Sri Shankara. According to legend, Shankara was walking down to the Tunga River for his daily ablutions when he witnessed a most unusual event. A cobra had spread its hood to provide shade for a frog that was experiencing labor pains. Struck with the sanctity of a place that could evoke love between natural enemies, he chose this location for a monastic center. It would be the first of four that he would establish.

211

Statue seated behind a Shiva-lingam,
symbol of Lord Shiva

At one end of the verandah is a small chapel; it sits behind an ornate iron gate that houses a three-foot-high Shiva-lingam sculpted from black stone. On a square base sits an oval pedestal; embedded in the center is a thick, cylindrical, round-topped form called the lingam. This popular and revered symbol represents the divine act of creation, the creative power of Lord Shiva, one of the three major deities in the Hindu trinity.

A white-robed pujari, the priest, kneels to one side of the symbol and performs daily rituals in honor of Shiva. Quietly chanting and praying, he pours libations of holy water, oil and, finally, coconut milk over the top of the lingam; they run down into an encircling channel carved into the stone below. Next, the priest carefully adorns the object, first with red and blue and yellow flower petals, then with garlands of delicate white blossoms, oblivious to those of us on the outside looking in, intrigued by the ritual.

Toward midmorning, the families begin lining up behind a long wooden desk, upon which sit empty, engraved silver trays and a large aluminum pot filled with blessed oil. I'm hesitant to join in, so I move to the back of the hallway, choosing a spot where I can watch events unfold.

Just as I settle my back against the wall, a tall Indian man leaves the line and starts toward me. He has short gray hair and a full beard; on his forehead are markings. The three white horizontal lines painted across the stranger's forehead, a *tilaka,* indicate his allegiance to Lord Shiva. Strung across the curly hair on his chest is the sacred thread, and an orange cotton wrap hangs from his waist almost down to his bare feet. He is a *sadhu,* a traditional Hindu monk or holy man. "Namaste," he greets me in Hindi, then switches to English, "You are going to receive the blessing from His Holiness, yes?" he asks, moving his face very close to mine and looking straight into my eyes. He seems curious rather than threatening, but I am surprised by his addressing me directly and in English.

"Namaste," I answer automatically, then, "Well, I, I thought I might just watch from back here."

"Oh my, no, no," he responds emphatically. "You have come all this way and must receive His blessing. Stay here a moment." He walks away into the crowd of people, and when he returns, he has some red paste on the index finger of his right hand. "Please face me and be still," he says. The words sound like a request, but his tone makes it a command. He places a dollop of the dark goo on my forehead just between my eyes.

"Yes, now this is better! This is your third eye," he exclaims with delight, taking my arm and escorting me to the end of the long line of people anxiously awaiting their blessings. The lanky sadhu stations himself behind me, where he remains throughout the ceremony.

Lord Shiva, to whom this Shankara Math is dedicated, is often referred to as the three-eyed god. Hindu mythology teaches that his third eye, when directed inward, is seeking knowledge. But when it is directed outward, it becomes a devastating fire, destroying certain negative human characteristics, like egotism, lust or envy. The faithful use paint to produce an imitation of this third eye.

The center of the forehead, where the "eye" is placed, is considered the most important psychic location on the human body — one of seven chakras, or psychic centers, known as the source of wisdom. Once the eye is opened, according to traditional Hindu teachings, the individual can reach a higher state of consciousness and ultimately attain union with Brahman, the Supreme Reality.

"I have nothing to offer His Holiness except some rupees," I confess to the sadhu.

"That is not important," he assures me, speaking slowly and distinctly. "It is not the worth of what you give, but what is in your heart when you give it."

Suddenly, the doors of the inner ashram are flung open. His Holiness emerges, escorted through the parting crowd by two assistants attired in red-and-gold-trimmed robes. Taking up a half-lotus position on the platform behind the desk is the revered Sri Bharati Tirtha. *Sri* is a title of respect used for a spiritual teacher or leader. The leader's short, heavy frame is emphasized by the folds of the orange-and-gold cloth he uses to cover his body and his head. His double chin is covered but not hidden by a bushy gray beard. Painted across Sri Bharati's forehead and both arms are five sets of white tilakas. And hanging from his neck is a circle of sacred Hindu prayer beads made from fruit pits believed to possess spiritual powers.

Slowly, the line begins moving as devotees offer His Holiness coconuts, fruits or flowers; some leave money. Smiling and talking with the people as they pass by, the spiritual leader uses a small silver ladle to dip out the blessed oil into their cupped hands. Upon reaching his desk, I deposit some of my rupees onto a silver tray then place my palms together

Shaivite Sri Bharati Tirtha

Ritual instruction from the pujari

at chest level, bow, and extend my cupped hands before him. Dipping the ladle into the container, His Holiness withdraws a measure of oil and slowly pours the golden liquid into my hands. I take a sip of the warm oil first then pour the rest onto the top of my head and rub it into my hair vigorously as the others have done before me.

For just a moment, I recall the anticipation I experienced years before while standing in line to have an audience with another revered Indian acharya. The setting was an ashram in Santa Monica, California. Every night the short, heavyset man would sit on a platform at the front of his circular, pale blue meditation hall and grant an audience to hundreds of his followers and ashram visitors. He would use a long, full peacock feather as his blessing tool. That night I had an audience with the acharya; he gave me his blessing by tapping me on the top of the head with his feather, leaving me with a feeling of slight euphoria.

Some of the families in the scene now before me stay, prolonging the excitement of the blessing, while others leave immediately. A few groups have requested that available pujaris perform special rituals for them. These rituals may be requested for various needs, such as healing the sick or improving annual income. The families sit on the tiled floor in groups of two, three or four, obeying the priests' instructions.

I turn my attention to one such ritual unfolding on the floor near me. A husband and wife are facing their pujari. The woman looks pensive, and her mate nervously tugs on the sacred thread pulled across his chest. Three circular silver trays, holding an assortment of fruit, coins and flower petals, are sitting in the center of the loose circle formed by the three, and beside the pujari is a small fuel lamp with an open flame. As he begins reading from a text, the couple begins chanting and performing specific tasks: First they stack all the coins onto one tray, then sprinkle flower petals on top of the coins and, finally, they rearrange the assorted fruits on another tray. To complete the ritual, the pujari picks up the lamp and moves the flame over the trays three times to purify the contents.

Before leaving the ashram, I ask the sadhu if he would join me on the steps of a nearby temple. "Certainly, if you wish," he says. "I will meet you outside shortly."

~~~~~~~~~~

In the late eighth century, the acclaimed Shankara was born into a Brahmin family living in southern India. At a very early age, according to the accepted story, the young man took on the life of an ascetic, traveling widely, studying and learning from Hindu scholars around the country. After years of such training, the young Shankara took it upon himself to strengthen the waning influence of Hinduism in two specific ways. First, he advanced a Hindu religious philosophy proclaiming the "oneness of all creation," where Brahman — the Supreme Being — is manifested through the Hindu trinity of Shiva, Vishnu and Brahma. In the trinity, Shiva is the dissolver and regenerator of the universe; the preserver of the universe is Vishnu; and Brahma stands as the god of creation.

His second major contribution was in organizing the various existing monastic sects, who primarily worshipped Lord Shiva. They were divided into four major groups, or monasteries, and headquartered in the north, south, east and west. Sringeri's Shankara Math, in the south, was the first to be constructed, and, thus, it became a major pilgrimage site for Orthodox Hindus. Comprehensive rules, as well as admission standards and training for novices, were codified for each center. And although each of the headquarters was assigned its own tutelary male and female deity, all the sadhus were devotees of the Lord Shiva.

Shankara then went a step further and arranged the Hindu sadhus into ten distinct orders, assigning two or more of the orders to one of the four monastic centers. To complete this incredible organizational scheme, he designated one of the four primary scriptures of Hinduism, the *Vedas,* to each of the four centers. The scriptures were to be emphasized in the training of novices.

During my stay at the Sringeri Shankara Math, a layman tells me a story that demonstrates just how aggressive and determined Shankara was in his successful attempt to revive Orthodox Hinduism and reorganize Hindu monasticism. The legend says that on his third pilgrimage around the whole of India, the leader made a stop in the sacred city of Bodhgaya, the place where Buddha was to have received enlightenment. There, Shankara and his followers took control of the major Buddhist temple, sealing up the altar behind a wall and replacing it with an altar of the Shiva-lingam, transforming the building into a Hindu temple. Whether or not the legend is true, the fact that it is circulated and widely believed reflects his influence. The man accomplished monumental organizational feats before dying in his early thirties.

By the time the sadhu joins me on the temple steps, the recently blessed devotees have dispersed, and the ashram is quiet once again. Before sitting down, the holy man leans his staff against one of the stone pillars. Made of a sacred ax-head covered by a sheath, the staff is the mark of a member of one of Shankara's monastic orders. All of them are known as *Shaivites,* holy men loyal to Lord Shiva. "Now, how can I help you, my friend?" he says slowly, lowering himself onto the temple steps.

"Well, you see, I want to ask questions about your life as a sadhu. I am working on a . . ."

He interrupts me in midsentence, "Excuse me, it is not often now that I am speaking English. You must talk slowly so I can understand and reply correctly."

I apologize and begin again, speaking slowly and explaining my reason for visiting India, and more specifically for my four-day stay in Sringeri. I give him my name and tell him where my home is in the United States, then I ask how he should be addressed.

"Yes, well, Bill, you may call me Dwarka for the purpose of our talk here," he says. "Dwarka is one of the four major Shankara Math, the one in the West. It is the place where I was initiated." The sadhu pauses for a moment, wrinkling his forehead, and asks, "Do you know what I am talking about?"

"What you say is clear. The Dwarka Math is one of four major Orthodox Hindu monastic centers that Shankara established in the eighth century. It is like the Shankara Math here in Sringeri, the one in the south."

"That is correct, that is correct," he says, smiling. "Good."

Unlike Christian monasteries in the West, Hindu math in India are primarily pilgrimage sites and education centers for devotees and sadhus. Here the sadhus do not take a vow of stability, like their Christian brothers and sisters, and they do not have permanent residence at the math. They stay there only during the months of the annual extended rainy season and when passing by on pilgrimage.

"Dwarka, can you tell me something about the family you were born into, where they lived, their professions?"

Looking puzzled, he answers, "Please understand what I am going to tell you," then he pauses for a moment. "During the initiation of a sadhu, there are certain steps or ceremonies that he must go through. Such rituals focus on leaving the old world and taking on a new life."

"You mean rites of passage?"

"Yes, yes, that's exactly what I mean. I think you understand." His expression tells me he is enjoying our interaction. "The first step, which is often done while standing in the sacred waters of a river, is a ritual to cleanse the devotee of impure things from his worldly life." The sadhu says a second step is the shaving of one's head and beard, sometimes all the body hair, in honor of leaving the past behind and welcoming the new spiritual life.

I tell him that I have read about some of these ceremonies.

He continues, "At the initiation, it is also common to perform one's own funeral rite, symbolizing death and rebirth, followed by a period of fasting and chanting of special prayers. It is very specific and takes a long time to perform. Finally, each devotee is given a number of items that he must honor for the rest of his life." He stops, giving me time to finish writing in my journal, and then continues. "One is this orange-colored garment, the clothing of a Shaivite sadhu. Another is this string of holy prayer beads to be worn around the neck." Dwarka fingers the one around his own neck. I hadn't noticed them until now, probably because the beads are much smaller than those worn by His Holiness at the blessing ceremony. "And finally, the sadhu receives a mantra from his spiritual teacher that he will use for the remainder of this lifetime. So you see, when I became a Shaivite sadhu, I left my worldly family behind. Therefore, I cannot talk about them. Do you understand?"

I do, but I cannot help hoping that he will answer one question about his past. I consider how to frame my question so as not to offend him. "Dwarka, because you speak English so well and seem to be an educated man, can I assume that you went to university?"

He hesitates but finally decides to offer some information — a window into his former worldly life. "Yes, I finished my academic work in philosophy at Benares Hindu University before joining the monastic order. Now, please no more questions about my past life."

I agree and shift to a new topic. "It's my understanding that there are ten Shankara monastic orders, each with a different title. Which order do you belong to?"

"Well, I am a member of the Tirtha order. And tirtha means one who lives near sacred waters," says the holy man.

I ask if tirtha implies that his mission is to make a pilgrimage around India and he replies yes.

"So the only things that you carry with you, or that you own, are your staff, your clothing, a water pot, the alms bowl and prayer beads?"

"That is right, but don't forget my mantra," he says, smiling.

Dolf Hartsuiker writes in *Sadhus: Holy Men of India* that

> . . . joining the brotherhood of sadhus is like going back in time, being reborn in a semi-nomadic "tribe" of the pre-agrarian age. It reflects a nostalgia for humanity's roots, for the simple, harmonious existence.

We talk about Dwarka's most recent travels and where he intends to make pilgrimage after leaving Sringeri. His next major destination will be a famous temple, further south, in the city of Tiruvannamalai, a pilgrimage site specifically for followers of Lord Shiva. When I ask about his daily life and schedule, he reveals some of the general religious duties that he has taken on as a Shaivite sadhu. Listening to him, I realize how self-motivated one must be to truly live the life of a sadhu; it is a strictly regulated life.

This is how author Ramesh Bedi describes the daily existence of Hindu ascetics in his book, titled *Sadhus: The Holy Men of India*:

> The religious duties that a sadhu is enjoined upon to perform . . . include: acts of self-purification, observing fasts, accepting the food taboos and living an ascetic life, acts of worship and meditation, participation in religious discourses, studying the scriptures, visiting pilgrim centers and performing the other religious duties ordained by the sect or the sub-sect to which he belongs.

Bedi finishes his lengthy description with a discussion of the sadhu's responsibilities to society at large:

> The social duties of the sadhu are to guide the common people on all religious and spiritual matters, preach the religious tenets, move among the people to mark the presence of the religious faith and create a religious atmosphere in society as a whole; console the afflicted, the frustrated and those in distress.

As in monastic traditions around the world, there is a reciprocal relationship between the sadhu and the layman.

"There are several hundred thousand sadhus in India, many of them pledged to an itinerant way of life, living on the bhiksha (alms) that

Sadhu in a pilgrimage city

people offer," writes Bedi when addressing the issues of numbers and gender of the ascetics. "The large majority of sadhus is composed of men, though women sadhus have also been accepted by many Hindu sects for some 2,000 years."

Getting up to leave, I ask Dwarka where he will be spending the night. "I am staying in one of the dormitories for pilgrims here at the math. In two days, I will leave to go further south." When he asks where I am staying, I tell him in a complex of simply furnished rooms at the other end of the village. All of my temporary neighbors are pilgrimage families. Offering Dwarka some bhiksha out of gratitude, I am pleased that the sadhu gladly accepts the money without reservation. I say good-bye, and he remains at the temple as I begin walking toward the arched bridge, built over the Tunga River, which connects the ashram to the temple complex of the Sringeri Shankara Math.

Earlier this morning, prior to attending the ceremony with His Holiness, I met briefly with the business manager and scheduled an afternoon appointment. It seemed necessary because the two most important and powerful men at each Shankara monastic center are the spiritual leader and the business manager. At no time are the duties and responsibilities of one position supposed to overlap those of the other. Informing me that his free time was limited, the businessman said the meeting might be brief.

Reaching the yellow brick building near the entrance to the math, I knock on the partially opened door, receive no answer and knock again. "Yes, yes, come in, come in," yells Radja Shankar from inside the room. Motioning me toward a seat near his desk, the business manager continues talking on one of his three telephones. Looking hot, frustrated and very much the man of business, Shankar sports a black mustache and thick, black-rimmed glasses. His tone indicates that his time is precious and shouldn't be wasted on anything but urgent matters. As he hangs up one phone, another rings, and he picks it up and starts a new conversation while I sit patiently waiting in the nondescript, pale green office.

"Yes, now what can I do for you?" he asks, slamming down the phone. "I believe you said you were interested in my role as business manager when we spoke this morning. So, what are your questions?" What a contrast to the cordial conversation I enjoyed with the sadhu.

"I am interested in knowing why you have taken on this job. Is the position volunteer, are you doing the work for religious and spiritual reasons, or is it strictly business?"

"Here, Mr., uh — will you please give me your last name again?"

"Yes, the last name is Claassen."

"Oh yes, Mr. Claassen. Here's one of my business cards," he says, handing over the blue-and-white identification card. "As you can see, I have a Master's in Business Administration. And yes, I am volunteering my time, and no, I am not doing this work for spiritual reasons." (During my stay in Sringeri, a local teacher tells me that working as a business manager at a math is an excellent way to make connections that will one day be very fruitful. The teacher guesses that those business contacts are the primary motivation for Mr. Shankar taking the job.)

I explain that most of my questions are about religious rather than business activities at the math and am surprised to hear him say he's willing to continue our conversation. So, I tell him about attending the ashram ceremony this morning and ask how often the position of His Holiness changes hands. He takes a moment to respond. "Well, the present spiritual leader could name a successor fifteen years prior to his departure or a few months before. It's up to his discretion and sense of organizational needs."

"What about the pujaris who assist His Holiness. Are they here indefinitely?"

"No. Training for the priesthood requires ten years of studying and practicing. They begin the course anywhere between the ages of fifteen and eighteen and live here until the course is finished."

"And then they are assigned to other temples or math once they graduate?"

"Oh, well, maybe. Some will remain here, depending on the needs of this math, and others will be assigned elsewhere," he states.

I inquire about the ritual blessing of food and special requests (of which I have recently been told) which take place in the inner sanctorum of the major temple.

"During the blessing, a pujari will take the items inside the sanctorum to be blessed by the deity," explains Shankar.

The businessman's comment about the temple practice sparks my curiosity, and I ask if the specific rules and regulations for the thousands of rituals are available for devotees to read.

"No, they are not," he replies, "partly because all the ceremonies are recorded in Sanskrit and are not translated into any other language." Thus, he explains, all the trainees must learn Sanskrit.

"Do both the young trainees and the sadhus have to be from the Brahmin caste?"

"Yes. Each must be of the Brahmin caste. But any person from any social class can come here to worship." A ringing telephone breaks into our conversation. Shankar sounds less harried as he begins talking into the receiver. Reviewing my notes, I jot down a few more questions before he hangs up the phone.

"Continue please," he says, looking up at me. Some of the harshness has left his tone, and he seems more receptive.

"Well, I am curious how a large religious institution like this supports itself financially."

"We, of course, receive a good deal of our money from the pilgrims who come all year round. And the government allots us a certain amount for subsidy, as with all religious math. We are all tax exempt."

The ringing of a phone interrupts us again, and it feels like an appropriate time to exit, so I say a quick thank-you and wave good-bye.

Back out on the temple grounds, I follow some visitors who are scurrying toward the other side of the ancient central temple, close to the arched walkway spanning the river. Standing nearby are two fully grown brown elephants awaiting the arrival of His Holiness. Each has a colorful tilaka on his forehead, extending down to the base of the trunk, which distinguishes him as a servant of Lord Shiva. Symbolizing the Hindu deity Ganesha — a half-man, half-elephant who is also the son of Lord Shiva — these animals reportedly have the power to remove spiritual obstacles and bestow success. They are holy animals in this culture.

Parading across the bridge to join the elephants and multitude of devotees are His Holiness and an entourage of pujaris. The spiritual leader, now wrapped in red brocade robes, wearing a crown and carrying a scepter, strides across the math grounds. He blesses excited pilgrims at each temple site. This is a ceremony enacted each time he returns from an outside engagement.

Later, when visiting another math office, I request an evening meal ticket, which I've heard is available to visiting pilgrims. Hours before the meal, I find a way to the refectory where thousands are fed weekly. After wending my way through an extended unlit hallway, I discover the dining hall. Instead of tables and chairs, there is a raised, extended, rectangular concrete slab with straw mats placed on either side.

Smelling something spicy cooking, I follow the scent to the kitchen and, without thinking, casually walk in to ask a question. Immediately, I am verbally assaulted. The workers yell and raise their arms to point their fingers toward the door. "Bahar jao, bahar jao, bahar jao!" Turning away from their ovens and looking at me, the cooks join the chorus, "Bahar. jao, bahar jao!" I flee, scurrying through the dining room in search of a quick exit. Once out where I can think, I realize what has just happened.

In most monastic traditions around the world, the kitchen is a sacred place and the preparation of food is regarded as a very holy and honorable activity. In fact, kitchen work assignments are usually reserved for the most trusted and dependable members of the community. By thoughtlessly walking into this Hindu temple kitchen, where outsiders, in general, and nonbelievers, in particular, are never, never permitted to go, I have just polluted not only the kitchen, but also the food that is being prepared. A pujari will now have to perform a series of rituals to purify the space and everything being cooked.

Reaching daylight, I immediately head toward the entrance gate of the math, gather my shoes and hurry out, making myself scarce until dinnertime. Only when the sun goes down and the lights go on inside the math do I meekly reenter the grounds, leaving my shoes once again at the gate and lining up with all the other pilgrims for the meal. I feel an irrational fear that someone will grab me from behind and throw me out the gate, but it never happens.

The hallway doors open, and we're herded into the refectory and directed to take seats on the straw mats. We each arrange the large green leaves in front of us that will serve as our plates. Down the long line of dinner guests, I spot Dwarka sitting with other sadhus. Seeing me, he smiles and nods. Sitting on either side of me are families, from grandchildren to grandparents, all very much occupied with their own business.

Walking in from the kitchen is a procession of young men, trainees for the priesthood, carrying deep pots filled with rice, vegetable curry and pickles. Working from both ends of the rows of pilgrims, they distribute to each of us a big spoonful of rice, a ladle of curry and a few

Main entrance into the Sringeri Shankara Math

Holy elephant at the Shankara Math

pickles. Everyone uses their fingers to roll their rice and curry into small balls, then eat them, quickly finishing the small but adequate portions. When the meal is over, each of us folds his or her leaves and takes them to the trash bins. It is a very efficient and environmentally friendly operation.

I go next to the main temple. Entering through an archway of carved stone, I move into a mixture of sounds, rituals and smells unique to this particular pilgrimage site. In the center of the long, pillared, soot-covered interior is the inner sanctorum, which only pujaris may enter. It is built of black marble.

Clutching folded pieces of paper on which they've written their special blessing requests, devotees are lining up outside the sanctorum. Periodically collecting and carrying the requests into the black vault, the pujaris present them to the iconic deity as the business manager had explained earlier. Returning soon, carrying burning lamps of oil, the priests slowly tread past believers, who wave their hands over the flames and wash their faces in the invisible purifying heat.

In one of the side chapels sit a dozen young pujari trainees, six on each side directly facing one another, dressed in white dhotis. Each boy, in possession of a medium-sized container of red cumin, is rhythmically transferring partial handfuls into a growing pile of cumin in the center of the space. At first they chant in unison, determining the speed of the movements. But soon they begin improvising, each voice taking on its own character and volume, creating movement at a self-determined speed. Then, without notice, they again return to chanting as one. Their rituals are an intriguing mystery.

Beside me on the rough, stone temple floor stands an elderly man facing the boys. Lightly tapping the sides of his head with his fingertips, crossing his arms over his chest, then pulling on his earlobes, he concludes by turning three circles. After repeating this ritual three times, he exits the temple with a satisfied look on his face, obviously cognizant of the meaning of their rituals.

Parading around the outside of the inner sanctorum is a continuous procession of worshippers moving on their own accord. I have heard that three revolutions is sufficient for the deity's blessing, and I observe many people performing sets of three, but most devotees continue walking around and around, praying and chanting at will.

Way down at the other end of the temple, sitting alone and quietly praying with his sacred circle of beads in hand, sits a middle-aged Brahmin. He has managed to create a private space in this cacophony of religious excitement and energy. Wandering over to the chapels on that end of the temple, I stand near a seated pujari, watching intently as he performs a series of rituals requested by some of the waiting devotees. Stopping his movements briefly and looking up, he hands me a delicate purple flower plucked from his aluminum tray, smiles, then returns his attention to the ceremony.

As I take it by the stem, a surge of energy moves into my hand, then up my arm, and finally spreads throughout my body, creating a hot tingling sensation. Suddenly, I am experiencing sensory overload. The movement around me seems to spin together into a kaleidoscope, and the sounds become indistinguishable from one another. I know that I must get out of here, now! Weaving in and out of the hundreds of worshippers, I begin moving quickly toward the entrance.

Swaying and chanting in unison, four tall, very heavy Brahmins are partially but unintentionally blocking the front exit of the temple. Prostrating themselves onto their bellies, then clasping their hands together when rising to their knees, they finally stand. Tapping their foreheads, then faces, ears and necks very lightly, the Brahmins close their ritual by circling around themselves three times.

Wedging myself between the crowd and the foursome, I find an opening and rush out into the cool night air. Outside, I collapse at the base of an ancient obelisk in front of the temple and remain there, exhausted, until closing time.

Chapter Twelve

UNITY IN DIVERSITY

A truly religious man should think that other religions also are paths leading to truth. We should always maintain an attitude of respect towards other religions.

Sri Ramakrishna
nineteenth century

When it convened at the new Chicago Art Institute in September 1893, the Parliament of Religions was the first of its kind anywhere in the world. Held as an adjunct to the World's Fair and organized by a Presbyterian minister, the conference brought together representatives from all the major world religions. Toward the end of the first day's session, Chicago's Catholic cardinal, who was serving as chairperson, introduced Hindu spokesman Swami Vivekananda to an audience of thousands. At that time, Vivekananda was practically unknown outside India, but that would soon change.

The Swami, a clean-shaven young man with large brown eyes and a cherubic face, wore an ochre cotton robe over a pair of long pants. On his head was a turban, and on his feet, a pair of Western-style shoes. The Christians in the audience may not have known what to make of his appearance, but his first words, "Sisters and brothers of America," brought everyone to their feet for a sustained cheer. Once the delegates quieted down, Vivekananda continued with his speech. The following are a few key passages, taken from the transcription of the speech kept by the Advaita Ashrama of Calcutta.

It fills my heart with unspeakable joy to rise in response to the warm and cordial welcome which you have given us. I thank you in the name of the most ancient order of monks in the world; I thank you in the name of the mother of religions and I thank you in the name of the millions and millions of Hindu people of all classes and sects.... I am proud to belong to a religion which

229

has taught the world both tolerance and universal acceptance. We believe not only in universal toleration, but we accept all religions as true. . . . I will quote to you, brethren, a few lines from a hymn which I remember to have repeated from my earliest boyhood, which is every day repeated by millions of human beings in my country: "As the different streams having their sources in different places, all mingle their water in the sea, so, O Lord, the different paths which men take through different tendencies, various though they appear, crooked or straight, all lead to Thee. . . ."

~~~~~~~~~~

A dozen years prior to his acclaimed trip to Chicago, Vivekananda had faced a personal and painful spiritual crisis when he questioned the existence of God. Out of desperation, he sought guidance from Sri Ramakrishna, who, despite a lack of formal education, would soon become his primary teacher and spiritual guide.

Having left his family at an early age, Ramakrishna had joined his brother, who was managing a Sanskrit school and serving as a priest at a Hindu temple in Calcutta. There he developed and applied a unique spiritual philosophy that integrated aspects of various religions, including Hinduism, Islam and Christianity. Ramakrishna believed that God, though one, is rightly called by many different names in many different religions throughout the world. And this is what he taught, using songs and parables as well as metaphors.

When the revered teacher was diagnosed with a fatal illness, his disciple, then simply Vivekananda, and more than a dozen other devotees moved him to a villa on the outskirts of Calcutta, where Ramakrishna soon established a new order of Hindu sadhus just prior to his death. After distributing ochre robes and turbans among his devotees, the teacher commanded that they all go out into the neighborhood and beg for food, then an act regarded as the traditional symbol of total renunciation. That ritual was his disciple's initiation and ordination.

Later, under the leadership of Swami Vivekananda, each of the monks also took formal vows, honored the ritual of receiving a new name — and, thus, a new life — and began living together as the first cenobitic Hindu monastic order in India. Performing social services for the masses — specifically in the areas of medical care, education and relief work —

was to be their mission. Unlike previous orders of Hindu sadhus, who advocated withdrawal from the world as the means to salvation, Vivekananda and his brothers perceived their social service work as a means to the realization of God.

~~~~~~~~~~~~~

I catch a crowded public bus on Old Court House Road in the heart of downtown Calcutta and am forced to stand in the aisle, swaying with the movement of the bus as it weaves its way through congested streets and over the famed Howrah Bridge spanning the murky waters of the Hooghly River. I'm finally able to claim a seat, although keeping it requires determination as the bus's movement is like that of a carnival ride but without the security of a safety bar. Continuing along a riverfront road, the route cuts through one of Calcutta's most notorious shantytowns. The bus hurtles through potholes and veers around sacred cows while the passengers cling to their seats and their belongings. Following an action-packed hour, the bus comes to a screeching halt at the last stop.

"Belar Math!" yells the bus driver.

Moving shakily down the steps, I experience a feeling of relief when my foot touches solid ground. I cross the street and buy a cold soda from a vendor so that I may have the luxury of sinking into a stationary wooden chair for a few minutes, thus permitting my internal organs time to rediscover their rightful places. A few blocks away is the entrance to the international headquarters of the Ramakrishna Order and Mission.

Once everything seems to have settled, I move down the street and through the guarded gates. I wander past well-kept lawns and blooming flower gardens. Next to the sidewalk, in front of the central headquarters, sits a neatly printed sandwich board propped up on the lawn. On both sides, red, blue and green lettering spell out "Relief and Rehabilitation Services — A Brief Report as of 1st May, 1996." Among the listed items are fire relief in West Bengal, assistance with the draught in Gujarat, and aid for flood victims in Bangladesh. Each line clearly spells out what kind of assistance was given, from drinking water to food and clothes.

In the building's entryway a young monk is on desk duty. "Namaste," he greets me and tells me in English to take a seat while he announces my arrival. Dressed traditionally in their habit of an ochre cotton pullover top and a wraparound that hangs down to his ankles, he is missing only the turban. I'm not surprised that he's speaking English; it is the first language

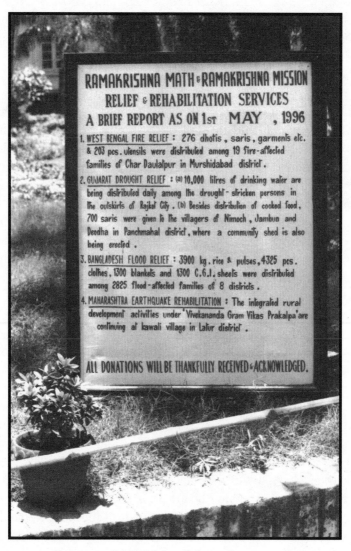

Monthly task board

of all the Ramakrishna monks, as established by Swami Vivekananda in the early days of the movement because he was building an international organization.

"I have been asked to show you the grounds as our first order of business," the young man informs me upon his return. "When we come back you may speak with one of the senior monks." He says to leave my shoulder bag on the chair. "You don't need to worry about theft here. It will be safe."

Towering over the entire monastic complex is the Ramakrishna Temple, standing many stories high. The substantial brownstone building is a curious architectural blending of different religious styles and traditions. "This house of worship represents a Christian cathedral, a Muslim mosque and a Hindu temple," says my guide. The domes topping the entrance and the altar could be from Mt. Athos, Greece or Turkey's Istanbul. There is an unusual circular emblem carved into the stone above the front entrance. "This was originally designed by Swami Vivekananda," he explains. "The rippling waters, the lotus and the rising sun are symbols of work, devotion and knowledge."

I notice that a cobra encircles the other elements in the design and ask what it represents.

"Well, the serpent symbolizes a number of things: the spiritual potential or power inside each of us and the path of meditation as a way to retrieve it."

"And the central character, the graceful swan?"

"It represents the supreme self — God, of course." A pamphlet from the order's publishing house summarizes the meaning of the emblem with a slightly different interpretation. "The emblem signifies that there are various paths to the realization of God, and an aspirant may follow any one or more of these paths according to his temperament and inclination for spiritual realization."

We leave our shoes outside and climb the stairs to the sanctuary. It is large and empty with a shiny marble floor. There's always something very inviting to me about a sanctuary that has been cleared of its pews and chairs, leaving only a bare space. It allows more room for the spirit to soar.

Toward the front, sitting in a meditative posture, is a polished, life-sized, white marble statue of Sri Ramakrishna. "This is where the sacred relics of the master have been enshrined," explains the young man.

Doorway into the Ramakrishna main temple

Major temple at Belar Math

Nearby is a white stucco dormitory for the monks, the front of which is protected by a multiarched porch. From the temple, I can see their sacred orange robes, hung just inside to dry, blowing gently in the breeze. The training center for the novices, built adjacent to the dormitory, holds a meditation hall, a library and classrooms. I ask what classes they attend as we continue over the grounds.

"Course work," continues my guide, "always includes studying the teachings of Sri Ramakrishna and Swami Vivekananda, as well as the scriptures and sacred books of Hinduism. But also, the monks spend much time studying the prophets and teachings of all the major religious traditions around the world."

Down along the riverfront we pass two small stone temples built in a style similar to that of their major house of worship. The first is the Holy Mother Temple where the wife of Sri Ramakrishna was cremated. "Although the marriage was planned and carried out by the two families when she was very young, it was never consummated later in her life," the monk explains. "Instead, when she came of age she joined Sri Ramakrishna as a student." He says she then became the only influential female presence within the Order. Next to her temple is that of Swami Vivekananda, also built on the location of his cremation.

Before we return to the administrative headquarters, the monk leads me down a narrow alley, through a green wrought-iron gate, to a path leading to the guesthouse. After introducing me to the house cook, the guide shows me to the dormitory on the second floor, where the interior is cool and breezy.

Once back at headquarters, the young man escorts me to a courtyard in the back of the building and through a screen door into the office of a senior Ramakrishna monk. Surprisingly, immediately following the introductions, the senior monk requests that neither his name nor title be used in my writing. He has been misquoted by Westerners in the past and does not want to be misrepresented again. I assure him that his request will be honored.

While slipping off his black-frame glasses and putting things in order on his desk, he makes it clear that the Ramakrishna Order of monks should always be distinguished from the Ramakrishna Mission, the social service center that the monks — and sometimes laymen — staff. "Too often the two are incorrectly referred to as the one Ramakrishna Mission.

You see, the Ramakrishna Order of monks is the religious order that views Sri Ramakrishna as an incarnation of God on Earth," he explains. "The Order needs to be distinguished from the Mission, as well as the other traditional Hindu monastic groups active in India."

"And what do you consider the other groups?"

"The first and oldest group includes the ten orders of Shankara," he replies. "They are called the Shaivites because their primary deity of worship is Lord Shiva." When I tell him of my recent visit to the Shankara Math in Sringeri, he seems surprised but does not pursue it. "The Vaishnavites, a second monastic group, worship Lord Vishnu as their primary deity, as you might already know, given your recent experience."

His remarks make me think of all the many different tilakas Hindu sadhus use to symbolize their allegiance. "There must be at least forty different vertical and horizontal markings to choose from," I say.

Nodding his head in agreement, the senior official makes it very clear that Ramakrishna monks do not use such markings on their foreheads or anywhere else on their bodies. "And the final group," he concludes, "are the Shaktas, worshippers of the Divine Mother, the Goddess Shakti."

I ask if Sri Ramakrishna was originally a member of one of the traditional groups.

"Well, technically speaking, he originally belonged to one of Shankara's ten orders," explains the senior monk. "But in reality, our more than one hundred communities here in India and abroad do not fit into any of the three groups I have just mentioned. Ours is a new kind of community, a new kind of monastic order." Pausing for a moment, and maybe recalling his manners, he offers me a glass of water, which I gladly accept.

He seems to welcome my next inquiry about what characteristics of the Ramakrishnas make the order so different from the others. "For one thing, we are a centralized institution. But unlike many Christian monastic orders, we do not take a vow of stability. Our superiors can move us around from one location to the next, according to the needs of the organization. And we also have a social commitment to the people around us. Our social work is an integral part of our philosophy."

"This combination of social work and monastic life is unique in India, isn't it?"

"Yes, it is," says the monk. "The primary focus of a traditional Hindu

236

sadhu is his spiritual development, not a commitment to bettering the material lives of those around him. Except, of course, he does offer spiritual counseling frequently requested by devotees."

~~~~~~~~~~~

I was introduced to the Ramakrishna Order and Mission months before during my stay in Bombay, now more frequently referred to as Mumbai. My first day in the community there began in the monk's refectory, sharing mid-morning tea and conversation with a few of the men. After the break, I was given a tour of the Mission's school and hospital complex and then delivered to the community librarian. The professional-looking man, who had been in the Order for more than twenty years, set aside several hours to talk with me about the Ramakrishna Movement and its respect for diverse paths to God. He then accompanied me to their late-afternoon worship service.

~~~~~~~~~~~

It's my understanding that a man from any religious tradition can join the Ramakrishna Order, and I ask if that's true.

"Yes. Men of all religious traditions are welcome to join the order without having to forfeit their religious beliefs." We're interrupted momentarily when another member of the order enters through the screen door. He whispers something to the senior monk, leaves some papers on the desk and exits.

Without missing a beat, the senior monk takes up our conversation: "As I was saying, the beliefs of our order are not in conflict with any of the major religious traditions, and we are quite modern. The robes we wear are of stitched material, unlike the traditional Hindu sadhu who is not permitted to wear sewn cloth. Our monks also wear shoes, use automobiles and make use of our extensive railroad system here in India." I notice that he frequently uses the word *monk* when speaking of the Ramakrishnas, because I've been thinking that the word sadhu really doesn't apply. The men here live in community, like Christian or Buddhist monks, rather than wander the countryside on constant pilgrimage like so many of the Hindu sadhus.

When I ask for a copy of the daily schedule, my acquaintance dictates to me the daily routine. "We awake a little before dawn and attend a meditation service in our temple. The monks are then given time for cleaning and bathing before breakfast. And after breakfast, time is set aside for studying and prayer; then we have lunch."

The work assignments are primarily in the morning and afternoon. "With our daily schedules, we try to integrate the search for knowledge, the practice of yoga, labor and worship in order to attain harmony," he explains as our conversation comes to an end.

Later, from my dormitory at the guesthouse, I hear the sound of bells announcing the late afternoon service, and I join the steady stream of men, women and children going to the worship center. This is the one service of the day that is open.

Spread across the marble floor are distinct seating areas for us all. In the front, near the white marble Sri Ramakrishna, sit the monks dressed in their orange robes and turbans, and immediately behind them are the white-robed novices, their bare heads seeming conspicuous. I find a place in the group comprising male visitors. At the very back is the area designated for women and children.

To the side of the statue, a few monks stand ready to play musical instruments, among them a small box with a keyboard about the size of an accordion called a *harmonium;* a two-piece drum set, the *tabla,* traditionally held between the legs; and a few sets of finger cymbals. Music has always been an important aspect of their worship services.

Two additional orange-robed monks, carrying dusters made of yak hair, position themselves near the flower-adorned statue of the master. A visitor sitting next to me explains, "The dusters symbolize the five natural elements of water, air, earth, fire and ether."

Monks and devotees soon join in chanting and reciting the Aratrika Hymns, inspired compositions written by direct disciples of Sri Ramakrishna. *Aratrika* literally means a vespers service conducted in a shrine or other holy place. As the musicians play, the worshippers chant, with one voice, simple praises to the Lord.

Thou art the Lord of the universe, manifested as the Incarnation for the modern age, for helping mankind in its spiritual endeavor.

Thy mind is above all fears, devoid of all doubts, and firm in its resolves.

Innocent of pride of birth and race. Thy universal love offers shelter to all devotees who seek it.

Light of all lights, ever resplendent in the cavity of the heart!

Adorning the statue of Sri Ramakrishna

Destroy the darkness of ignorance therein. O Lord! Destroy the darkness!

Aratrika Hymn (verses 1, 3, 4, 6)
composed by Swami Vivekananda

The monks with the feather dusters begin a detailed and choreographed ceremony at the base of the statue. Sweeping over its feet, then gradually up over the body and eventually to the head, the dusters never disturb the colored blossoms decorating the white marble. In the beginning, the chanting is soft, but it gradually builds in strength, filling the hollow sanctuary with a soothing and repetitious Hindi melody. As it draws to a close, lay visitors exit out the front doors into the darkness. The monks and white-robed novices leave through the side doors and migrate toward the two smaller temples near the river, setting off on their nightly pilgrimage rounds.

Remaining on the cool marble floor for a short while, I am reminded of my initial spiritual experience within a Hindu community. Rather than in India, it took place in my old neighborhood on the Upper West Side of Manhattan in New York City. St. John the Divine, reportedly the largest Gothic cathedral in the world, was hosting a dawn-to-dusk concert led by Ravi Shankar, the famed Indian sitar player. I'll never forget my surprise when I entered the sanctuary that evening to discover thousands of Hindus spread out on the floor. There was not a chair or pew in sight. That night I was temporarily adopted by a family of seven; they welcomed me into their inner circle and insisted that I share their meal of rice and spicy curry and chapatis. The evening was a joyous occasion that opened with the sweet music of the harmonium and cymbals, anchored by two women playing the tabla. Chanting was continuous throughout the night.

Returning to the house, I join a few other guests in the dining room for a light vegetarian supper. Sitting next to me is another middle-aged American, who introduces himself as an active member of the Ramakrishna Vedanta Society in Southern California. He is a tanned, dark-haired businessman who has made many retreats to Belar Math. Across the table is a teenage male devotee from Mumbai (Bombay) and two European women in their early thirties.

Excusing myself from the table right after the meal, I go upstairs to begin reading an article on the Ramakrishna Movement titled "Ramakrishna Monasticism and the Charisma Hindu Ethos." The piece was written by one of the monks who lived in their Bangalore Mission back in the late

240

1970s. Most of the article is a review of material that I have gleaned from past research or from conversations with Ramakrishna monks in my travels throughout India. However, toward the end of the article, the author presents a short and concise explanation of how this monastic movement has managed to present Hinduism in a more contemporary and universal light.

> What the Ramakrishna monks did was to reinterpret the basic tenets of Hinduism in order to provide the people with a practical, positive philosophy of life ... unity in diversity was emphasized ... experience was stressed more than revelation; the struggle for ... "liberation" was interpreted as the existential problem of freedom. The result of all this chiseling was to give a new profile to the Vedanta (Hindu religious writings).

Returning to the temple again before dawn, I take a seat on the floor among the other men just as the service begins. Only the men inside the monastic complex are permitted to participate in this morning meditation, where the worship of God integrates flowers with incense and fire. At the front of the sanctuary, the master's statue is now adorned with two necklaces of delicate flower blossoms, and at his feet are an array of red and orange flower petals; the aroma of burning incense fills the temple.

As the lights are lowered, a lone monk, carrying a large oil lamp with a single flame symbolizing purity and the spiritual essence of the individual, slowly approaches the statue while sweeping the lamp back and forth in broad, dramatic strokes. Beginning around the head, then moving to the body and finally the feet, he moves the lamp according to the rhythm of the harmonium and tabla in this daily ceremony of purification.

Our silent meditation begun in darkness ends after daybreak. I feel tremendous spiritual support from the men sitting around me, and the strong sense of our becoming one strengthens my focus. It's a feeling I've frequently experienced over the years during silent Quaker worship meetings.

Quakers often speak of the "inner light," the light of God in each of us. This morning I have the unmistakable feeling that the "inner light" is shared and magnified a hundredfold by the men around me.

When I join the senior official after breakfast, he seems much more comfortable and less businesslike than he had the day before. Maybe he feels that he can trust me now. "I want you to know that although admission into this Order is open to all men, regardless of caste or religious tradition," he explains as we begin our discussion, "he must accept that Sri Ramakrishna is an incarnation of God, as are other recognized religious prophets."

Once a novice completes his probationary period, which can last more than three years, he will relocate to Belar Math and continue studies in Hindu scriptures, the Bible and the Quran. If he successfully completes his studies there, he takes vows and is ordained as a *bramachari,* a celibate brother, the monk tells me.

"What vows does a bramachari take?"

"There are a dozen vows in our order, of which the most important are chastity and obedience, poverty and service." As a bramachari, the man is required to maintain the brother status for an additional span of years until he is finally eligible for the monkhood. Once deemed acceptable, the candidate is ordained on Ramakrishna's birthday and given his ochre robe, the honored turban and a new name.

But the man is not officially a monk of the order even after the birthday ceremony, according to the official. A final condition must be met.

"There is one more requirement and that is that he begs food in the neighborhood as the symbolic act of renunciation. That has been a tradition since the ordination of Swami Vivekananda." It is the culmination of almost a decade of preparation.

When the subject of women devotees comes into our discussion, he informs me that there are no official women's Ramakrishna Orders in India. However, there are a few orders of nuns active in Australia and the United States. "But they wish to remain independent," says the official.

"Before you leave, I want to invite you to visit our Vedanta Society in St. Louis," says the senior monk, getting up to show me out. I am suddenly feeling rushed. "As you know, we have many centers in your country. They will be pleased to know of your interest and will welcome you into their home."

When I return to the guesthouse to pick up my gear, I stop to thank the cook for his hospitality and discover the Californian sitting in the dining room. I join him for coffee and tell him about my recent interviews with the senior official and my reactions to the past two days. Interested in his perceptions of the Ramakrishnas in India and elsewhere in the world, I ask what he sees as the greatest strength of this unusual order of monks.

"I believe there are a number of strengths," he says after thinking a moment. "One is that civic responsibility is emphasized by the Order. This is really counter to traditional Indian culture, where responsibility has usually been limited to family members. They are broadening the concept of community beyond the front yard."

He says that another strength is that the Ramakrishna monks break with the widely held tradition that they should only attend to 'monkly' duties, not social service work. Their presence forces Indian society to look at their monastic community in a different light.

I point out that monks around the world are frequently faced with the problem of acceptance, regardless of their duties. Certainly, I say, that's true in the West. He agrees, although hesitantly. I ask him if he perceives other major strengths in the order here.

"Oh, yes," he answers. "A third strength would be their work as an international organization. As you know, their missions even extend to the United States. Their message is worldwide; not solely confined to the Indian continent."

The man pauses for a moment. "But the most important, in my opinion, is their belief in the oneness of God. Within this philosophy, as you must know, is the assumption that every major culture has created its own unique way of finding and expressing God, a way that must be honored, respected and recognized as true." He emphasizes that "this is their greatest strength and the most important message they can share with the world."

I am grateful for the opportunity to talk with the American before my departure. His clarity of thought is important for me to hear at this time. He helps me refocus on my initial attraction to Sri Ramakrishna's philosophy. It is one that honors and respects my and others' individual spiritual journeys in search of truth, one that affirms the value of my pilgrimage.

AFTERWORD

A friend recently suggested that silence rather than English is my first language. Initially, I dismissed his comment. Later, I realized that he spoke a truth. It was this native tongue that I recognized in Peter Matthiesson's words quoted in Chapter One:

> To this day, I am drawn joyfully to cathedrals in every land — mosques and temples, too — the stone, the light, the soaring naves, the murmuring and mystery and quiet. With gratitude I kneel and lose myself amidst the bent humanity crouched in the pews. In the great hush, we breathe as one.

These words speak of a reverence for the oneness of creation that I have heard called the "chain of being." I prefer to think of it as the "bigness of God." Throughout my journeys to monasteries as diverse as the countries I visited, I was repeatedly reminded of God's bigness, that unmistakable sense of unity. Each community spoke a language I understood, the language of silence. In the process, each offered me the opportunity to move beyond my already explored domains into the bigness. My personal religious boundaries were expanded in my conversations with the monks, both men and women, through my participation in their daily prayers and rituals and with my better understanding of their individual traditions.

I came to recognize that each monk I encountered had willingly entered into a disciplined journey of losing self or, more aptly stated, of dying to self. In a manner of speaking, they had reached their destination with the taking of final vows. Those vows, which assume a total commitment to God, or in some cases to "no God," firmly established the monk's primary life relationship. It was a commitment to live alone in community.

Day-to-day, in each monastery, I witnessed universal practices that helped acclimate me to monastic life. Common to each tradition was the use of prayer beads, prayer books and the frequent chanting of scriptures. Daily worship schedules and the veneration of religious figures and icons also bound these communities together. Practices of offering libations and purifying rituals using incense and fire further demonstrated a common thread among these communities. Yet perhaps the most striking shared element was the simplest. It was one I perceived at the foundation of these disparate traditions: In almost all the communities I witnessed there was a constellation around *three* primary concepts.

In the *Dictionary of Symbols* Jean Chevalier and Alain Gheerbrant state that the number three has historically been an expression of the "intellectual and spiritual order in God" and has frequently been referred to as the "number of heaven." David Fontana, in his *Secret Language of Symbols*, reminds us that the number three "underlies all aspects of creation — mind, body, spirit; birth, life, death; past, present, future." He writes that in humanity's vast range of religious and spiritual traditions, the number three is symbolic of unity in diversity.

Buddhist temple communities express this unifying symbol in the Triple Jewel — the Buddha, the Dharma and the Sangha. In Christian monasteries, this unity is revealed in the Holy Trinity — Father/Mother, Son and Holy Spirit. In the Indian math, the Godhead of Hinduism unfolds with Brahma the Creator, Vishnu the Preserver and Shiva the Destroyer. And Jain ascetic life has always stood on the foundation of Right Faith, Right Knowledge and Right Conduct, their intrinsic interpretation of the Three Jewels.

This "threeness" was so pervasive in my travels that it became a unifying motif in this text. Each chapter title is comprised of three words, as is the book's title. In fact, I even discovered within myself three active players along my journey: pilgrim, traveler and writer.

There were times when I found a balance among these three players, each complementing the other. At other times, however, I experienced the tension of walking a tightrope when trying to maintain that equilibrium. There were certainly days, for example, when I was less a pilgrim than a curious traveler — what Timothy Ware, the Eastern Orthodox Bishop, might call a tourist or a "two-legged wolf." On days when I tried too hard to maintain journalistic objectivity, I realized I lost sight of the pilgrimage. But then, as a pilgrim, there were times I neglected my practical goal as a writer. Yet, when I lost my balance, I was almost always caught in my hosts' supportive net of hospitality, patience and tolerance.

It was repeatedly clear that I was an outsider peering only briefly into a chosen way of life, one that, in each tradition, has evolved over the centuries. And I never presumed my introduction into the life of a particular community would capture its essence or fully convey the spirituality found there. My observations and impressions — colored by myriad factors, ranging from ignorance to insight — were a fast-moving series of images. For me, these images show that each of these monasteries, apart from their common elements, was also unique even within its particular order. In the course of my journeys, I became convinced that each of the communities was ultimately its most reliable representative within the bigness of God.

When I consider my own spirituality within this scope, I am keenly aware of what binds me to the whole. Sometimes this awareness is a revelation; at other times it can be overwhelming.

I wonder where my journey will go from here. Will it take the form of additional miles, experiences of new traditions and the witness of more expressions of faith — including, for example, more contact with women living a monastic life — or perhaps a fuller picture of traditions I've already visited? Whatever my next step, I have found a key. That key is my willingness to "die to self." Indeed, that is what my monastic brothers and sisters have shown me. It's just that simple. It's just that difficult.

I do not know what you have received from my travels, but if they enrich your own spiritual journey, then this book will have accomplished its end. As my Sufi friends from Istanbul would say, "May your time be happy."

Glossary

abbot – Religious leader in a Christian monastic community.

abuna – Coptic monk.

acharya – Spiritual teacher in the Hindu tradition.

agamas – Hindu and Jain sectarian scriptures.

ajahn – Spiritual teacher in a Thai **wat**.

ajari – Literally, "saintly master"; similar to the Zen Buddhist **roshi;** high-ranking **Tendai** priest who has successfully completed demanding tasks established within the Buddhist order.

Allah – Arabic word for God.

alms – Donations of food or money.

Ambedkar, Bhimrao Ranyi – Significant twentieth-century leader of India's "**Untouchables**," the lowest class in traditional Hindu society, and Law Minister of the Indian government. He played an important role in drawing up the Indian constitution.

Amida Butsu – Buddha of Infinite Light and Life. Lord of the Western Paradise, he vowed to save all those who invoke his name.

anapanasati – Buddhist form of meditation in which one focuses on the breath moving in and out of the nostrils.

anba – Religious official of the Coptic Church, equivalent of a Catholic **bishop**.

anchorite – One who renounces the world to live in solitude. In Eastern (particularly Orthodox and Coptic) Christian traditions, **hermits** who live in wilderness areas, desiring to be "anchored" to God.

arahant – Pali term reflecting the spiritual ideal of early Buddhism — a monk or perfected being who has attained enlightenment and escapes from the cycle of rebirth.

ashram – 1) Religious retreat for a colony of disciples under the leadership of a **guru;** 2) center for religious study and meditation.

Bahubali, Lord – Son of King Rishabha, the first Jain **Tirthankara;** worshipped as the Jain ideal.

Basil, Saint – Also known as Basil the Great, he lived during the fourth century in what is now Turkey; a leader in the early Christian church and influential in the development of monasticism in the East.

batsi – Jain temple; the dwelling of a deity.

Benedict, Saint – Sixth century hermit and founder of the great abbey of Monte Cassino; his **Rule** was instrumental in the development of monasticism in the West.

Benedictine – Member of a Christian monastic order founded in the sixth century and noted especially for its liturgical worship and its scholarly activities.

bhat – Unit of Thai currency.

bhiksha – Alms.

bhikkhu – Fully ordained monk in the Thai Buddhist monastic tradition.

bhote – Official ordination hall in a Thai **wat**.

Bible – Hebrew and Christian Scriptures; also sacred to Islam.

bindabhat – Daily rounds for gathering food as practiced by Thai **bhikkhu** in a tradition established by Buddha.

bishop – High-ranking Christian clergyman with authority over a church district or diocese.

Black Death – Form of bubonic plague that spread over Europe in the fourteenth century and killed an estimated quarter of the population.

Bodhidharma – Twenty-eighth Patriarch in line from the Buddha. The first Patriarch of Zen in China, he is reported to have lived in the sixth century.

bodhisattva – Enlightened being who dedicates himself/herself to helping others attain liberation. The person represents a high stage of Buddhahood.

Brahman – Cosmic Absolute in Hinduism; the ultimate principle underlying the universe.

Brahmin – Member of the priestly class in traditional Hindu **caste** society.

bramachari – Hindu who has taken a vow of celibacy.

Buddha – 1) Sanskrit word meaning ultimate truth or absolute mind; 2) one awakened or enlightened to the true nature of existence; 3) Indian philosopher and founder of Buddhism with the given name of Siddhartha and family name of Gautama who lived in the fifth century B.C.E.

canonical hours – Seven periods of the day assigned to prayer and worship in the Roman Catholic Church. They are matins (with lauds), prime, tierce, sext, none, **vespers** and **compline**.

Carmelite – Male or female member of the Roman Catholic mendicant Order of Our Lady of Mount Carmel founded in Palestine in the twelfth century.

caste – Division or class of Hindu society comprising persons within a separate and exclusive order.

cenobitism – Form of monastic life in which monks live in a community in obedience to a superior.

chakras – Seven psychic centers of life and consciousness within the human spine and brain.

charnel house – Particularly in the Christian Orthodox tradition, a building or chamber in which bones are deposited.

Chih'i – Eighth-century Chinese Buddhist master.

Cistercian – Member of an austere order of Christian monks founded on the **Benedictine** rule as adopted by Robert de Molesme at Citeaux, France, in the eleventh century. See also **Rule of St. Benedict**.

cloister – 1) Covered walk or arcade connected with a Christian monastery, often around the open court of a quadrangle; 2) place of religious seclusion.

compline – Final liturgical prayer of the day, said after nightfall or just before the Christian monks retire.

Copt – Native of Egypt descended from the ancient inhabitants of that country.

Coptic – Ancient Hamitic language of the Copts, now used only in the rituals of the Coptic Orthodox Church.

curry – Mixture of savory and hot spices used in the preparation of most South Indian dishes.

dair – Coptic monastery.

Daphni – Port of entry for Mt. Athos located on the southern coast of the peninsula in the Aegean Sea.

dervish (darwish, darwesh) – Literally, "seeking doors," from the Persian; synonymous with **Sufi.**

devotee – Follower of a religious path dedicated to a particular deity or saint.

dharma (Sanskrit) – 1) Doctrine and teachings of the **Buddha**; 2) Buddhist term meaning truth, universal law, condition, phenomena; Buddhist doctrine, teachings of Buddha. Also, **dhamma** (Pali).

dhoti – Loincloth worn by Hindus.

diamonitirion – Official permit to visit Mt. Athos and seek the hospitality of the various monastic communities there.

Digambara – 1) Jain muni or Hindu **sadhu** who is sky-clad (naked); 2) one of two major monastic sects in the Jain religion.

disentailment – Act of divestiture; to free (as property) from entailment.

divine office – Roman Catholic expression indicating the complexes of prayer **services** that mark out the hours of the day and night for monks who join in the official prayer of the church.

dojo – 1) Zen Buddhist training monastery; 2) a place to clarify the Buddha nature.

ecumenical movement – Chiefly twentieth-century movement toward worldwide, interdenominational Christian unity originating in Protestantism and now focused in the World Council of Churches. It is supported by many Protestant and Eastern Orthodox church bodies. Since the Second Vatican Council, in the 1960s, the Roman Catholic Church has taken an active role in ecumenical dialogue.

enlightenment – Awakening to one's true nature, prior to ego.

esonarthex – Inner narthex of an Eastern Orthodox **katholikon**.

exonarthex – Outer narthex of an Eastern Orthodox **katholikon**.

farang – Foreigner, usually refers to a Westerner in the Thai language.

Fayyum – Division of northern Egypt with an area of approximately 670 square miles.

forest monastery – Traditional Thai monastic community where the **bhikkhu** live in individual **kuti**.

French Revolution – Beginning in 1789, it overthrew the absolute monarchy and the system of autocratic privileges, and ended with Napoleon's seizure of power in 1799.

fresco – Painting executed on freshly spread, moist plaster, using pigments that have been mixed with water.

full lotus – Cross-legged sitting meditation posture in which each foot is placed on the opposite thigh, with the soles of the feet facing upward.

gakki – Literally, "hungry spirits"; people who have died and not yet realized Buddhahood.

Gandhi, Mohandas – Often called "Mahatma," literally "great soul"; twentieth-century Indian philosopher and patriot; leader of the struggle against the British for Indian independence.

Ganesha (Ganapati) – Hindu deity worshipped as the god of success and remover of obstacles. In Hindu mythology, he has the head of an elephant and is the son of Lord Shiva.

gassho – Buddhist gesture; raising the hands, palm to palm with fingers pointing toward self, to indicate respect, gratitude, humility, or all three.

ghee – Semifluid, clarified butter commonly made in India and neighboring countries, usually from buffalo milk; frequently used in Hindu religious ceremonies.

Goma – Fire ceremony incorporated into Tantric Buddhism, symbolizing the fire of wisdom that consumes all passions and purifies the world; a central element of the **Tendai** practice.

gommatesa – (Prakrit) good, handsome; benefactor.

Gregorian chant – Ritual plainsong introduced in the Roman Catholic Church under the influence of Pope Gregory I; unharmonized, oftentimes unaccompanied, and without meter.

guru – Religious teacher; spiritual guide; spiritual master who has realized union with God.

gyoja – 1) **Tendai** who undergoes strict Buddhist training; 2) an ascetic.

habit – Distinctive religious costume; a robe.

half-lotus – Cross-legged sitting meditation posture in which one foot is placed on the thigh of the opposite leg, which rests on the floor.

Heart Sutra – Buddhist scripture considered the decisive statement on the nature of ultimate wisdom.

henot – Coptic amulet filled with sweet herbs and perfumes that have had contact with the holy dead, carried on one's person to keep one safe and in the spirit of God.

hermit – One who lives alone, in solitude or seclusion.

Hiei-san – Mount Hiei, near Kyoto, Japan, site of the Koji-rin **Tendai** Training Center.

Hinayana – Literally, "small vehicle"; one of two main branches of Buddhism; often referred to as the conservative branch; originated in southern India and spread to Sri Lanka, Myanar, Thailand and Cambodia. The spiritual ideal, in Hinayana, is a human being who attains enlightenment and escapes from the cycle of rebirth.

Hindu trinity – Lord Brahma, the creator; Lord Vishnu, the preserver; and Lord Shiva, the destroyer.

Hmong – Mountain tribe, originally from Laos.

hojo-san – Head priest of a Buddhist temple or monastery; commonly used in place of **roshi.**

hondo – Main temple in a Zen Buddhist monastery; where **dharma** teachings and ceremonies are held.

Hundred Year's War – Series of wars between England and France, lasting from 1337 to 1453, in which England lost all its possessions in France except Calais.

icon – Sacred image venerated in a variety of religious traditions; Christian icons depict Christ, the Virgin Mary, a saint or some other religious subject; typically painted on a small, wooden panel often with a metal cover.

iconostasis – Partition, usually covered with icons and having three openings, that separates the sanctuary from the nave of a Christian Orthodox or Coptic church.

idiorrhythmic – Lifestyle formerly practiced by some of the Athonite monasteries in which monks received an allowance from the common income, retained their own property and did not have a common superior or lead a common life.

Iviron – One of twenty ruling monasteries on Mt. Athos, located on the northern coast.

Jesus Christ – Christian Messiah, as foretold by the prophets in the Old Testament of the **Bible**. As expressed in the **Nicene Creed**, Jesus Christ is truly human and truly divine, the Second Person of the Holy Trinity.

jikijitsu – Head training monk of the **zendo** in a Zen Buddhist monastery.

kaihogyo – Literally, "practice of circling the mountains." Mt. Hiei kaihogyo is a **Tendai** Buddhist pilgrimage to the sacred sites of the mountain and an honoring of the principles represented in each respective station of worship.

kalogeros – Informal Greek term for monk.

kalyva – Isolated cottage or hut in the Christian Orthodox tradition.

karma (Sanskrit) – Hindu and Buddhist concept of cause and effect that transcends individual lifetimes. Also, **kamma** (Pali).

Karyes – Civil capital of the Holy Mountain, Mt. Athos.

katholikon – Principal church of an Orthodox monastery; a basilica.

Kawaguchi, Ekai – Twentieth-century **Rinzai** Zen Buddhist master who lived and taught in Tokyo. He was the first Japanese person to enter Tibet. Ekai disguised himself as a Chinese monk and entered at a time when foreigners were prohibited. He was seeking the fundamental teachings of Buddhism.

keisaku – Staff or stick used in Buddhist monasteries to administer discipline during meditation.

koan – A training tool, often in the form of a riddle, containing words and experiences of the ancients that cannot be solved by logic; used by Zen Buddhists to cut dualistic thinking, awaken to their **Buddha** nature, and rid themselves of ego.

kuti – Living quarters of **bhikkhu** monks in a Thai **forest monastery**.

lectio divina – Meditative scriptural reading undertaken by Christian monks to lead them into contemplative prayer.

little hours – Minor prayer **services** observed throughout the day in Christian monastic communities. In Roman Catholic communities: prime, tierce, sext and none; in Eastern Orthodox communities: first, third, sixth and ninth hours.

liturgy – Rite or series of rites, observances or procedures, prescribed for public worship in the Christian tradition in accordance with authorized or standard form.

Lord's Prayer – Christian prayer beginning "Our Father," which **Jesus** taught his disciples.

Lotus Sutra – Said to date from the first century; influential among Buddhists of China and Japan; the final discourse by **Buddha**, offering a vision of infinite Buddha worlds.

mae-chii – Buddhist woman renunciate in Thailand; nun.

Mahavira – Twenty-fourth and most influential Jain **Tirthankara**, who lived in the sixth century B.C.E.

Mahayana – Literally, "great vehicle"; one of two main branches of Buddhism; often considered highly speculative and mystical; originated in northern India and spread to Tibet, Mongolia, China, Korea and Japan. The spiritual ideal, in Mahayana, is a human being who, having attained enlightenment, is motivated by compassion to remain within the cycle of rebirth and further the liberation of all living beings.

mantra – Divine name, sacred syllable, word or verse, used for worship and prayer in the Hindu spiritual tradition.

Mara – Buddhist equivalent to Christianity's Satan.

math – Religious establishment or monastery in the Hindu and Jain faiths.

Mecca – (in Saudi Arabia) Birthplace of **Muhammad**; yearly pilgrimage site for Muslims.

Megisti Lavra – Senior of the twenty ruling monasteries on the Holy Mountain, Mt. Athos; founded by Saint Athanasius in 963.

merit – Karmic benefit gained through performance of good deeds, which results in better rebirth in future lives.

mesnevi – A form of poetic compositions of any length dealing with epic, romantic, ethical or didactic themes. This poetic form probably originated in Persia.

Mevlevi Order – **Sufi** order known in the West as the "Whirling Dervishes"; devotees of Mevlana **Rumi**.

mihrab – Niche in the wall of a mosque indicating the direction of **Mecca**.

miso – Fermented, salty bean paste used for soup and flavoring.

mizuko – Literally, "water baby"; a fetus.

Mizuko Jizo – Japanese Buddhist god of children who watches over aborted fetuses.

moksha – Liberation from transmigration; the birth, life, death cycle of reincarnation, and becoming one with God.

mokugyo – Wooden drum used to accompany sutra readings in a Japanese Buddhist temple.

Monophysite – 1) One who believes that Christ had but one nature, a divine nature, or a composite human and divine nature; 2) a tenet of the Coptic Church.

Muhammad, Prophet – Seventh-century prophet of Allah and founder of Islam; a native of Mecca.

muni – Jain monk or Hindu **sadhu**.

mureed – **Sufi** novice preparing to enter a dervish order.

namaste – Hindi greeting; literally, "I bow to the divinity in you."

narthex – Western part of an Orthodox church, in front of the nave, which extends from the north to the south side of the building; used originally by persons (such as women, penitents or catechumens) not permitted to enter the church itself.

nave – Main part of the interior of a church.

ney – Wooden flute.

Nicene Creed – Confession of faith for Christians, adopted at the first Nicene Council in the fourth century.

nirvana (Sanskrit) – Literally, "de-spirited," like a candle that has been extinguished; state of enlightenment, freedom from desire, often misrepresented as a place like heaven. Also, **nibanna** (Pali).

novice – Probationary member of a religious community.

oblate – Layperson dedicated to a religious or monastic life.

Om (Aum) – Most sacred symbol of Hinduism, symbolizing both the personal and the impersonal aspects of the Supreme Reality; the first sound of the universe.

pahkow – One who takes the eight precepts and lives in a Buddhist monastery.

Panagia – Holy Virgin Mary.

Pansa – "Rains retreat," lasting the three months of the monsoon season as determined by the lunar calendar. Buddhist monks must not spend a night away from their monastery at this time of the year.

Panteleimon, Saint – Fourth-century martyr popular in Eastern Orthodoxy because of his many miraculous interventions.

Pantokrator – Majestic image of Christ as the creator; common icon in the Eastern Orthodox Church.

Patimokkha – The 227 monastic disciplinary precepts accepted by an ordained Buddhist monk.

patriarch – 1) Great master who has received and formally transmitted the Buddha's teachings; 2) title of reverence given an outstanding master, both Chinese and Japanese; 3) the head of one of the Eastern (including Coptic) Christian Churches; 4) a bishop of one of the major Orthodox Christian sees.

Pentecost – Christian feast celebrated on the seventh Sunday after Easter (literally, the fiftieth day), marking the Holy Spirit's descent upon the apostles.

phiale – Sacred fountain of a Christian monastery, found near the main church, consisting of a basin covered by a dome resting on columns.

Philotheou – Monastery in the hills on the northern side of Mt. Athos.

pitchi – Whisk broom made of peacock feathers or woolen tufts carried by Jain ascetics; used to brush aside — unharmed — living organisms.

Portaitissa – Literally, "doorkeeper"; title of a famous icon of the Holy Virgin in a special chapel by the entrance gate of Monastery Iviron on Mt. Athos.

post – Sheepskin dyed a dark red, used in the **Sema Ritual** of the **Mevlevi Sufis**.

poste restante – Office, found within major urban post offices around the world, that holds mail for international travelers.

postulant – 1) Candidate for admission to a Christian monastic order; 2) stage preliminary to the novitiate.

practice – The ongoing confirming and clarifying of the same awakening attained by the **Buddha** to a human's true, original nature; working creatively and inventively and with one's own experience.

Prakrit – Any of the ancient Indian languages or dialects other than Sanskrit.

precepts – Vows taken by Buddhist devotees to develop moral purity. Laypeople take 5; mae-chii, 8; male novices, 10; monks, 227.

Protaton – Oldest church on the Holy Mountain, Mt. Athos, located in Karyes; has served the Holy Community for nearly ten centuries.

Psalter – Book of Psalms, separately printed or specially arranged for liturgical or devotional use.

pujari – Hindu or Jain temple priest.

Quran – (Koran) Sacred writings of Islam; revelations made to **Muhhammad** by angel Gabriel.

Ramakrishna, Sri – Nineteenth-century sage of India, now worshipped as an incarnation of God on Earth; guru of **Swami Vivekananda** and founder of the Ramakrishna Order of monks.

raki – A clear liqueur made from grape juice and grain.

relic – Object, such as a bone, article of clothing or possession, venerated for its association with a saint or martyr.

reliquary – Small box, casket or shrine in which relics are kept.

Rinzai Gigen Zenji – Ninth-century founder of the Rinzai Zen sect; the twenty-eighth **patriarch.**

Rinzai Zen Buddhism – Line of Zen teaching, begun by Rinzai Gigen Zenji, which uses **koans** as training tools.

roshi – Zen master.

Rule of St. Benedict – Guidelines directing the life and prayer of Christian monks and for organization of monasteries, adopted by **Benedictines** and **Cistercians,** or **Trappists**.

Rumi, Mevlana Jalaluddin – Thirteenth-century Persian poet, teacher and spiritual leader for whom the Mevlevi Order of **Sufi** dervishes is named.

rupee – Unit of Indian currency.

sacred thread – White thread worn across the chest of a **Brahmin** male to indicate his membership in Hindu society's "priestly **caste**."

sadhu – Hindu religious ascetic.

Saicho – **Patriarch** of Japanese **Tendai** Buddhism who studied with the Chinese master **Chih-i** in mainland China on Mt. T'ien-t'ai. He lived in the late eighth and early ninth centuries.

sala – 1) Usually an open-sided assembly hall on Thai temple grounds; 2) main temple of a **wat**.

sallekhana – Jain ritual of absolute subjugation of human passions; death through gradual abstention from food and drink.

sammon – 1) Official entrance gate into a Buddhist monastery; sometimes referred to as the "mountain gate"; 2) symbolic passageway between the secular and the sacred.

Samsara – Interminable cycle of rebirth, the Wheel of Life, from which the Buddha's teachings provide a means of escape.

samu – Temple work practice in Japanese Buddhism.

san – Japanese honorific attached to a name, indicating Mr., Mrs., Miss or Ms.

sanctuary – Most sacred part of Christian churches; in the Orthodox **katholikon**, located behind the **iconostasis**, where only the priest and his assistants are permitted.

sangha – 1) Community of Buddhist practitioners; 2) the monastic community.

Sanskrit – Ancient Indian language; the classical language of India and of Hinduism, as described by Indian grammarians.

sarcophagus – Stone coffin, often embellished with sculptures or bearing inscriptions.

sari – Garment worn chiefly by Hindu women, consisting of five to seven yards of lightweight cloth that is draped gracefully and loosely to form a skirt and leave an end free to cover the head or shoulder; worn with a blouse.

Scetis – Northwestern desert of Egypt.

Sema Ritual – **(Sufism)** 1) listening to music, singing, chanting and measured recitation designed to elicit religious ecstasy; 2) performances by voice or instrument designed to inspire religious excitement; 3) whirling dance of the **Mevlevis.**

semantron – Board (usually about eight feet long and ten inches wide) that is struck rhythmically with a wooden mallet to announce **services** in an Eastern Orthodox monastery.

service – Orthodox term for daily prayer period laid out by the constitution; similar to the Roman Catholic **divine office.**

Shaivite – One of three principal Hindu sects of **sadhus**; votaries of the Lord Shiva.

Shakta – Sect of Hindu **sadhus** worshipping the Goddess **Shakti.**

Shakti – Eternal energy in the form of "Great Goddess"; Hindu deity.

Shamsi Tabriz – **Sufi** spiritual guide of **Rumi** living in the seventh century.

Shankara, Sri – Ninth-century Hindu saint and scholar, known as the spiritual genius of Hinduism.

sheikh – Name given the spiritual teacher of a **Sufi** lodge or association.

shikan – **Tendai** meditation of "calming the mind and discerning the real."

Shiva-lingam – Symbol of the divine act of creation; the creative power of Lord Shiva.

shojin ryori – Literally, "food for practice"; vegetarian Buddhist fare.

Shvetambara – One of two major Jain monastic sects; its monks dress in white unstitched cloth.

skete – Settlement of Eastern Orthodox monks inhabiting a group of small cottages around a church and dependent upon a parent monastery.

songthaew – Literally, "two rows"; common name for small pickup trucks with two benches in the back, used as buses/taxis in Thailand.

sri – Indian term of respect for a spiritual teacher or leader.

starchestvo – Confessional practice whereby the Orthodox monk reveals to his Spiritual Father his inner thoughts, intentions and temptations, and then receives counsel; usually done daily in the postulant stage of monastic life.

Stations of the Cross – 1) Series of fourteen (as in the Roman Catholic and Anglican Churches) or more (as in the Eastern Orthodox Church) images or pictures that symbolize scenes of suffering in the successive stages of Christ's passion; usually located in a church or on the road to a church or shrine; 2) series of events that occurred as Christ carried the cross through Jerusalem to his place of crucifixion.

Sufi – 1) Name given to an Islamic mystic; 2) from the Arabic word *suf,* meaning wool, from the wool cloaks worn by the holy mystics.

sura – Chapter in the **Quran**.

sutra – Discourse, dialogue or sermon by the **Buddh**a or a disciple; literally, "a thread on which jewels are strung"; sutras are the Buddhist scriptures.

swami – Title of respect and reverence for a spiritual teacher or holy person in Hinduism.

takuhatsu – Literally, "carrying the bowl." Religious mendicancy in Japanese Buddhism, practiced by groups of monks. Devotees offer sustenance either in the form of money, which they place in the monks' wooden bowls, or uncooked rice, which the monks receive in a cloth bag carried for this purpose.

tatami – Thick, tightly woven straw mats used for seating and to cover the floor; common in Japan, Korea and China.

tekke – Central prayer lodge in Sufism, sometimes referred to as the "Hall of Celestial Sounds."

Tendai – Japanese sect of Buddhism founded in the early ninth century. Term comes from T'ien-t'ai, a mountain in mainland China, where the Chinese Buddhist master **Chih-i** lived and taught. Doctrines and practices of the sect are based chiefly on the Lotus Sutra and the teachings of Buddha as laid down by the Chinese founder.

tilaka – Markings usually found on the foreheads of Indian **sadhus** and Hindu religious leaders indicating allegiance to a particular deity.

Theraveda – Old school of Buddhism, now practiced in Thailand, Burma, Sri Lanka and on the Indian subcontinent, called the "small vehicle" (**Hinayana**) by **Mahayana** Buddhists.

tirtha – One who lives near sacred waters.

Tirthankara – 1) Guide on the path to salvation of the soul; 2) one of twenty-four prophets in the Jain religion.

Trappist – Member of a reformed branch of the Roman Catholic **Cistercian** Order established in the seventeenth century at the Abbaye de la Trappe in Normandy, France. See also **Rule of St. Benedict**.

tudong – Buddhist monk's pilgrimage; literally, traveling on foot and living in the open.

tusker – Elephant.

Typicon – Constitution for the monasteries of Mt. Athos; determines details of daily life and structure of services and ceremonies.

Untouchables – "Outcastes" from traditional Hindu society; members do not belong to any of the four main **castes** and are regarded as impure.

Vaishnavite – Order of Hindu **sadhus** loyal to Lord Vishnu.

Vedas – Four canonical collections of hymns, prayers and liturgical formulas that make up the earliest Hindu sacred writings.

vespers – One of the principal Christian monastic **services**, typically celebrated a few hours before sundown.

vihara – Buddhist temple in a Thai monastery.

Vinaya – Book of discipline for the Buddhist monastic community.

Vivekananda, Swami – Nineteenth-century disciple of Sri **Ramakrishna** and founder of the Ramakrishna Mission.

Wadi'n-Natrun – Phrase referring to a group of four Coptic monasteries in the northwestern Egyptian desert between Cairo and Alexandria.

Wars of Religion – Series of civil wars, more than a half dozen, fought in France from 1562-1598. The struggles were characterized by fighting between Catholics and Protestants but were complicated by conflicts between the French crown and the nobles.

wai – Greeting of respect in Thai culture, expressed by putting the hands together, palm to palm with fingertips touching the forehead.

wat – Thai Buddhist monastery.

wun phra – Lunar observance day, celebrated on the new, half and full moon; a time for confession by Thai **bhikkhu**.

xenodochus – Guestmaster in a Coptic monastery.

yin and yang – Principle of polarity in Chinese cosmology, e.g., heaven and earth, male and female, hot and cold

yaza – Period of sitting meditation in a Zen Buddhist monastery practiced at night by a training monk outside of the **zendo**. It varies in length of time.

yurt – Circular, domed tent consisting of animal skins or felt stretched over a collapsible lattice framework; traditional dwellings for nomadic tribes.

zafu – Pillow, usually round and black, on which one sits during Zen meditation.

zazen – Sitting Zen meditation.

zendo – Building where Zen Buddhist monks practice meditation by day and sleep by night.

zikr – The remembrance of **Allah** in the **Sufi** tradition, expressed through repetition of His name.

Recommended Reading

Buddhism

BREITER, PAUL. *Venerable Father: A Life with Ajahn Chah.* Bangkok: Funny,1993.

CHADWICK, DAVID. *Thank You and OK! An American Zen Failure in Japan.* New York: Penguin, 1994.

KAPLEAU, PHILIP. *The Three Pillars of Zen.* New York: Anchor Books, 1989.

The Meditation Temples of Thailand: A Guide. Concord, Calif.: Wayfarer Books, 1990.

NISHIMURA, ESHIN. *Unsui: A Diary of Zen Monastic Life.* Honolulu: University Press of Hawaii, 1973.

POWELL, ANDREW. *Living Buddhism.* London: British Museum Press, 1994.

ROSCOE, GERALD. *The Monastic Life: Pathway of the Buddhist Monk.* Bangkok: Asia Books, 1992.

ROTH, MARTIN, AND JOHN STEVENS. *Zen Guide.* New York: John Weatherhill, 1985.

SATO, KOJI. *The Zen Life.* New York: John Weatherhill, 1972.

STEVENS, JOHN. *The Marathon Monks of Mt. Hiei.* Boston: Shambhala Publications, 1988.

SUZUKI, DAISETZ TEITARO. *The Training of the Zen Buddhist Monk.* New York: University Books, 1965.

TATE, AJAHN. *The Autobiography of a Forest Monk.* Chiang Mai, Thailand: Amarin Printing and Publishing, 1993.

WARD, TIM. *What the Buddha Never Taught.* Berkeley, Calif.: Celestial Arts, 1993.

WEIR, BILL. *A Guide to Buddhist Monasteries and Meditation Centres in Thailand.* Bangkok: Horatanachai Printing, 1991.

Christianity

ATHANASIUS, St. *Life of Saint Anthony.* Cairo: Nubar Printing House, 1992.

BENEDICT, ST. *The Rule of St. Benedict.* New York: Cooper Square, 1966.

BIANCO, FRANK. *Voices of Silence: Lives of the Trappists Today.* New York: Anchor Books/Doubleday, 1991.

BYRON, ROBERT. *The Station – Athos: Treasures and Men.* New York: Alfred A. Knopf, 1949.

CAVARNOS, CONSTANTINE. *Anchored in God: Life, Art, and Thought on the Holy Mountain of Athos*. Athens, Greece: Astir, 1959.

DALY, LOWRIE J. *Benedictine Monasticism*. New York: Sheed and Ward, 1965.

LEMEE, KATHARINE. *Chant: The Origins, Form, Practice and Healing Power of Gregorian Chant*. New York: Bell Tower, 1994.

LOCH, SYDNEY. *Athos: The Holy Mountain*. New York: Thomas Nelson and Sons, 1962.

LOUF, ANDRE. *The Cistercian Way*. Kalamazoo, Mich.: Cistercian Publications, 1983.

MEINARDUS, OTTO F. A. *Monks and Monasteries of the Egyptian Deserts*. Cairo: American University in Cairo Press, 1989.

MERTON, THOMAS. *New Seeds of Contemplation*. New York: W.W.Norton & Co., 1974.

MERTON, THOMAS. *Seven Storey Mountain*. New York: Harcourt, Brace, 1998.

MERTON, THOMAS. *Waters of Siloe*. New York: Harcourt, Brace, 1979.

MORISON, E. F. *St. Basil and His Rule*. London: Oxford University Press, 1912.

NOUWEN, HENRI J. M. *The Genesee Diary: Report from a Trappist Monastery*. Garden City, N.Y.: Doubleday, 1976.

PENNINGTON, M. BASIL. *Monastery*. New York: Harper & Row, 1990.

PENNINGTON, M. BASIL. *O Holy Mountain: Journal of a Retreat on Mount Athos*. Garden City, N.Y.: Doubleday, 1978.

ROFAIL, FARAG. *Sociological and Moral Studies in the Field of Coptic Monasticism*. Leeds, England: Leeds University Oriental Society, 1964.

SHERWOOD, PHILIP. *Athos: The Holy Mountain*. Woodstock, N.Y.: Overlook Press, 1982.

SOPHRONY, ARCHIMANDRITE. *The Monk of Mt. Athos*. Crestwood, New York: St. Vladimir's Seminary Press, 1991.

TUNINK, WILFRID. *Vision of Peace: A Study of Benedictine Monastic Life*. New York: Farrar, Strauss, 1963.

WAKIN, EDWARD. *A Lonely Minority: The Modern Story of Egypt's Copts*. New York: William Morrow, 1963.

WARE, TIMOTHY. "Athos after Ten Years: The Good News and the Bad." *Sobornost,* 1993:15.

WARE, TIMOTHY. *The Orthodox Church*. New York: Penguin, 1993.

WARE, TIMOTHY. "Wolves and Monks: Life on the Holy Mountain Today." *Sobornost,* 1983:5.

Hinduism

BEDI, RAJESH. *Sadhus: The Holy Men of India.* New Delhi, India: Brijbasi Printers, 1991.

BHAJANANANDA, SWAMI. "Ramakrishna Monasticism and the Changing Hindu Ethos." *Journal of Dharma,* April/June 1978:3.

GHURYE, G. S. *Indian Sadhus.* Bombay: Popular Prakashan, 1995.

GROSS, ROBERT LEWIS. *The Sadhus of India: A Study of Hindu Asceticism.* Jaipur: Rawat Publications, 1992.

HARTSUIKER, DOLF. *Sadhus: Holy Men of India.* London: Thames & Hudson, 1993.

PANDIT, BANSI. *The Hindu Mind: Fundamentals of Hindu Religion and Philosophy for All Ages.* Glen Ellyn, Ill.: B and V Enterprises, 1993.

SINGH, DHARAM VIR. *Hinduism: An Introduction.* Jaipur: Travel Wheels, 1994.

Swami Vivekananda's Addresses. Calcutta: Advaita Ashrama, 1993.

TAPASYANANDA, SWAMI. *Aratrika Hymns and Ramanam.* Madras: Sri Ramakrishna Math, 1993.

TAPASYANANDA, SWAMI. *Swami Vivekananda: His Life and Legacy.* Madras: Sri Ramakrishna Math, 1994.

TRIPATHI, B. D. *Sadhus of India: The Sociological View.* Bombay: Popular Prakashan, 1978.

VIVEKANANDA, SWAMI. *The Complete Works of Swami Vivekenanda.* Calcutta: Advaita Ashrama, 1944.

VIVEKANANDA, SWAMI. *Ramakrishna As I saw Him.* Mylapore: Sri Ramakrishna Math, 1970.

Jainism

DOSHI, SARYU. *Homage to Shravana Belgola.* Bombay: Marg Publications, 1981.

KHADABADI, DR. B. K. *Gommatesa-Thudi: Hymn of Gommatesa.* New Delhi: Sri Kundakunda Bharati, 1990.

SITTAR, S. *Inviting Death: Indian Attitude towards the Death Ritual.* Leiden: E.J. Brill, 1989.

SITTAR, S. *Shravana Belgola.* Bangalore, India: Ruvari, 1981.

WARREN, HERBERT. *Jainism.* New Delhi: Crest Publishing House, 1993.

Sufism

BAYAT, MOJDEH, AND JAMNIA, MOHAMMED ALI. *Tales from the Land of the Sufis.* Boston: Shambala Press, 1994.

BURKE, O. M. *Among the Dervishes.* London: Octagon Press, 1993.

FRIEDLANDER, SHEMS. *The Whirling Dervishes.* Albany: State University of New York Press, 1992.

GARNETT, LUCY M. J. *The Dervishes of Turkey.* London: Octagon Press, 1990.

HALMAN, TALAT SAIT, AND METIN AND. *Mevlana Jalaladdin Rumi and the Whirling Dervishes.* Istanbul: Dost Yayinlari, 1992.

INAYAT KHAN, PIR VILAYAT. *The Call of the Dervish.* Santa Fe: Sufi Order Publications, 1981.

OZTURK, YASAR NURI. *The Eye of the Heart.* Istanbul: Redhouse Press, 1988.

The Rumi Collection: An Anthology of Translation of Mevlana Jalaluddin Rumi. Kabir Helminksi, ed.. Brattleboro, Ver.: Threshold Books, 1998.

SCHIMMEL, ANNEMARIE. *Selected Poems: Mevlana Jalaluddin Rumi.* Ankara: Donmez Offset, 1994.

TURKMEN, ERKAN. *The Essence of Rumi's Mesnevi: Including His Life and Works.* Konya, Turkey: Misket, 1992.

TURKMEN, ERKAN. *Rumi: As a True Lover of God.* Hyderabad, India: Islamic Culture Press, 1988.

Comparative Religions

BOWKER, JOHN. *World Religions.* New York: D.K. Publishing, 1997.

The Circle of Life: Rituals from the Human Family Album. Hong Kong: Cohen, 1991.

CREEL, AUSTIN B., AND NARAYANAN VASUDHA. *Monastic Life in the Christian and Hindu Traditions: A Comparative Study.* Lewiston, N.Y.: Edwin Mellen Press, 1990.

FRACCHIA, CHARLES A. *Living Together Alone: The New American Monasticism.* San Francisco: Harper and Row, 1979.

GRIFFITHS, BEDE. *Return to the Centre.* Springfield, Ill.: Templegate, 1976.

GRIFFITHS, BEDE. *Vedanta and Christian Faith.* Middletown, Calif.: Dawn Horse Press, 1991.

INAYAT KHAN, PIR VILAYAT. *Toward the One.* New York: Harper & Row, 1974.

MERTON, THOMAS. *The Asian Journal of Thomas Merton.* New York: New Directions, 1975.

Monasticism: Ideal and Traditions. Madras, India: Sri Ramakrishna Math, 1991.

PENNINGTON, M. BASIL. *Monastic Journey to India.* New York: Seabury Press, 1982.

The Religious World: Communities of Faith. New York: MacMillan, 1988.

World Religions: Information Now Encyclopedia. New York: MacMillan, 1998.

Miscellaneous

CHEVALIER, JEAN AND GHEERBRANT, ALAIN. *Dictionary of Symbols.* New York: Penguin, 1997.

FONTANA, DAVID. *The Secret Language of Symbols.* San Francisco: Chronicle Books, 1993.

MYDENS, SETH. "Nomads of Laos: Last Leftovers of Vietnam War." *New York Times,* March 12, 1997, sect. A, p. 3.

Index

A

abbot, 249. *See also* specific religious community

ablutions, holy, Hindu, 211; Sufi/Muslim, 108, 109

acharya, Jain, 199, 203

Adams, Ansel (photographer), Coptic architectural forms reminiscent of, 104

Aegean Sea, 52, 54, 82

Agamas. *See* sacred texts

AIDS, Bhikkhu Yantra's work with, 168; Lopburi's program on, 157; project working with, 165. *See also* Tham Krabok, Wat, AIDS work at

Aishegul (Sema Ritual attendee), conversation with, 109; description of, 108-109

ajahn, Christian abbot compared to, 186; reference to, 185

ajari, Tendai Buddhist, chopsticks lesson by, 136; dress of, 136, 137; lecture by, 136; meditation led by, 134-135; video narrated by, 133; visit permission granted by, 120-121

Ali (Whirling Dervish member), conversation with, 115; description of, 114, 115

Ambedkar, Dr. B. R., India's constitution written by, 149; "untouchables" movement founded by, 149, 152-153

amulets, author's possession of, 100-101; reference to, 136

Anchored in God. See Cavarnos,Constantine

anchorite, 249; Egyptian desert history of, 88-89, 100, 104; Mt. Athos history of, 54, 82

Andres (American Monastery Philotheou asst. guestmaster), acknowledged, 10; conversations with, 65, 67-68; description of, 65;

Anne, Skete of Saint, description of, 81; skeleton at, 82; transportation from, 82

Anthony, Saint, biography about, 89; cave of, 87-88, 94, 95; life of, 88-89; quote from, 87. *See also* icons

Antunius, Dair Anba: architecture of, 91-92, 94-95, 100; ceremonies in, 94-95, 97; chanting at, 97; Church of St. Anthony in, 101; Church of the Apostle in, 94; dress at, 92, 97; gardens of, 98, 100; icons at, 95; introduction to, 91-92; keep at, 101; labor at, 98; location of, 91; population of, 99;

resurgence of interest at, 98-99; schedule of, 89, 94, 98; tour in, 94, 100,101; training at, 98; transportation to, 91; tribal attacks on, 101; visitor's quarters, 94

Arabian Sea, 211

architecture. *See* specific religious community

Arijika, "mother," 204; photograph of, 204

aritrika, 238

Aritrika Hymn, 238, 240

art, religious. *See* specific religious community

Ashram, Sringeri's Shankara, author's introduction to, 211; ceremony in, 213, 214, 216; description of, 211; devotees at, 211; location of, 211

Ataturk, Mustafa Kemal, Turkish Republic founder, 107; Sufi brotherhoods closed by, 107

Athanasius, Saint, biography of Saint Anthony written by, 89; Megisti Lavra construction directed by, 84; Megisti Lavra Monastery founded by, 84; Typikon written by, 82

Athos after Ten Years: The Good News and the Bad. See Ware, Timothy

Athos, Mt., description of, 52, 54; edict of,54; geography of, 51, 52; history of, 54-55; legends about, 54; mentioned, 151; military interference forbidden on, 54; pagan history of, 54; "republic of monks," 55; resurgence of interest in, 66; trails on, 56, 64, 68, 75, 85; transportation to, 52; whistling forbidden on, 62; women forbidden on, 54

attacks, desert tribal. *See* specific Coptic monastery

authority, Thai traditional. *See* "pu noi" and "puyai"

B

Belar Math. *See* Math, Belar

baptism, author's collective vision of, 26

Bahubali, Lord: description of, 194, 195; history of, 194, 195; hymn dedicated to, 195; icons of, 206; postcards of, 200; Tirthankara's son, 194

Bakara Sura 2/115 (Quranic scripture), 112, 114. *See also* sacred texts

Basil, Saint (Basil the Great), description of, 84; quote from, 51; relic of, 72 bathhouse, Koji-rin. *See* Koji-rin, bathing at

Bazaar, Istanbul's Old Book, meeting Sufis at, 116; mentioned, 11

Bedi, Ramesh (author), 220, 222

Benares Hindu University, 219

Benedict, Saint, grotto of, 48; life of, 47; quotes from, 19, 27, 50; relic of, 28; rural location advocated by, 42; vows advocated by, 19, 32; writing Rule of, 47

Benedictines, Roman Catholic monastic order of, 19, 32; American communities at Conception Abbey, 10; at Weston Priory, 14, 46; mentioned, 35, 40

Beth (Irish Sogenji trainee), conversation with, 140, 142-143; description of, 140

bhat, Thai currency, 176

bhikkhu, duties of, 156-157, 192-193; interdependence with nearby villagers, 188; ordination process of, 170, 177-178; possessions of, 192

bhiksha, practice of, 221-222

bhote. *See* Pah Nanachat, Wat, bhote in

bindabhat, author's experience with, 190, 192; description of, 182, 188-189. *See also* Pah Nanachat, Wat, ceremonies at

bishop, Coptic (anba), 90. *See also* specific religious community

Black Death, European plague of, 32

Blue Highways. See Heat Moon, William Least

Bosphorous Straight, 107

Brahma, Hindu creation god of, 217; holy trinity member, 217

bramachari, 242

Brahman, Hindu supreme reality of, 214

Brahmin, Hindu priestly class of, 211, 216, 224

Bridge, Galata, 107, 117

brotherhoods, Sufi. *See* Sufi

Buddha, addict's vow to; 168, 173; broken vow to, 168; enlightenment of, 180-181, 217; icons of, 129, 131, 132, 142, 163; mantra, 133; mentioned, 121, 147, 166, 187; nature of, 148; refuge to, 189; rules of, 178; statue of, 121, 165, 180-181; teachings of, 156, 188

Buddhism, four basic vows of, 147; Heart Sutra of, 146, 147; integral to Thai culture, 156, 173; introduced to U.S., 145; major types of, 16; Tendai sect of, 122, 124; "untouchables" conversion to, 152

butoh, Japanese contemporary dance of, 152

C

calendar, Julian, 55

calisthenics. *See* Koji-rin, calisthenics at

calligraphy, Japanese, Koji-rin place cards printed in, 131-132; practice of, 135-136. *See also* Koji-rin, calligraphy at

canonical hours, Coptic monastic observation of, 97, 103; Orthodox monastic observation of, 62

Carmelites, Roman Catholic monastic order of, 31. *See also* Therese de Lisieux, Saint

caste, Hindu social, 211, 224

Cavarnos, Constantine (author), 60, 61, 75

cave, religious, at Ajanta and Ellora, 149, 153; on Mt. Athos, 82; of St. Anthony, 87, 88, 89, 94; of St. Benedict, 47. *See also* Anthony, Saint, cave of

Cenobitism, 52, 54, 66, 84. *See also* monasticism, Orthodox, types of

Chadwick, David (author), 147

Chah, Ajahn, quote from, 175; spiritual leader, 181, 186-187; unquestioned authority of, 186; Wat Pah Nanachat founder, 179, 186-187

chakras, 214

Chalcedon, Christian Council of, 90

Chandragiri Hill. *See* hills, sacred Jain

chant, Abbaye de la Trappe practice of, 27, 31; Dair Anba Antunius practice of, 97; Hindu pujari practice of, 213, 227, 228; Jain devotees practice of, 195; Koji-rin practice of, 132, 137; Mevlevi Sufi practice of, 110, 119; Monasteri di Sacro Speco practice of, 48; Monasterio de Santo Domingo practice of, 35, 36, 44; Ramakrishna practice of, 238, 240; Sogenji practice of, 144, 146-147; St. John the Divine practice of, 240; Wat Tham Krabok practice of, 159, 166; Wat Pah Nanachat practice of, 180, 182, 184, 189-190, 193

Chant, lyrics from, 35; mentioned, 45; Santo Domingo's recording reviews of, 36. *See also* LeMee, Katharine

charnel house, 101

Chih-i, Chinese Master, teacher of, 126; quote from, 135

Chi-san (Sogenji guestmaster), conversations with, 144, 149, 151; description of, 140, 144, 149; correspondence from, 140

Chile, Valle de Elqui, retreat at, 14-15, 94

268

Chris (Monastery Panteleimon visitor), conversation with, 79; description of, 79

Christ, Jesus, abbot as symbol of, 31; Coptic Orthodox belief about, death of, 37, 40; 90, 97; guests received like 19, 86; icons of, 58, 72, 75; Jain ascetic statement about, 209; Lazarus raised by, 54; passion of, 50; St. Benedict's reference to, 27; stone carvings about life of, 40; symbols of Jerusalem crucifixion walk by, 28

Christopher, Frere (Abbaye de Citeaux guest master), conversation with, 33-34; description of, 33; family history, 33; teaching style, 33

Church, Coptic Orthodox, 90

church. *See* specific religious community

Circle of Life: Rituals from the Human Family Album, The. See Matthiessen, Peter

Cistercians, Roman Catholic monastic order of, clarification of, 19; first monastery of, 21; repurchase of Citeaux land by, 32

Cistercian, order of the Strict Observance, Roman Catholic monastic order of. *See* Trappist

Citeaux, Abbaye de: anniversary of, 34; architecture of, 31, 32, 33; author's flashback at, 34; author's reference to while at Santo Domingo, 41, 44; daughterhouse of, 31; description of, 31, 32, 33; dress at, 33; founding of, 32; history of, 32; introduction to, 31; meal at, 32, 33; population, 34; refectory in, 32; transportation to, 31

Clan, Ikeda, Sogenji founder, 145

cloister, description of, 38, 40-41; history of, 38. *See also* Santo Domingo, Monasterio de

Communism, Mt. Athos fear of, 78

confession, Orthodox monastic practice of. *See* starchestvo; Thai Buddhist practice of. *See* wun phra

Constantine IX, Emperor, edict proclaimed by, 54; monastic control accomplished by, 54

convents, Coptic, 99

Coptic, original meaning, 90

Costas (Monastery Koutloumousiou asst. guestmaster), conversations with, 58-60, 62-64; description of, 58

cremation, Thai Buddhist grounds of, 187; Thai Buddhist rules about, 181; Swami Vivekenanda site of, 235

D

Dair as-Surian Monastery Saints, 106

Daphni, Mt. Athos port, arrival at, 55; transportation from, 55

David, Abuna (Dair as-Surian monk), conversation with, 103, 104, 106; description of, 103

Dervish, Whirling. *See* Mevlevi

detoxification center, demonstration at, 159. *See also* Tham Krabok, Wat, detoxification program at

dhamma, 156; Buddha's teachings and doctrines of, 188. *See also* Tham Krabok, Wat, dhamma talks at

dharma talk, at Koji-rin, 121, 136

dialogue, Christian/Buddhist, 45, 133

Dialogues, 47. See also Gregory 1, Pope

diamonitirion, acquisition of, 52; obtaining extension for, 61-62; reproduction of author's, 53

Digambara, belief about women, 203-204; description of, 202-203; hair plucking practice by, 204-205, 208; history of, 202; mentioned, 16; "sky clad," 203; traditional ritual death practice by, 198, 199, 205; training of, 202-205

Dionysiouu, Monastery, 83 *(not in text)*

disentailment, act of. *See* Santo Domingo, Monasterio de

Divine Mother. *See* Shakti, Goddess

divine office, worship periods of, 21; Orthodox services similar to, 59

Doi-san (Sogenji guesthouse keeper), 142

dojo, Sogenji designated as, 145

Doshi, Sanya (author), 200

Dwarka, Sadhu (Hindu ascetic), conversations with, 213-214, 216, 218-220, 222; description of, 213, 218, 219; meal taken by, 225; temporary residence of, 222

E

Ecumenical Movement, Monastery Philotheou rejection of, 66

edict, Mt. Athos. See Athos, Mt., edict of. *See also* Constantine IX, Emperor

Egypt: Alexandria, 90, 102, 103; Cairo, 91, 99, 101, 102, 103; Suez, 91; Zefarana, 91

Eizan Station, arrival at, 120

El Camino de Santiago, pilgrimage trail of, 15, 16, 40; symbol of, 42

elephants, holy, 224. *See also* Ganesha

enlightenment, mentioned, 188; Shodo Harada Roshi's receiving of, 143

"evening medicine," practice of, 143

"eye of God," Christian symbol of, 67; Monastery Philotheou portrayal of, 67

F

farang, 176

Farid (Whirling Dervish novice), conversations with, 115, 117-119; description of, 114

fasting, Orthodox monastic practice of, 81

Fayyum, monastic history in, 100; region of, 87

"food for practice." *See* shojin ryori

footwashing, author's experience of, 196

forest monastery, discussion of, 156-157; mentioned, 16; Wat Tham Krabok's differences from, 157; Wat Pah Nanachat, 176

France: Citeaux, 21; L'Aigle, 19; Normandy, 19; Nuits St. George, 31; Paris 22, 31, 33

Francis, Saint, fresco of, 48

French Revolution, 32

frescoes. *See* specific religious community

Friedlander, Shems (author), 116

G

gakki, Sogenji offering to, 144

Gandhi, Mohandas (Mahatma), reference to, 184

Ganesha, 224

gardens, monastic. *See* specific religious community

gassho, 122

Gethsemani, Abbey of, author's retreat at, 13-14

gift, from Abuna David, 106; from Ashok Kumar, 204; from Bhikkhu Yantra, 172; from Frere Gregoire, 29; from Haythem,100; from Monastery Panteleimon guestmaster, 79; from Tendai monk Ryoei, 126

Girosimos, Kalogeros (Mt. Iviron monk), conversation with, 75-76, 78; description of, 75-76

Glass, Philip (composer), Sema Ritual music reminiscent of, 109

Goma, fire ceremony of, 137

Gommatesa, another name for, 195

Gommatesa-Thudi, hymn of, 195

Gordon, Bhikkhu (Wat Tham Krabok monk), conversation with, 155-157; description of, 154; history of, 156; mentioned, 172-173; speech by, 154, 155

Great Lavra, Monastery of. *See* Megisti Lavra, Monastery

Greece, Oureanopolis, 51; Thessaloniki, 51

Gregorian chant, Abbaye de la Trappe practice of, 27; Abbaye de la Trappe recordings of, 29; contrasted with Rinzai Zen Buddhist chanting, 146; founder of, 36; Gethsemani Abbey practice of, 14; history of, 36; lyrics from, 35; Monasteri di Sacro Speco practice of, 48; Monasterio de Santo Domingo practice of, 35, 36, 42, 44; Monasterio de Santo Domingo recordings of, 36, 45. *See also* chant, and *Chant*

Gregoire, Frere (Abbaye de la Trappe monk), conversation with, 27-29; description of, 27

Gregory 1, Pope, 36, 47

grotto, Saint Benedict. *See* Benedict, Saint, grotto of

gyoja, "spiritual athlete," 124

H

habit. *See* specific religious community, dress at

"heavenly gate." *See* iconostasis

Hagit (Israeli Wat Tham Krabok visitor), bargaining by, 160; conversation with, 159; description of, 159

Hall of Celestial Sounds. *See* Tekkesi, Sufi Galata Mevlevi

halls, Tendai sacred, of Perpetual Practice, 129; of Lotus, 129

Haney (Dair Anba Antunius guest), conversations with, 89-90, 95; description of, 89

Hartsuiker, Dolf (author), 220

Haythem (Dair Anba Antunius guest), conversations with, 89-90, 95, 100; description of, 89

Heart Sutra, 146, 147. *See also* sacred texts. *See also* Buddhism

Heat Moon, William Least (author), 25

henot, 100, 106

hermit, Athonite, 66, 82; Coptic monastic life as, 99, 103; Coptic monastic training as, 99; St. Anthony's life as, 87, 88, 89; St. Basil's comments about, 84; St. Benedict's life as, 47

hermitage, Bhikkhu Yantra's, 172; compared to kuti at Wat Pah Nanachat, 182; Nova Nada use of, 14; Thomas Merton's, 14

Hiei-san, cloud forest on, 127; description of,

Jewels, Three, 202, 205, 246. *See also*
    Jainism, religious beliefs of
jikijitsu. *See* Hi-san
Johnson, Tim (American academic at
    Monastery Philotheou), conversation with,
    65-66; description of, 65-66
Jo-san (American Sogenji trainee), 152
Justinian, Emperor, Dair Anba Antunius keep
    built by, 101

K

kaihogyo, Koji-rin's schedule of, 125, 130;
    participation in, 135
Kakushan (Koji-rin's primary trainer), conver-
    sations with, 129-130, 136-137; description
    of, 129; memory of warning from, 144
Kallistos. *See* Ware, Timothy
kalyva hut, mentioned, 82
Kan'ei-ji. *See* temples, Tendai, Kan'ei-ji
Kapleau, Philip (author), 148
karma, Jain concept of, 204
Karnataka Fortnightly, 199, 200
Karnataka, state of, 199
Karoulia, 82
Karyes, author's observation of, 55-56; bus
    trip to, 55; description of, 55-56; lunch in,
    78; monk's dress at, 55; obtaining
    diamonitirion extension at, 61-62; Protaton
    in, 56; whistling incident in, 62
katholikon. *See* specific Orthodox
    monastic community
keep. *See* specific Coptic religious community
keisaku, mentioned, 134; physical experience
    of, 152; purpose of, 134
koans, Ajahn Panchand's style of, 162, 170, 173;
    Rinzai Zen, 148-149; examples of, 148-149
Koji-rin (Lay People's Training Center):
    architecture at, 129, 130, 131; author's
    food incident at, 136-137; bathing at, 133;
    calisthenics at, 135; ceremonies in, 130-132,
    133-135, 136, 137; chanting at, 132, 137;
    description of, 129, 130; dress at, 129, 130,
    136, 137; introduction to, 127, 129; labor at,
    135; lecture at, 136; letter from, 120, 123;
    location of, 127, 129; meals at, 131-132,
    136-137; meditation in, 131, 134-135;
    organized retreats at, 120-121; refectory at,
    131-132, 136-137; schedule at, 130; sutra-
    copying at, 121, 135-136; population, 130;
    training at, 136; transportation to, 120,
    126, 127; video at, 133; visitor's quarters,

129, 133-134
Koutloumousiou, Monastery: architecture of,
    56, 58, 59, 60, 61; ceremonies at, 60, 61;
    confession at, 63; description of, 56; dress
    at, 58, 61; frescoes in, 60; gate closing at,
    61; hike to, 56; icons at, 58; introduction
    to, 56, 58; katholikon at, 58, 59, 60, 61;
    labor at, 63; meal at, 60-61; refectory at,
    60-61; refreshments in, 56, 58;
    schedule of, 63; semantron use at, 60;
    training at, 62; visitor's quarters, 58, 60
Kolzom, Mt., 87, 94
kuti. *See* Pah Nanachat, Wat, kuti at
Kumar, Ashok (Jain newsletter editor),
    conversation with, 200, 202-205;
    description of, 199; gifts from, 204-205;
    house of, 199; telephone call to, 199
Kundakunda Bharati (Jain research center):
    architecture of, 206; introduction to, 206;
    thatched hut inside of, 260; recommendation
    to make visit to, 205

L

laboratory, botanical, Bhikkhu Yantra
    working at, 168-169; description of, 165;
    mentioned, 160, 172
Last Judgement, mentioned, 115
Laura (Whirling Dervish associate), conversa-
    tions with, 114, 118, 119; description of, 114
lavra, early desert monastic community
    called, 100
Lazarus, bishop of Cyprus, 54; risen from the
    dead, 54; Virgin Mary received invitation
    from, 54
lectio divina, 28
legends, Mt. Athos. *See* Athos, Mt., legends
    about. *See also* specific religious communities
LeMee, Katharine (author), 36
libations, Hindu practice of, 213; Jain practice
    of, 195, 196. *See* Ashram, Sringeri's
    Shankara, ceremonies at. *See also*
    Shravana Belgola.
lingam. *See* Shiva-lingam
Little Way. *See* Therese de Lisieux, Saint
liturgies, Coptic, Saint Basil's, 97; fourteen
    original ones, 97
lodge, Sufi: description of, 118; sheikh's
    attendance at, 118, 119; author's second
    Sema Ritual experience in, 118-119; zikr
    ceremony at, 119
Lord's Prayer, mentioned, 97

M

possessions of, 204; Sanskrit term, 200; training of, 200, 202-205; two major types of, 202

Mureed. *See* Sufi, training of

Mydons, Seth (newspaper writer), 160

mystics, Islamic. *See* Sufi, Islamic mystics

N

National Geographic, Sufi photograph in, 118

Neil (Sri Vidyanandji's lay asst.), conversation with, 206, 209-210; description of, 206

ney, Sufi symbol of, 109

Nicene Creed, mentioned, 97

nibanna, reference to, 166

Nishimura, Eshin (author), 148

Nivard, Saint, description of, 21; room named after, 20-21

Nikos (Monastery Panteleimon guest), conversation with, 79-81; description of, 79

Noah, Biblical figure, semantron symbol of, 60

Nomads of Laos. See Mydons, Seth

Nova Nada, Monastery, author's retreat at, 14

nuns, Coptic, 99; Jain, 203, 204

O

O Holy Mountain. See Pennington, M. Basil

oblate, Ashok Kumer similar to, 200; Roman Catholic monastic term of, 22

O'Keeffe, Georgia (artist), Coptic architectural forms reminiscent of, 104

Old Book Bazaar, Istanbul's: *See* Bazaar, Istanbul's Old Book

Om (Aum), 114

"Opium-Pipe Cave Monastic Center." *See* Tham Krabok, Wat

opus dei, 21. *See also* divine office

O'Shaunnesy, Padre (Monasteri di Sacro Speco guest master), conversation with, 48, 50; description of, 48

P

Pablo, Padre (Monasterio de Santo Domingo monk), conversation with, 44-46; description of, 44; meeting arranged with, 42

Pah Nanachat, Wat: ajahn (abbot) at, 185, 186, 189, architecture of, 177, 179, 180-181, 182, 185; bhote at, 185; ceremonies at, 182, 184, 189-190, 193; chanting at, 180, 182, 184, 189-190, 193; daughterhouse of, 186; dress at, 177, 178, 185, 192; hair shaving practice at, 177, 178, 193; history of, 179, 185, 186-187; iguana incident at, 190; introduction to, 176, 177; kuti at, 182; labor at, 182, 192-193; location of, 176-177, 187; meal at, 184; population of, 187; refreshments at, 181, 189; salas at, 180, 182, 184, 193; schedule at, 180; training at, 177-179; transportation to, 176; visitor's quarters, 179; vows at, 178

Pah Pong, Wat, daughterhouse of, 181

Pali, Jain sacred texts written in, 203

Panaghia Portaitissa. *See* Iviron, Monastery

Panasaro, Bhikkhu (Canadian Wat Pah Nanachat monk), conversation with, 182; description of, 182; kuti of, 182; walk with, 182

Panchand, Ajahn Chamroon (Wat Tham Krabok abbot), conversations with, 161-162, 170, 173; author's letter to, 155; description of, 161; final advice from, 173, 174; mentioned, 174; poem by, 154

Pansa, ordination time of, 185; Thai Buddhist observation of, 157

Panteleimon, Monastery: architecture of, 78, 79, 81; ceremonies at, 79, 81; chanting at, 81; fasting at, 81; gift from, 79; history of, 78; icons at, 79, 81; introduction to, 78; katholikon at, 79; location of, 75, 78; meal at, 81; refectory in, 81; relics in, 79; special chapel in, 79; tsar's room at, 78

Pantokrator. *See* Iviron, Monastery, Pantokrator in

Parry, Robert Lloyd (Monastery Megisti Lavra volunteer), conversations with, 84-85; description of, 84

Patimokkha, 178

Patriarch, Orthodox, in Constantinople (Istanbul), 66

Patriarchate, Coptic, visit to, 102; mentioned, 90, 92, 99, 106

Patrick, Bhikkhu (Dutch Wat Pah Nanachat monk), conversation with, 177-180; description of, 177

Pennington, M. Basil (author), 62-63, 81

Pentecost, color symbol of, 74; Mt. Iviron celebration of, 74

Peter, Bhikkhu (Swiss Wat Tham Krabok monk), conversation with, 170; description of, 170

Philotheou, Monastery: ceremonies at, 67; dress at, 65; "eye of God" at, 67; history of, 65, 66; "hotbed of conservatism," 66,

home of, 108; mentioned, 115, 116; *Mesnevi* authored by, 109; prayers offered to, 110, 114; quote from, 107; Sufi spiritual guide, 116
rupee, Indian currency, 214
Ryoei (Tokyo Tendai monk) conversation with, 124-126; description of, 124; gift from, 126

S

sacred texts, Agamas, 194; Bakara Sura 2/115, 112, 114; Bible, 21, 41, 242; Heart Sutra, 146, 147; Gospel, 97; Matthew 19:21, 89; psalms, 21, 97; Psalm 150, 74-75; Quran, 108, 112, 242; sutras (Tendai), 121, 130, 132, 135; sutras (Rinzai Zen), 144, 146, 147, 148, 166, 184; Ten Commandments, 178; Vedanta, 241; Vedas, 217; Vinaya, 178
"sacred thread," Brahmin symbol of, 211, 216
Sacro Speco, Monasteri di: architecture of, 47; art in, 47, 48, 50; ceremony in, 48; chanting at, 48; dress at, 47, 48; garden of, 47; grotto in, 48; introduction to, 47; labor at, 47, 50; location of, 46-47; mentioned, 10, 46, 180; population, 50; schedule at, 50; transportation to, 46
sadhu, alms collecting by, 222; author's meeting with, 213-214, 216, 218-220, 222; description of, 213, 219; religious duties of, 220; social duties of, 220; ordination of, 218-219; population of, 220; possessions of, 220; women's participation in, 222
Sadhus: Holy Men of India. See Hartsuiker, Dolf
Sadhus: The Holy Men of India. See Bedi Ramesh
Saicho, Tendai Patriarch, Hiei-san's first temple not established by, 122; eternal flame legend of, 127; quotes from, 131, 132; teacher of, 126, 135; tomb of, 135
Saint John the Divine, 240
sala. *See* specific Thai Buddhist community
Salgado, Padre (Monasterio de Santo Domingo guest master), conversations with, 37, 40, 42; description of, 37
sallekhana, ritual death, 198-199, 205
Salve Regina, Mater Misericordiae, Trappist traditional singing of, 26
sammon. *See* Sogenji, sammon at
Samsara, Tibetan Buddhist Wheel of, 179-180
samu, 135. *See also* Koji-rin, labor at
Sangwaro, Bhikkhu (Wat Pah Nanachat guestmaster), conversations with, 184,

185-189; description of, 184
Sanskrit, Buddhist sutras written in, 144; Jain scriptural texts written in, 203; Hindu pujari rituals printed in, 224
Santiago, El Camino de. *See* El Camino de Santiago
Santo Domingo, Monasterio de: architecture of, 35, 36, 37, 40-41; art in, 37, 38, 40-41; ceremonies at, 35-36, 40, 42, 44; chanting at, 35, 36, 44; cloister of, 38, 40-41; comparison to Abbaye de la Trappe, 40, 41; daughterhouses of, 44; disentailment of, 41; dress at, 35-36, 38, 44; economy of, 36, 45; garden at, 41, 42; history of, 40, 41, 44; introduction to, 35-36; labor in, 45; location of, 35, 42; meals at, 37-38, 41; pharmacy of, 41; population, 40; refectories at, 37-38, 41; schedule at, 37; transportation to, 35; visitor's quarters, 37
sari, Indian women dressed in, 195, 211
Scetis, Egyptian desert of, description of, 102; history of, 102. *See also* Wadi'n-Natrun
School, Italian Sienese, art institute of, 48
scripture house. *See* Sogenji, scripture house of
Second Vatican Council, 23
selam, 112, 118. *See also* Sema Ritual
Sema Ritual, chanting in, 110, 119; chorus in, 109; dress at, 108, 109, 110; musical instruments in, 108, 109; musicians in, 109; post in, 110; selam in, 112, 118; spiritual leader of, 110, 112, 114, 118, 119; two stages of, 109; whirling in, 110, 112
semantron, sound of, 60; symbol of, 60; use of, 60, 61, 74
services, Orthodox monastic, clarification, 59, 63, 81; "low," 70
settlements, refugee. *See* Hmong
Seven Storey Mountain, The. See Merton, Thomas
Shaivite, mentioned, 16; monastic order of, 217-218, 236; oldest Hindu monastic order of, 236; Shankara's ten divisions of, 217, 236
Shaka-do, 129, 130, 131, 134, 135. *See also* temples, Tendai
Shaktas, Hindu monastic order of, 236
Shakti, Goddess, 236
Shankar, Radja (Sringeri's Shankara Math business manager), conversation with, 222-224; description of, 222
Shankar, Ravi, 240
Shankara, Sri, Bodhgaya incident caused by,